Consciousness,
Brain Evolution and
The Atomic Science of Minds

FIRST EDITION

Library of Congress Control Number:

ISBN No. 9781096863786

Mamoun, John Sami, 1976-
Consciousness, Brain Evolution and the Atomic Science of Minds

Cover design by J.Mamoun, using public domain clipart, and an anatomical brain specimen engraving from the anatomical atlas De Humani Corporis Fabrica, published in 1543 by Andreas Vesalius.

Includes bibliographical references

1. Cognitive neuroscience. 2. Neuropsychology 3. Natural selection
4. Human evolution 5. Psychology I.Title.

☞ When you are done reading me, please donate me to a university library! 🕮

❧ Contents ❧

Introduction

Can the functionality of the human mind, or any other organic mind, be explained in reductionist, atomic or molecular terms? Are all human minds, whether the minds of a Winston Churchill, a Pablo Picasso, a William Shakespeare, or a beloved grandmother, who warms the hearts of family members with her delicious, homemade apple pie, automated in their operation, like a fax machine? The homo sapiens mind appears to be too "inventive," "emotional," "consciously aware," "motivated," or "creative" to be an automated machine. Many books and articles have been written about various aspects of how the mind works, and no one publication (including this one) provides definitive answers to this question. In all of these books or articles, at some points or another, the authors digress with arguments that seem to make sense from a common-sense standpoint. However, just as common sense has little to do with mathematical proofs, common sense has little to do with explaining how a human mind, consisting of 100 billion neurons, with up to 1,000 connections each, of which about 16.5 billion exist in the "intelligent" cerebral cortex of the human brain, generates what is called "conscious awareness."

It is not possible, using current scientific knowledge, to explain, in a rigorously reductionist way, how a human mind, or any other mind, works (Nagel, 1974; Turing, 1950). Such an explanation would require knowledge of how the brain works at the molecular and probably at the sub-atomic level, which can only be determined using scientific investigation that is beyond the current state-of-the-art approaches to such investigation. However, there exists enough science or evolutionary psychology understanding to explain some general ideas about how a mind works. In addition, other laws of physics, such as the laws of thermodynamics, are applicable to understanding how minds work, and will be explored here.

The purpose of this book is to give some idea of how the mind works. From where do our motivations and thoughts originate? Can the cause of any thought that any human can conceive of, whether rational or irrational, be explained as originating purely from the laws of physics? What determines what ideas become installed in a mammalian, insect or other animal mind, and which ideas become excluded? What is the difference between a homo sapiens brain computer and a man-made computer? More fundamentally, what is a mind? What is a thought? What is a question? What is information? What is this entity that is commonly called "consciousness" or "conscious awareness?" And, of course, who can omit the age-old question, "does free will exist?" Terms such as "mind," "thought," "intelligence," "information," "knowledge," or "question" need to be defined as sub-atomic, atomic or molecular mechanisms. A philosopher sometimes uses such terms in a common sense explanation of how some aspect of the mind works, without defining what these terms mean in atomic or sub-atomic terms. People then might agree with the philosopher's arguments on common sense grounds, but nobody, including that philosopher, would be able to precisely explain what the philosopher means.

Terms like "human soul" or "human mind" are too anthropocentric. Minds do not have to be only human minds. There exist computer minds, frog minds, solar-powered calculator minds, as well as human minds. A complete theory of mind should encompass or explain how all minds can be grouped into some kind of general category. Statistically, earth-like planets, possibly containing lifeforms with minds, are calculated to exist in abundance in the known universe, with 30 billion earth-like planets statistically posited to exist just in our Milky Way galaxy alone, which is among hundreds of billions of galaxies in the human-observable universe. The generalized distribution of minds in the universe, which is statistically suggested, suggests that a theory of mind must be generalizable to all forms of minds.

The word "soul" has a well-defined meaning in philosophical literature as being a "spiritual" thinking mind, created by God, constituting a spiritual entity that is separable from a physical body (Musolino, 2015; Foster, 1996; Descartes, 1988 edition). To provide a scientific rationale for how an organic brain works, an organic brain should be thought of as a "mind," or as a thinking device in general, that is one of many possible thinking devices existing on the planet earth, as opposed to a "soul," which is a thinking entity with more "spiritual" properties. If the human brain contains a God-created "soul," scientific explanations of where human motivations come from are irrelevant, because human motivations simply come from God. According to the most popular god paradigms that have become established within the popular culture of homo sapiens civilization on the planet earth, God created the universe and all that is in it, and created people, and endowed them with the free will to make morally good or bad decisions while alive on the planet Earth, and when people die, their souls leave the body and pass into a judgement phase where they will be judged deserving of spending eternity in either heaven or hell, depending on how morally they behaved while making their own free will decisions of whether to behave rightly or wrongly.

It is sometimes said that conscious awareness results from neurons, made of inert matter, being combined into vast numbers of logic gates, which are perhaps structured as Boolean logic gates, and that these neurons "process information," such as to make "consciousness" possible. This is like saying that a computer mind works because it is made up of millions of transistors. Yes, but many dozens of PhD's are needed to figure out how to connect the transistors together, and other PhD's are needed to figure out how to manufacture the microprocessors that contain these millions of connected transistors. It is also sometimes said that, since humans know how to design the minds of computers, that humans can use this insight to understand how the human brain works. To some extent this is true, although the human brain is not a computer in the sense that a computer is a computer. It is not entirely obvious what human minds are trying to compute or optimize. Much of human thinking is not particularly mathematical, so how can the human mind be compared to a purely mathematical calculating device like a computer?

It is intellectually risky to ask the questions, "what is consciousness" or "what is conscious awareness?" The problem with this question is that it presumes that there is some kind of definitive form of "conscious awareness." However, every mind thinks differently and is "consciously aware" in a different way. "Conscious awareness" is likely an arbitrary construct in any mind, consisting of intellectual or emotional components that exist arbitrarily. This book will provide some answers to, but not definitively answer, the question of what is "conscious awareness?" One of this book's posited generalizations, which is not original, is that all thoughts in all minds originate from or are caused by atomic and molecular phenomena (Crick, 1994; Penrose, 1989). One of this book's approaches for understanding how the human mind works, is to show that much of a human mind's thinking is due to the human body being a thermodynamically unstable cohesion of atoms and molecules, requiring a continuous input of food energy in order for this body to maintain its thermodynamically unstable body form (Vandervert, 1995). This reality, caused arbitrarily by the laws of physics, is the cause of the thought, continuously recurring in human minds, that one is hungry and wants to find food to eat. The motivation to find food is also a cause of a vast array of different thoughts that a mind may have.

Another of this book's "intellectual attack points" for understanding how the human mind works is to demonstrate that the thermodynamically unstable body form of a human forces the human to engage in reproduction activities, or else that human's genes will not reproduce. Death, which is a state of catastrophic instability in an organic body form, that causes the atoms and molecules of that body form to disintegrate into the infinity background of the universe, apparently cannot be avoided in a thermodynamically unstable body form such as that of the human body, due to the arbitrary laws of physics. Reproduction of genes is the only way to ensure continuation of a species after the deaths of individual members of a species. This need to reproduce, caused arbitrarily by the laws of physics, is the origin of the vast array of thoughts and behaviors associated with human reproduction activities.

Of course, these food-locating and reproduction-activity-locating thoughts also originate in the minds of non-human mind-containing organisms for essentially the same reasons that they have evolved to exist in human minds. Of course, different minds think thoughts, belonging to these two general categories of thoughts, in different ways, depending on the life-support requirements of different minds, and the life-support niches that different minds occupy on the planet earth.

It is impossible to write a book about how minds work without "reinventing the wheel," probably many times over. Many ideas contained in this book, and in many other books on the topic of how minds work, have been explored previously by numerous philosophers, scientists, psychologists and armchair theorists. The author does not claim originality for most of the ideas contained here, but hopefully, the overall "synthesis," or how these "wheel-reinvention" ideas come together into a coherent paradigm, is itself relatively original. A bibliography is included in this book, that provides sources of some of the ideas contained here, although this bibliography is not necessarily a complete representation of the vast numbers of books and articles, encompassing multiple fields of expertise, that have been published on topics related to "how the mind works." Those who wish to explore this topic via other avenues are encouraged to search for and read other books on the topic of how the mind works, written by scientists and psychologists, and also to read original scholarly papers in the field of philosophy. Professional philosophers have written vast numbers of articles on topics such as, can the mind understand reality, what is reality, how accurately can human language describe reality, and what is morality? Understanding the intricacies, complexities and ambiguities of these topics is essential for anyone who wishes to understand how the mind works.

A major caveat of any book on how the mind works is that it is not possible to prove that the human brain is capable of rationally understanding the universe. A human mind's understanding of the universe may consist of a non-rational constructs conceptualized by the mind. It is also not possible to prove that objects exist in reality, as real objects separate from a mind's perception of the object (Jackson, 1986). However, this book, perhaps arbitrarily, works along the assumption that objects exist independently of minds. If you pound your fist on a table, the table probably exists, at least in some physical way.

If an organic mind's evolution is a product of the laws of physics, that mind must possess at least some rational beliefs about physics and reality. Otherwise, that mind would not be adaptive, and the genes of that mind and the body to which that mind is attached might eventually be wiped out of the gene pool. One major evolutionary reason why conscious awareness evolved is to make minds think thoughts and feelings, and implement behavior patterns, that facilitate the propagation of the genes of the bodies to which those minds are attached. Such thoughts do not necessarily have to be rational, and do not necessarily have to consist of rational understandings of the reality of objects in the real world. Actually, irrational thoughts, emotions and behavior patterns can in some contexts be adaptive.

One demonstration that the mind possesses a rational physics understanding of at least one facet of reality is that organic minds know that if they eat foods, they can avoid starving to death. If a starving person eats an apple, and eating this apple delays the person from starving to death for a longer amount of time than if the person did not eat anything, the fact that eating the apple temporarily prevents the person from starving to death is not due to any beliefs in the person's mind. Instead, this is due to the unseen effect that the apple has on that person's body after the apple is eaten and digested, and is also due to the apple providing enough energy to temporarily prevent the person from starving to death. This temporary prevention of starvation is a purely physical phenomenon, that exists independently of what the person's mind thinks. One could argue that it is an illusion that a table exists, or that the mind does not understand exactly in what sense a table exists. However, it is probably not an illusion that eating an apple prevents a starving person from starving to death, or that the belief in this idea is false.

Any theory of how organic minds work, and any theory of what is conscious awareness, should provide insights that a computer programmer could use to program a computer to think like a "consciously aware" mammal. This is perhaps the ultimate critical judgement of whether or not a theory of mind is truly scientific. If a philosopher and scientist makes a claim about how the human mind works, how can a computer programmer use this claim as an insight that helps in programming a simulated human mind? For example, if philosophers Richard Dawkins or Daniel Dennet claim that consciousness consists of a system of acquired human cultural memes, how can a computer programmer use this claim to design a computer mind that simulates an organic human mind? No book or article on conscious awareness, including this one, has succeeded completely in providing such insights to such computer programmers. It is thought that organic minds evolved from scratch, or from precursor amino acids that somehow concatenated into precursor single-celled organisms, that somehow over eons evolved into organic minds such as humans. These organic minds evolved in the context of a universe consisting of repetitive patterns of sub-atomic, atomic and molecular movements and matter-attraction and matter-repulsion phenomena, and these organic minds evolved to be optimized for performing various life-support and gene-propagation activities. How can a computer be programmed to evolve, from virtual precursor molecules, virtual minds that exist as virtual evolving structures in a virtual world driven by repetitive patterned behavior of many different simulated, virtual sub-atomic particles, in the context of a virtual universe operating according to the virtual laws of thermodynamics? How can a computer evolve such a diverse set of virtual organic minds, that are collective assembled into a virtual food chain, which is essentially a virtual energy equilibration system, from scratch, such as by starting with cellular automata oriented to a virtual, simulated universe like the universe in which humans inhabit?

Some questions explored in this book include: Why do biological minds exist? What are the forces of natural selection trying to optimize by evolving biological creatures possessing biological minds? Is the mind immortal and separate from the body, so that if the body dies, the mind somehow lives on forever? Or is the mind a part of the body, dying forever when the body dies? What makes us "aware" of things? Are we more aware of reality than is a frog or a dog? Is consciousness some kind of miracle, that separates us humans from inanimate objects like rocks, or "dumb animals" like frogs or houseflies? Is it rational to have opinions or attitudes? Where do our motivations come from? Why are human personalities or minds so diverse in attitudes, intelligence levels, opinions, and knowledge containment? What makes a thought enter into a person's mind and become remembered? Why do some thoughts exist in some peoples' minds but not in other peoples? Is reincarnation possible? Do the lives of humans on the planet earth have a purpose? What is morality and do human minds behave morally? Is it rational to have political viewpoints? Where, or when, are we in the universe? What is the difference between a computer brain and a human brain or a frog brain? This book will explore these basic questions, from both scientific and religious perspectives, but cannot provide a complete answer as to how the mind works at a molecular level, since only experimental scientific investigation can provide that.

The Origins of Thoughts

Generally, life can only be born from other previously existing lifeforms. "Spontaneous generation," or the generation of life from inanimate matter, is generally impossible. It was once thought that flies spontaneously generated from raw meat left out in the open, but an experiment was performed where fresh raw meat was placed in a jar and the jar covered with dense cloth, and no insects ever came out of that meat, no matter how many times the experiment was repeated. It was later realized that flies need to be able to access the raw meat to lay eggs on the meat. Flies appeared to spontaneously generate from the uncovered meat because no one observed the flies landing on the meat to lay their eggs there to begin with. However, a single reproducing cell, spontaneously generated from inanimate matter, is thought to have been the origin of life on earth. Of course, it is astronomically unlikely for such a spontaneous generation event to occur due to chance, within any specific time point or volume of space on the planet earth.

The first cells ever to exist on the planet earth, if we assume that life on earth was not seeded by space aliens or originally created by God (these hypotheses cannot be proven wrong), had to have been created out of inanimate atoms and molecules on the planet earth. In other words, the earth had to be the "original womb" from which the first living cell was assembled or concatenated from inanimate atoms and molecules. Given that a cell consists of many trillions of atoms and molecules that must be assembled in precisely parameterized ways for the cell to function and reproduce, the probability of the earth spontaneously generating an initial cell, in any one particular volume of space on the planet earth, at any one particular moment of time, is astronomically low. Yet, the probability of this happening at least once over many millions of years is not zero.

Physicists do not know what the "physics access point" is by which a mixture of atoms and molecules, that could be statistically likely to occur, could be brought together within a tiny volume, such as to spontaneously generate an initial functional and reproducing cell, such that this event has enough of a probability to occur for this event to probably occur within a long but not infinite timespan, such as one or two billion years, which is a fraction of the total time (approximately four billions years) that earth has been in existence. Physicists have not created yet a model of what kinds of atoms and molecules, that exist or can generate spontaneously in nature on planet earth, could generate a functional, reproducing cell if the earth brought these ingredients together simultaneously within a tiny cubic volume, under specified conditions of temperature and pressure and energy inputs, and the specific probability of such a physics event occurring.

There is no way to prove that the earth as a womb originally generated an original reproducing cell from inanimate matter. Experiments show, however, that the building blocks of life (simple amino acids, for example) can be generated from simple precursor atoms and molecules in a chemical reaction chamber containing an atmosphere similar to that of the pre-biotic earth, and energized by small voltage sparks of electricity (Eschenmoser, 2007; Johnson, 2008; Miller, 1953 and 1955). If the pre-biotic earth generated a vast quantity of a diverse range of amino acids and simple peptides in a sterile "organic soup," (Sagan, 1980), this increases the probability of the "earth as a womb" concatenating spontaneously an initial reproducing cell.

If the atoms and molecules, that can be brought together by the "earth as a womb" to create a cell, exist within a volume of space of (let's assume for argument's sake) one cubic millimeter, and it is within this volume of space that the atoms and molecules are close enough together to assemble together into a functional and reproducing cell, and that the earth contains countless quadrillions of cubic millimeter volumes where such atomic and molecular interactions could occur within each second of time on the planet earth, then over an extremely long timespan, perhaps one or two billion years, then the probability of an initial cell being spontaneously generated by the "earth as a womb" may closely approach 100%, even if the probability of such a spontaneous assembly event occurring per any particular second per any particular millimeter of volume would be itself astronomically miniscule.

The origin of the first reproducing cell by the "earth as a womb" represents the origin of the manifestation, on the planet earth, of the physics fact that lifeforms are thermodynamically unstable and require a constant input of energy in order to maintain their atomic and molecular cohesive body forms. The origin of this physical fact then provides the foundation, on the planet earth, for the evolution of minds that are capable of realizing that this physical fact exists, such that the forces of natural selection evolve (and therefore create originally) minds capable of thinking that one of the central ideas in the mind's thinking is that the mind must locate food to prevent the body attached to the mind from dying of starvation (i.e. disintegrating due to the intrinsically thermodynamically unstable nature of the atomic and molecular cohesive form of that mind's body). This concept, the thinking of which is adaptive universally for all organic minds, is one of the central motivators of the behavior patterns that are directed by thinking organic minds.

The automatic generation, over a timespan of probably 1-2 billion years, of the first functional, reproducing and surviving cell line, is also the origin of the reality, on the planet earth, that organic lifeforms exist, and that organic lifeforms need to reproduce, because all cells eventually disintegrate, and the inevitability of cell disintegration forces members of a species to continuously reproduce in order to maintain the survival of the gene line of that species. It is arbitrary that the laws of physics permit

3

the automatic generation of an original, functioning, reproducing cell by the "earth as a womb." It is also arbitrary that the laws of physics result in all organic cells being thermodynamically unstable and requiring a constant input of energy, and result in the reality that eventually all organic cells die through disintegration, which forces cells to continuously reproduce over time to maintain the survival of the species represented by the cell line.

The temperature, presence of water, typical types and proportions of atoms and molecules, and other parameters within the environment of the planet earth make it possible, in earth's natural environment, for plants to exist. A plant is a thermodynamically unstable cohesion of organic carbon-based polymers that requires the input of solar energy, in the form of sun photons, to obtain the energy needed to keep the plant body form thermodynamically stable. The laws of physics seem to dictate that, in this universe, plants can only exist on a planet with an environment similar to that of earth.

The laws of physics arbitrarily allow the spontaneous evolution of thermodynamically unstable plant body forms on the planet earth, given the parameters of the environment of the planet earth, such that these plant body forms require photon energy originating from a star in the vicinity of the planet earth to provide the energy input that keeps the plant body form continuously cohesive as an aggregate atomic and molecular structure. In this sense, a plant might be thought of as an energetically unstable energy structure in the universe.

The energy range of the quantum energy states of the plant's atoms and molecules are approximately within the energy ranges of the freezing point of water and a temperature where water is very hot but not boiling. There are also examples of lifeforms being able to live outside of these ranges. These are "mild" energy ranges, compared to the more extreme energy ranges that can be found in the universe, such as the extremely hot energy level of the sun, or the extremely low energy level of a planet like Pluto, which is billions of miles away from a star energy source. In other parts of the universe, energy equilibration reactions occur at temperatures that are far more extreme than is found on the planet earth. Black holes or super-novas are energy equilibration reactions occurring at colossally large scales of mass and energy. There are also ultra-cold environments in the universe where energy equilibration reactions occur at ultra-cold temperatures, One example is Saturn's moon Titan, where the average temperature is about -179 centigrade, leading to phenomena like frozen lakes made out of methane and rain cycles involving liquid methane as the raining liquid. On planet earth, with more moderate temperature ranges revolving around the melting point of water, water rain occurs instead.

The molecules within plants can exist because energy from the sun provides an energy input that allows these molecules to be chemically synthesized. The sun is a colossal nuclear reactor in space, that generates vast amounts of light energy by nuclear fusion of hydrogen to helium. Somehow, arbitrarily, vast amounts of hydrogen concatenated into a gigantic ball, and the gravitational force of this ball condensed the hydrogen until the sun "ignited" into a colossal nuclear power plant. Each second, the sun fuses vast quantities of hydrogen atoms (about 550 million tons of hydrogen atoms per second) into helium atoms, releasing colossal amounts of energy due to the sun's nuclear fusion process converting about 4 million tons of matter into energy each second. Energy from the sun travels to earth in the form of photons, and these photons are captured by plant leaves on earth, that use the energy from the photons to power chemical reactions that result in creation of carbon polymers called carbohydrates, that store the energy of the sun in the form of the energy contained within the atomic bonds within the plant's molecules.

The storage of the sun's energy within plants' molecules makes possible the fact that if an animal eats a plant, the animal can extract energy from the molecular bonds of the molecules contained within the plant, to help the animal to maintain the cohesion of the atoms and molecules of the animal's thermodynamically unstable body form. This results in the molecules within the animal being a store of energy. This fact in turn originates the reality on the planet earth that an animal can kill and eat another animal to gain that other animal's energy. The energy from the sun is then converted into the energy contained within food molecules, and ultimately powers the energy of life forms on the planet, since the energy of the sun can "travel up" the "food chain" towards the "apex predators" at the top of the food chain.

Predation may be thought of as an energy equilibration phenomenon occurring in the universe. A predatory animal's body becomes more unstable or dis-equilibrated thermodynamically due to a continuous decline in its body's energy level without a food energy input, which induces the predator's mind to feel the emotional pain associated with hunger or starvation. This motivates the animal to kill and eat another animal to use the energy stored within the molecules of that eaten animal to restore that predator's own energy equilibrium. If a mountain lion caught a rabbit, and the mountain lion and the rabbit could have a conversation, the conversation might go something like this:

Mountain Lion [to rabbit]: I've caught you!

Rabbit: Please don't eat me!

Mountain Lion: Don't worry. Eating you would not be anything personal. My body is a thermodynamically unstable energy form that is hungry for energy from food, and therefore is at risk of thermodynamic disintegration. Your body contains stored energy that I can consume that will help me to maintain the atomic and molecular coherence of my thermodynamically unstable body form. Therefore, eating you is simply an automated energy equilibration reaction occurring in the universe.

Rabbit: But if you eat me alive I will scream in horror!

Mountain Lion: It would not be adaptive for me to care about that. [bites rabbit]

Rabbit: [screams in horror, then, after a few more bites, dies.]

Mountain Lion: [after eating rabbit] Well, that rabbit's suffering is over. His body is now disintegrated to the point where its atoms are not coherent enough to be conscious of anything. Briefly, his body passed through moments of Planck time when the quantum energy states of his body's atoms and molecules were configured such as to make the rabbit scream with feelings of horror. But now that these Planck time moments and their corresponding quantum energy states have passed, he is too disintegrated for his existence to any longer be relevant. He was so delicious! It was merciful of the forces of natural selection to have evolved my gene line such that as an offspring of that gene line I would not feel feelings of guilt every time I ate a rabbit this way, or else I would soon become exhibit A in the psyche ward.

The pre-biotic earth was continuously bathed in energy contained within photons coming from the sun. The laws of physics seem to cause lifeforms to automatically generate if a solar power source provides photon energy to a planet such that the temperature range on the planet is within the range of the freezing point of water and the temperature range where water is hot but not boiling. Without this "free solar energy," these initial lifeforms, generated by the "earth as womb," could not emerge into existence. The apparent fact that all lifeforms need a free solar energy input, or some other source of free net energy, in order to originally come into existence, implies that life is intrinsically thermodynamically unstable without a continuous input of energy. No life-form is known that can exist without a continuous input of energy to power its existence. This implies that life in general is thermodynamically unstable, which shows why all motile life forms must show a behavioral or thinking pattern that makes the life forms position themselves where there is an energy source.

Since all matter consists of forms of energy, and since matter, according to string theorists, is made up of incredibly tiny bits of vibrating strings of energy, then living cells, themselves being made up of vibrating strings of energy, are themselves clusters of energy. These living cell energy clusters might arise spontaneously in the universe in local environments in the universe where the universe is locally in a state of energy disequilibrium, such that the universe can only re-equilibrate itself in that local volume of space by spontaneously concatenating an energy cluster in the form of an organic reproducing cell. Ironically, that cell itself is thermodynamically unstable, even though the cell emerges as part of an automated tendency of the universe to equilibrate itself in response to a local state of energy disequilibrium. Through a continuous input of energy, probably solar energy, but also possibly chemical energy, that original thermodynamically unstable organic cell was able to maintain its thermodynamically unstable energy-matter form, and then reproduce that energy-matter form to ensure the survival of that form.

DNA, the genetic blueprint of lifeforms, is commonly thought of as an information source, that provides information determining which protein synthesis reactions occur in a living organism to create that organisms's structures. However, DNA might also more fundamentally thought of as a director of the energy structure of the organic body energy form, or an "informational director of energy structure," more fundamentally than an "informational director of protein structure." A structural protein, by being made of matter, is also a form of energy, and protein structures that help to form the body are part of a cohesion of sub-atomic particles that may be thought of as a thermodynamically unstable energy cluster. DNA directs protein synthesis, but more fundamentally, it directs the structuring of the thermodynamically unstable energy cluster that forms a living being's body. DNA not only directs the protein structure of an organism, but affects how this protein structure absorbs, from the environment, the water molecules and inorganic minerals that are needed to complete the formation of the organism as a matter cluster with its own specific thermodynamic energy equilibrium properties.

If the resulting thermodynamically unstable energy cluster, or specimen of a species, located at a specified epoch and range of position points on the planet earth, cannot locate and occupy a life-support niche on the planet earth, by which the energy cluster can extract energy from the environment to maintain the cohesion of its thermodynamically unstable body form, and then use the time while surviving to reproduce that specimen's genes, then that specimen will die (or, more technically, disintegrate due to its body's intrinsic thermodynamic instability not being counter-acted by a continuous input of typically food energy) before reproducing its genes. If enough specimens of that species containing a specified gene in that species die before

8

propagating that specified gene, that gene itself may be wiped out of the gene pool (Darwin, 1859; Gould, 2002; Mayr, 1982). This process is known as "natural selection," and is really a process by which the forces of evolution select which forms of thermodynamically unstable body energy forms are optimally suited for being able to occupy life-support niches on the planet earth for long enough of a time to propagate the genes that direct the plan of the thermodynamically unstable energy form, prior to the death of the body propagating the gene.

Natural selection, as a mechanism facilitating the gene evolution of a species, is essentially an energy equilibration phenomenon in the universe. The automatic movement force in the universe that is automatically driving natural selection consists of the automatic tendency of the universe to evolve towards energy equilibrium. The planet earth is a local area in the universe with an environment such that, given the laws of physics (Penrose, 2005), energy equilibration reactions in the form of natural selection phenomena can occur. Since natural selection operates on energy structures that are made of carbon-based organic molecules, natural selection can only exist, according to the laws of physics, in planetary environments where long chains of organic carbon molecules are possible, and this requires that the temperature range of the planet generally hovers between the freezing point of water and a temperature where water is very warm but not boiling, with some extremes of temperature allowed in either direction outside of this range.

Without a constant input of energy from food, those atoms and molecules of an organism's body form will not be able to maintain the numerous intra-molecular and inter-molecular bonds that keep the body together. The body will rapidly disintegrate, resulting in the death of the person's body form, followed by the rapid rotting of the body. The proof of this is simply that almost as soon as an animal dies, its body begins to disintegrate. Some of the molecular structures within the body disintegrate automatically if there is no energy input to maintain their molecular forms. Other molecular structures within the body are disintegrated within days by billions of bacteria and by large numbers of insects, and perhaps larger animal predators, eating the large amounts of stored energy contained within the molecules inside that body.

These eaters want to transfer the energy from that rotting body to their own bodies to enable their own thermodynamically unstable body-forms to maintain their atomic or molecular cohesiveness. These eaters also use this energy to reproduce their own selves, using the energy inputs from the food to concatenate atoms and molecules into their own offspring.

The digestion of the food by the body releases the energy stored within food molecules, which can be used to enable thermodynamically unstable molecular structures within the body to continue to exist, and powers the heart, which pumps blood that distributes nutrients to the body's cells, and which also powers the immune system, which is the body's intelligent process of attacking and destroying any bacteria or viruses that try to attack the body's molecular structures to siphon the body's energy that is stored in those molecules.

The chemical reactions that occur in the human body that result in proteins and fats to be synthesized, and that allow the body to perform work, such as pitching a baseball, tend to be energetically unfavorable. These unfavorable bio-chemical reactions can occur, however, if another chemical reaction occurs simultaneously that releases energy, and then this energy can be used to power the unfavorable chemical reaction. The basic energy-providing molecule in the body is called Adenosine Tri-Phosphate, or ATP. Solar power from the sun ultimately powers the synthesis of ATP molecules, that then can move around the body to locations where energy is needed locally to power a bio-chemical reaction, to provide energy for that reaction. This one major rationale as to why the body requires solar energy to be able to function, and is also the origin of the concept that the human (and all other mammalian) minds must continuously search for food, because food molecules store in their atomic bond energies the solar energy of the sun, which can then be harnessed to produce ATP. ATP is the main unit or "currency" of energy within the human body.

The sun that warms planet earth arbitrarily exists at the position in the universe where it exists. The earth's sun also arbitrarily exists at the specific time, after the birth of the universe, that the sun exists. The distance of planet earth from the sun (approximately

93 million miles) is also arbitrary. The wattage or energy output of the sun is also arbitrary. By coincidence, the wattage from the sun that reaches earth keeps the planet earth at a temperature range makes possible the chemical synthesis of chains of carbon-based molecules such as carbohydrates and fats, or chains of protein molecules consisting mostly of carbon, hydrogen, oxygen and nitrogen. The laws of physics make it possible for brains, which are thinking devices, to evolve, that are made up of these organic molecules. The earth also, by coincidence, is of a gravity that allows the earth to retain an atmosphere, which protects these organic molecules from cosmic radiation that would normally destroy the molecules, and also possesses a magnetic field that also protects these organic molecules from cosmic radiation that can also blow away earth's atmosphere.

These physics parameters result in the planet earth being like an "isolated chemical reaction vessel" in space that continuously generates chains of organic carbon-based molecules, using carbon, nitrogen, oxygen and hydrogen atoms that exist on the planet earth, with such chemical generation activity being powered mostly by the watt energy of the sun. These organic molecules also differ from one another by tiny, gradual differences in the energy levels of their molecules, which results in subtle "shades of energy" among the molecules of the planet earth. One basis of this gradation is that a single sugar molecule can combine with another sugar molecule to form a simple carbohydrate, and another sugar molecule can be added to this, over an over again, with each added sugar molecule slightly changing the total energy content of the carbohydrate. A similar gradation due to molecular sub-unit addition exists with fats and proteins. These result in subtle differences in the energy content, and therefore the nutritional value, of various living organic plants and animals on the planet earth. This leads correspondingly to subtle or precise differences among plants and animals in terms of how they seek out food and what foods they eat. The isolation of the earth as a point-mass consisting of a chemical reaction vessel of specified parameters of atomic proportions, temperature ranges and solar energy input, with a gravitational force that pulls these atoms in proximity with one another, causes the synthesis of the specific range of molecules on the planet earth, and this range of molecules found on the planet earth in turn dictates much of the "chemistry environment" or "natural environment" of the planet earth. The general common sense phenomena that trees exist, the sky is blue on a clear day, insects buzz around, etc., result from these parameters and the resulting natural environment.

The environment of the planet earth can be described (very generally and simplistically) as one where the temperature range of the planet revolves around the freezing and melting points of water, with an average temperature ranging from -40 to +45 degrees Celsius, give or take, with an atmosphere consisting mostly of nitrogen with some oxygen, with a magnetic field and atmosphere that protects the planet from most ultra-violet rays, which allows organic polymers of carbon, called carbohydrates, proteins and fats to exist, and a phenomenon called photosynthesis to exist, which makes plants, that appear green to the human eye, possible. Sun photons provide energy that enables plants to maintain their thermodynamically unstable body forms, and animals also exist, that eat the plants to get the stored energy in the plants, so that the animals in turn can maintain the existence of their own thermodynamically unstable body forms. The organic polymers of carbon that make life possible exist due to the high amount of raw atomic materials (particularly carbon, nitrogen, oxygen and hydrogen) existing on the planet earth, and these polymers can be synthesized and be molecularly stable due to the ambient temperature range of planet earth, which hovers around the freezing and melting temperature ranges of water. The planet earth is such that the atmosphere appears blue to the non-color-blind human mind, which makes possible writings and poems by humans in which the blueness of the sky is emphasized. Trees are also possible on this planet, due partly to the existence of wood, which consists mostly of vast quantities of molecular cellulose, which makes possible the common perception that trees exist, and poetic statements such as "I think that I shall never see a poem lovely as a tree." Essentially, all of the chemical reactions and physics phenomenon that typically occur on the planet earth, given the atom and molecule types and proportions on the planet and the various temperatures and pressure ranges at which these reactions occur, create the informational environment of the planet. Each planet has different parameters that affect which chemical

12

reactions and physical phenomenon occur on the respective planet, such that each planet has its own informational environment, and these environments can be predicted systematically by scientists when the scientists are given the parameters.

There are big differences between the environments of the planet earth versus, as an example, the planet mars. Mars has a minimal atmosphere and a minimal magnetic field, so it is bombarded by ultra-violet radiation. Carbon polymers cannot exist on mars due to the radiation that prevents organic carbon polymer formation. Carbon polymers might in theory exist in the soil below mars' surface, where the soil may be thick enough to protect the carbon polymers from disintegration due to ultraviolet radiation from the sun. The daily temperature range of mars is very wide, ranging from -125 to 20 degrees Celsius, which prevents organic life from occurring on mars, unless there is some bacterial life living deeply in martian soil. Much of mars is covered by iron oxide rust, giving the planet's soil and atmosphere a red color. The poem "roses are red and violets are blue" would not be conceivable as a literally plausible concept on the planet mars, where the laws of physics prohibit the existence of flowers in the natural environment of the planet, but can be conceived as such on the planet earth, where flowers can exist given the earth's natural planetary chemical and physics parameters.

Minds must exist on planets, because planets are the only environments in the universe that, so far as is known, are parameterized such as to permit liquid water to exist, and to permit the synthesis of the long-chain carbon-based molecules (proteins, fats and carbohydrates) that, so far as is known, are required for bodies and the minds attached to these bodies to exist and to function. Planets are essentially isolated point masses in space, formed due to gravity pushing vast amounts of matter towards the center of the mass, and concatenating vast amounts of matter into spherical or ellipsoid matter clusters in space. The chemical reactions that occur on the planet dictates the informational environment of the planet, or what informational inputs the planet projects to whatever minds exist on the planet.

An interesting fact about the environment of planets is that relatively few parameters determine the informational environment on planets. The gravity force, atmosphere presence, types and proportion of atoms and molecules on the planet, magnetic field presence, distance from a nearby star, and the energy watt output of that star (or stars), essentially dictate the entire informational environment of that planet. These few variables can be described and quantified, which allows a scientist to understand the environment of a planet in a reductionist way. Chemists and physicists can predict what chemical and physical reactions occur on the planet using this information, and can predict what kind of planetary environment that will result from these reactions. The environment of the planet provides the energy inputs, in the form of information, that minds can detect, and that form the "conscious awareness" that a mind possesses of various facets of the information environment of a planet. A substantial amount of "conscious awareness" can be understood in a reductionist way because the planetary informational inputs projected to minds on the planet can themselves be understood and predicted in a reductionist way.

A Technical Definition
of Thought

What is a "thought?" George Boole, the inventor of Boolean algebra, entitled his 1854 book, that introduced his ideas of logic, as "An Investigation into the Laws of Thought." This book was perhaps viewed by the readers at the time as being a pompous, impractical theoretical exercise due to the book's presumptuous implication that Boole's logic gates could explain, or be used to replicate, human thought. However, a century later, Boole's logic system became the basis for designing electronic computers, when it was realized that electric circuits or microscopic transistors could be arranged into thousands or millions of physical manifestations of boolean logic gates, that channel electrons such that the electrons generate computational results (Shannon, 1948). Of course, as complex as computers seem, they do not seem to exactly replicate human thought.

To define what a "thought" is in a reductionist way, a thought should be defined as a phenomenon of the laws of physics, and defined in terms of the behavior of molecular, atomic or sub-atomic particles. A "thought" is a result of a flow of particles, which can be atomic, sub-atomic, molecular, or macroscopic particles, through a circuit or conduit or a relay pathway, such that the particles flow to some kind of node or location within the circuit or conduit or relay pathway, such that a "movement or motion" of some kind results due to the flow of particles at that node point within the circuit or conduit or relay pathway. A "thought" is that "movement or motion" that occurs as a result of particles flowing through a specific node in a circuit, conduit or relay pathway.

Technically, according to this definition of what is a thought, an electric light bulb lighting up is a thought. Electrons, powered by a voltage differential, flow through a closed circuit to the light bulb, which is a node in the circuit, such as to cause motion in the lightbulb, with the motion manifesting as light emanating from the light bulb, caused by the friction of electrons crowding through the filament of the lightbulb. The thought, which is the light bulb's light-projecting "motion," is the result of the electrons flowing through the node. Also, if water flows in a river, and the water flows into a large rock in the river, and the rock divides the flow of the river water in two, this division of the water flow where that rock is in the river is also a thought. This would imply that it is possible to design a calculator or other Boolean logic gate circuit using water flowing through conduits that are inter-connected like a circuit. A relay-chain of dominos falling onto one another, such that dominos at one point in the chain fall onto a ball, and make the ball roll around the floor, generates a thought, in the form of the rolling ball occurring after the dominos contact the ball and make it roll. Technically, this definition of a thought also implies that a Boolean logic gate is also a thought-generating entity. For example, a light bulb circuit can be designed as a Boolean logic circuit with two parallel switches, such that if either switch is connected, the light bulb lights up, illustrating a Boolean "OR" logic gate. By this definition of what is a thought, Boole was right after all; his laws really are the laws of thought.

A matter-based thought-generating mechanism can generate mathematical patterns. A Galton Board is one example. This is a device where there is a top column where tiny balls are inserted. At the bottom of the column, the balls hit a metal spoke, which makes the balls either fall to the left or to the right, with a 50/50 chance of either outcome. On either side, left or right, there is another metal spoke that the ball hits, which also gives the ball the ability to fall either to the left or the right, with a 50/50 chance of either outcome occurring. After the ball hits the second spoke, on either the left or right sides of that second spoke there is another spoke, and so on. The many balls fall through many vertical levels of spokes, until each ball ends up at the bottom of the board, in various positions from the left side to the right side of the board, depending on where the spokes made the balls move. This device statistically tends to make the balls fall so that the balls form a statistical Bell curve distribution pattern of balls at the bottom of the Galton board. The balls fall through conduits and nodes to eventually form a mathematical pattern in this thought-generating mechanical device. Another example of a thought-generating machine that generates mathematical patterns is Charles Babbage's Difference Engines Nos. 1 and 2, which were mechanical calculators, made up of large numbers of metallic gears and other parts, that Babbage invented in the 19th century.

More complex thoughts, such as a computer playing chess or backgammon, or a shark thinking that it wants to kill and eat a mackerel, require more complicated thought-conducting circuit and node architecture than a simple lightbulb circuit. However, the basic principle is the same, that the thought results from thought-conducting particles moving through a node (or multiple nodes) within circuits.

In order for a thought "motion" to occur, energy is required. Energy is also required for the motion to be continually occurring. Hence, a light bulb only lights up as long as electrons, driven by energy, continue to flow through the circuit to the light bulb node. For example, to calculate that 2+2=4, an electrical energy potential is required to enable a computer to send electrons continuously through the nodes in its circuits that generate the "4" answer, and then the computer must send electrons continuously to a computer monitor, in order for the monitor to display the answer "4" to communicate that answer to a homo sapiens mind. If the electricity is turned off, the flow of electrons stops, no more electrons continue to flow through the nodes, and both the calculating thought of "4" and the displayed answer of "4" vanish.

17

How does the matter that conducts thoughts (such as the matter associated with synapses in the brain, or the electrons in a computer central processing unit) relate to itself such as to create a "unified thinking entity?" Thought-conducting particles, like the electrons in a computer's central processing unit, are individual, lifeless matter entities, that are dissociated from one another, except for the coincidence that they are part of the same cloud of particles that flows through the same circuit towards the same node. Yet, these electrons function as a "cohesive thinking whole" where the individual electrons are "inter-related with one another" such as to create a computer mind that is a "unified thinking entity," made up of a cloud of electrons flowing across the logic gates of the computer's central processing unit, all along one single electric circuit. Where does the "unity of the electron cloud as a thinking entity" come from fundamentally? What happens to this electron-cloud thinking unity in a computer when the computer is turned off? A similar question might be, how can the electrons that flow across a simple lightbulb electric circuit make the lightbulb illuminate, and have a cohesive unity as a "cohesive cloud of electrons that functions to make a lightbulb illuminate?"

With respect to the lightbulb circuit and the corresponding lightbulb lighting up to create a "thought," the "cohesiveness of the electron cloud as an entity causing the lightbulb to light," comes from the fact that a continuous flow of electrons, powered by the energy of a voltage difference between the positive and negative terminals of the circuit, moves through the circuit. Each electron is an individual entity, but each electron is related to the other electron because each electron is being "pushed forward" by another electron behind it. Electrons flowing across the lightbulb filament will randomly bang into atoms and molecules in the filament, generating friction that generates light photons emanating from the filament. As soon as one electron moves through the entire filament and exits from the filament, that one electron no longer participates in the "functionality of making the filament generate light photons." However, because another electron is behind that one, and more electrons behind that other one, there is a continuous flow of electrons, each connected with one another because each is "pushing" one another, and the continuous flow of the electrons is the factor that makes the filament continuously emit light. Once the flow of electrons stops, the filament stops emanating light. The "cohesiveness of the electron cloud as an entity causing the lightbulb to light" may be an illusion. The electrons are not communicating with one another. They are simply being "pushed along" the circuit, with the result of the lightbulb lighting, without the electrons being "coherent," in the sense of being a "unified, soulful lightbulb-lighting team."

A computer central processing unit, like the lightbulb circuit, is also one continuous electric circuit. Like the lightbulb circuit, the computer can only generate thoughts, in this case mathematical computer thoughts (compared to the thought of emanating light as with the lightbulb), as long as electrons continuously flow through the computer's silicon logic gates. As with the lightbulb, each electron flows only once through the circuit and then must be replaced by another electron pushing that electron from behind. A continuous flow of electrons is required for the computer to continuously keep in mind a computed result. Each electron is its own particle, being pushed along by a voltage difference or by the electron behind it. The cloud can result in computerized mathematical results or thoughts, but the matter particles making up the computer's thinking cloud are fragmented or isolated from one another. The only rationale that one can think of for defining this cloud of electrons as a "unified computer-thought-generating entity" is that the electrons are all related to one another because they are all being pushed along the computer silicon logic gates by the same basic voltage differential or by "an electron behind each other electron." This is not a convincing rationale.

Given that there may be no way to define how thought-conducting molecules forming a "unified thinking entity or cloud," there may not be a difference in the "conscious awareness" of a computer that outputs its responses based on a vast database of pre-programmed responses, and a pattern-thinking computer. For example, a computer can be programmed to optimally play backgammon by memorizing every one of the 10^{20} backgammon board patterns and responses to the backgammon dice, and then choosing the best play of the dice by matching a current position and dice roll to the database that shows the best way to play the dice. Or, the computer can use a patterned way to calculate what would be the best move in a position, given the roll of the dice. In either situation, the electrons that generate the computer's optimal backgammon thought move are individually isolated from one another, and may not be functioning as a "cohesive thinking cloud." In other words, a computer that generates outputs by using patterned thought is no more "consciously aware" than one that generates outputs by using brute force.

A Technical Definition
of Mind

A "mind" is a thought-generating mechanism made of matter. A mind is a mechanism that sends energy, of some form, through a conduit, circuit or a relay pathway, to a node or a position point within the conduit, circuit or relay pathway, such that, when energy passes through that node, a movement or motion of some kind results, and this movement is by definition a "thought." This definition of mind is broad. A lightbulb circuit, such as where electrons flow from a negative battery terminal to a positive battery terminal in a copper wire circuit, and pass through a lightbulb and cause the lightbulb to emanate light photons, is technically a "mind," and the light bulb lighting up is a "thought." Electrons flowing through a computer central processing unit (CPU) generate large numbers of thoughts, which are often complexly mathematical, and the "system" by which there is a flow of electrons through silicon logic gates in a CPU, is itself a "mind." A relaying chain of dominos falling onto one another, that relays the energy of the previous domino to the next, such that the terminal domino falls onto an unsprung mousetrap, and makes the mousetrap snap, is a mind, and the snapping mousetrap is a thought resulting from that mind. A single bacterium of E. coli contains a mind if, for example, that when a molecular detector on the outside surface of that bacterium detects a ribose sugar molecular, this detection results in energy being relayed from that detector to a motion-inducing flagellum in the bacterium, and then this causes the bacterium to swim towards the direction of increasing concentrations (Montagnes, 2008) of ribose sugar molecules, to consume the nutritious ribose molecules.

Another example of a mind is a common children's toy where a marble is dropped at the top of the toy, and the marble travels down a pathway, and eventually passes into and through a plastic paddle-wheel, and makes the paddle-wheel spin, after which the marble drops down into a holder bin at the bottom of the toy. Here, the toy is a mind because it is a thought-generating entity, and the thought that it generates is the spinning plastic paddle wheel. The thought-conducting particle is the marble, which travels down a tubular plastic conduit or pathway towards the nodes in the pathways that contain the plastic paddle wheel. The thought-generating mechanism is powered initially by the child raising the marble to the top of the toy to drop the marble into the toy, and then gravitational energy powers the marble down the plastic conduit, and provides the marble's energy that spins the paddle-wheel. The toy mind has no memory structure, and to keep its thoughts being generated (i.e. to keep the paddle wheels spinning), the child must continuously pump marbles into the toy.

With an organic mind like the human brain, the thought-conducting particles are not so much electrons but calcium and sodium ions at synapses, and neurotransmitter molecules, although there is also an electron cloud of electricity flowing across neurons between each synapse node. Somehow, these independent molecular particles develop a "unity of a thinking cloud" that generates thoughts, but the thought-functionality of a human brain is not understood as precisely as is the thought-functionality of a computer mind, given that human engineers know exactly how to design a computer, but not how to design a human brain. However, given that the ions, electrons and neurotransmitters that conduct mammalian brain thoughts are also made of

22

individual particles of lifeless matter, how can this "thinking cloud of lifeless matter particles" in the organic brain by any more "unified" as a thinking entity than the electron cloud in a computer mind? Both the organic mind and the computer mind consists of a "thinking cloud" made up of individual particles, and with the case of the computer, it is difficult to define how these individual electron clouds are cohesively unified into a thought-generating mind. If the computer electron cloud is not unified, how can the organic mind neurotransmitter/electron cloud be unified?

A single bacterium of E. coli can have proteins called methyl-accepting chemotaxis proteins (MCP) on the surface of the bacterium (Salah Ud-Din, 2017; Galperin, 2018). If a molecule that can be a nutrient to the E. coli, such as a sugar molecular like a ribose or galactose molecule, touches an MCP molecule on the E. coli surface, the MCP molecule will in an automated way change shape. This molecular shape change alters the energy level of the MCP molecule, such that the MCP molecule sends a signal to the inside of the E. coli bacterium. That signal then causes other bio-chemical reactions and changes that ultimately cause the E. coli flagellum, which is the molecular motor of the E. coli, to molecularly move such as to create a force that makes the E. coli move towards the source of the nutrient. The E. coli bacterium could have evolved such that, when an MCP molecule detects a ribose molecule, the E. coli does not do anything. Or, the E. coli bacterium could have evolved such that, when an MCP molecule detects a ribose molecule, the E. coli flagella pushes the bacterium towards great concentrations of the nutrient. If the E. coli bacterium moves towards the nutrient, the E. coli bacterium will be able to absorb more molecules of the nutrient, which will provide energy to the E. coli bacterium. The E. coli bacterium can use this energy to prevent its thermodynamically unstable body form from disintegrating and dying.

With a domino relay chain "mind," the energy that initially powers the domino chain comes from a human finger pushing the first domino of the chain, so that the first domino tips over. After the first domino tips over, gravitational energy provides the power to keep the relay chain of dominos tipping over, such that the first domino falls into the next domino, which also tips over, and so on, until the chain of falling dominos reaches a node within the chain of falling dominos where a thought or some kind of matter movement results. A manual typewriter is also a mind mechanism, that generates thoughts in the form of a letters inked on a page, such that a human finger both originates the energy that starts the thought-generating mechanism, and also provides all of the energy that powers the mechanism that generates the thought.

However, a human finger power source is not the only kind of power source that can provide the initial energy that is needed to originate the generation of a thought, and/or the total energy that is needed to result in the thought. Different power sources can initiate power to minds, and continue to power the minds, such as a voltage differential that powers an electric light bulb circuit mind. With a computer mind, the energy that initiates a computer thought consists of an electronic input of some kind, such as where a human inputs "2+3=?" on a computer keyboard, and then a human-created electrical power source powers the transition from the initial input to the generation of the thought answer of "5." An organic mind is different from these other mind examples, in that the energy that originates a thought often comes from the environment of the planet on which the organic mind exists. For example, light energy emanating from a nearby banana may be inputted by light energy inputting molecular photoreceptors in an organism's eye, and this ultimately may result in a thought that the person seeing the banana wants to eat the banana. Energy within the body may amplify this initial light energy signal to power that signal's movement to the brain processing nodes within neuron circuits that generate the thought to eat a banana.

A mind can be a molecular structure capable of object awareness. Object awareness is the ability of an energy-receiving mechanism to react, in an atomically or molecularly or sub-atomically patterned way, to an energy fingerprint (or a distinctive pattern of energy) that emanates from an object, such that the specific unique energy fingerprint emanated from and associated with that object causes the sensory mechanism to relay energy to a node within a circuit, conduit or relaying mechanism. Objects in the environment of the planet project energy, such as when photons of various light frequency values emanate from objects, or sound energy emanates from objects. The

24

energy that emanates from specific objects may be patterned in such a differentiated way such as to be an "energy fingerprint" that is uniquely associated with that object or category of objects.

Light energy, that hits photoreceptors in organic organisms, results from photons, of different combinations of frequency values and intensities, reflecting off of objects in the environment, and projecting energy to the photoreceptors in organic organisms. When photons, which mostly originate from the sun, reflect off objects, the objects reflect combinations of different photon energy levels. These combinations of photon energy levels, which the mind perceives as combinations of colors of various brightness levels, tend to form a light energy pattern or "fingerprint" that enables identification of specific objects, reflecting specific patterns of light energies, at a distance from the mind observing the objects.

Although the energy difference between two colors may be extremely small, the molecules in the eye that detect light energy can be energetically influenced by these tiny energy levels. These photon energies are too small to influence more than the sight molecules that the photons contact, so the body must expend energy to amplify the signals to relay the visual signals to the brain, and then the brain must expend energy to process the signals. All of these energy interactions involved with inputting a light energy "fingerprint" from an object alter the energy levels or the quantum energy states of the atoms and molecules in that organism and in that organism's brain, in ways that, theoretically, are precisely and predictably parametrizable by the laws of physics. Energies that cause signals to be generated at taste receptors, touch receptors, ear ossicles, or smell receptors are also similarly tiny and require energy expenditure by the organism to amplify the signals to send them to the brain for processing, and also affect the total quantum energy state of the organism and the organism's mind, in strictly parametrizable ways.

The light energy fingerprint that emanates from two different objects, such as a rock and a banana, are both tiny in energy and similar in energy magnitude. Because of this, the amount of usable food energy in an object does not necessary correlate with the amount of energy emanated from its light fingerprint. For a human, a banana contains far more usable food energy compared to a rock, since the human digestive system cannot digest rocks but can digest bananas. Therefore, the visual system does not directly detect the food energy contained within an object, and does not detect the total nuclear energy contained within the atoms and molecules of the object. Instead, the visual system detects the specific light fingerprint of an object, and this light fingerprint can be used to visually identify the object, but then this object must cognitively be associated with an axiomatic understanding of whether or not, as an axiom, this object can be consumed to obtain food energy from the object.

Sound is also a form of energy, that emanates from vibrating atoms and molecules and is conducted through a non-vacuum medium, typically air, to an animal ear, where the sound energy, which is small in magnitude, vibrates ear ossicles that are sensitive to tiny amounts of sound energy. These ossicles then conduct the sound energy signals to nerves that then expend energy to relay the signal to the sound processing centers of the brain. Sound energy can emanate from an object with enough uniqueness of a sound energy pattern and intensity to also function as a sound energy "fingerprint" that can help to distinguish one object from another. If a species of animal cannot speak, but can hear, that animal can use the natural sounds emanated from objects in its environment as sound energy fingerprints to help identify an object based on the sound that the object makes under various physical circumstances. Birds have distinctive singing patterns that can be used to identify the type of bird, and various insects and toads emanate differentiating sound patterns. Being able to identify an object's sound fingerprint can be adaptive, because this can alert a creature of the existence of a predator, a food item, water, or other life support assets.

Organic minds can identify specific objects on the planet if those objects emit sound energy such that the sound energy is unique enough in its mathematical characteristics as to be uniquely associated with the object emitting that sound energy fingerprint. A waterfall emits a unique sound fingerprint continuously, as do rivers, and oceans when they emit a sound as waves oscillate at the beach. A rock can emit a unique sound identifying it as a rock if the rock is in motion, but a rock standing still does not emit a uniquely identifying sound. Many birds emit sound energy fingerprints that a mind can use to identify the species of bird emitting the sound fingerprint. However, not every object in nature emits an identifying sound energy fingerprint, or emits that sound fingerprint continuously.

A species of animal that can speak is at an advantage, since that talking species does not have to rely exclusively on natural sound energy fingerprints, which are infrequently and inconsistently generated in the natural earth environment, to be able to identify objects based on their sound. Instead, the talking species can use language to generate its own set of sound fingerprints that the species associates with different specific objects. A talking species can alert one another of the existence of a non-sound-emitting object, such as a table, by speaking the agreed-upon standard sound fingerprint that has been assigned to that object. Otherwise, the existence of that object cannot be known based on its sound energy fingerprint, if there are no natural forces inducing that object to emit a sound. Talking mimics and expands upon the natural phenomena of sound fingerprints being emanated from objects in the environment. After evolving the ability to detect natural sound fingerprints, a foundation of a sound energy fingerprint detecting structure exists in the genes of a species, which can be used as a foundation for evolution of a sound-assigning or language capability, if a physical ability to generate a wide range of sound patterns also evolves in a species, such as by possessing vocal chords and a hyoid bone.

A common-sense perception among humans is to think of thoughts as "words or sentences that appear in the either the conscious or the sub-conscious." However, words and sentences are not the thinking thoughts themselves but are thoughts resulting from the thinking thoughts. Those thinking thoughts are intuitively generated. That is, thoughts, due to particles flowing to certain nodes within a human neural network, may represent a result or conclusion of some kind, but the flow of particles at those "result-generating or conclusion-generating nodes," itself triggers a motion in the form of a flow of thought-conducting particles to other neural network nodes that generate the verbal representation of the thinking thought. The purpose of language, or the translation of intuitive thoughts into words, is mainly to facilitate

27

communication between members of the same species. People also use language to articulate in words what they are thinking intuitively, so that they can repeat to themselves the thought represented in words, so that they can think in a more concentrated way about whether or not this articulated thought makes sense. This is because the intuition is sometimes wrong, but intuitive thoughts are produced too quickly for the mind to be consciously aware of if they are incorrect or not; by articulating some of those thoughts in words, a person can think more precisely about whether or not these articulated thoughts are incorrect. The mind does not convert most intuitive thoughts into words because this is more energy-consuming than simply generating thoughts intuitively.

Odor molecules, and food molecules, can fit into odor detecting and taste bud molecular detectors, respectively, such as to induce an energy level change in odor or taste detecting energy inputting molecular mechanisms. The magnitude of this energy level change can also be relatively unique for the type of odor or taste molecule, providing an energy fingerprint that can help to identify a specific objects.

Touch energy can also be uniquely associated with different objects, and provide a touch energy fingerprint that helps a mind to identify the object. Touch energy can be relayed to touch sensitive nerves in the skin. Organic minds have evolved to feel a pointy touch to be painful, because a pointy touch is associated with a dangerous breaking or penetrating of the skin, which can lead to infection. A pointy touch can be associated with the sensation of a stinging or biting insect, or a predator biting a creature using sharp teeth. Touch energy tends also to be small in magnitude, but the body expends energy to amplify the touch signal and relay that signal to the brain for processing.

All of these energy inputs directly change the quantum energy states of a body's atoms and molecules by directly applying energy to the body, and by inducing the body to expend energy to amplify the resulting sensory signals to relay those signals to the brain. The process of the signals also requires energy and alters the quantum energy states of the body and the mind attached to the body. These alterations are in theory predictable and strictly parametrizable, based on how the laws of physics govern what possible quantum energy states are possible in the atoms and molecules of an organic body that contains a mind.

The general rationale as to why the five senses evolved is that the objects in the environment that emanate energy can be detected based on the energy fingerprints that these objects project to the sight, sound, taste, touch and smell energy receptors of the five senses; these energy fingerprints help an organism's mind to estimate the energy level of that object, and also to predict, to some extent, if the object can be eaten and become a source of energy to enable the organism's thermodynamically unstable energy form to maintain its atomic and molecular cohesiveness. Also, the organism can detect if the object is in fact another organism that wants to eat it, to know to get away from that predator.

In a mind that is capable of object awareness, the pathway of thought-conducting particles can consist of a relaying chain of atoms and molecules that connects to a node, or a conduit or circuit through which sub-atomic particles or atoms or molecules move toward that node. When a node is energetically altered due to particles passing through the node, or due to a relaying chain of atoms or molecules sending energy to that node, some kind of atom-based or sub-atomic-particle-based "motion," that is, a "thought," results. This motion is ultimately induced by the specific energy fingerprint emanated by that specific object to the sensory mechanism, that initiated the signal that ultimately reached the node in the circuit.

The molecular mechanism in the E. coli bacterium, that receives an energy "fingerprint" from a ribose molecule, relays the energy from that fingerprint through a molecular relay or conduit to a node within a circuit, such that energy passing through that node within the circuit causes the E. coli flagellum to move the E. coli bacterium towards greater concentrations of ribose molecules, is itself a "mind." The activation of the E. coli flagellum is itself a "thought."

An object-detecting "mind" might be defined as an atomic, molecular or sub-atomic mechanism, powered by energy, that contains an atomic, molecular or sub-atomic energy receiver mechanism, that receives an energy input, where said energy input causes a change in the quantum energy state of the energy receiver, where this change in the energy state of the energy receiver occurs in an automated, patterned way, as is dictated by the laws of physics, and where this change in the energy state of the energy receiver is differentiated enough for that degree of change in the energy state in that type of energy receiver to be associated uniquely with the type of object that generated the energy input that caused the change in the energy receiver, such that this energy signal is relayed, in a relaying way that may or may not require inputs of energy beyond the energy inputs imparted by the energy fingerprint of the object, such that the relaying of the signal causes energy to flow across a node within a molecular relaying pathway or circuit, such that a "thought" of movement of some kind is generated as a result of energy passing through that node.

The energy input that initiates the passage of thought-conducting particles through conduits to nodes such as to generate a thought consists of the energy fingerprint emanating from objects, in a mind that is capable of object awareness. This energy source, that initiates the thought of the object-aware mind, is different from, for example, the energy source that powers an electric lightbulb circuit "mind" mechanism that generates a thought in the form a of a lightbulb lighting up, since the energy source initiating the lightbulb lighting up consists of the energy that powers electrons through the lightbulb circuit. This is also different from the energy source (the energy from a human finger push) that initiates a domino-relay-chain "mind" that generates a thought when a ball rolls when a domino bumps into the ball.

The effect, or the result, of the awareness of a mind to a specific kind of object consists of the thought or motion that results from energy passing through a node in a circuit within that mind, as a result of that mind's inputting of the energy fingerprint of that object. "Object awareness" does not mean awareness of an object in any specific way. Instead, "object awareness" consists of the ability of an object, emanating an energy fingerprint, to induce any thought, or movement occurring as a result of energy or thought-conducting particles flowing through a node, in reaction to a mind's inputting of an energy fingerprint emanating from a specific object. A mind is aware of a specific object simply if it has any arbitrary thought reaction to detecting that specific object.

A mind can consist of a set of sensory inputting molecular mechanisms, that can, collectively, receive energy fingerprint patterns from a set of objects existing in the environment of the mind that is made up of this set of sensory inputting molecular mechanisms, such that the energy fingerprint emanating from any specific object, capable of being detected by a molecular mechanism within this set, causes the molecular mechanism that inputs an energy fingerprint from that object, to relay energy through a molecular pathway (either via a conduit of thought-conducting particles or via a molecular relaying mechanism) to a node within that pathway, such that a thought, that is, some kind of molecular movement, possibly leading to a macroscopic physical movement by the body attached to that mind, results from energy passing through that node within that pathway. It would be evolutionarily adaptive if the thoughts resulting from the inputting of specific object fingerprints contributed to the improvement of the ability of the body attached to that mind to survive and reproduce.

Also, the passage of energy through the node, in response to the detection of the object energy fingerprint, may result in energy being relayed through another pathway to another node, such as to result in an emotional reaction being experienced by that mind in response to detection of that object fingerprint. It would also be evolutionarily adaptive if the emotions resulting from the inputting of the respective object fingerprints contributed to the improvement of ability of the body attached to that mind to survive and reproduce.

In addition, the passage of energy through the node, in response to the detection of the object energy fingerprint, may also result in energy being relayed through another pathway to another node, such as to result in a thought pertaining to an object that does not exist in reality nearby the organism. It would also be evolutionarily adaptive if the abstract or imaginary thoughts resulting from the inputting of the respective object fingerprints improved the ability of the body attached to that mind to survive and reproduce.

An organic mind's thought reaction to a specific object, that is, the "motion" resulting from that object's energy fingerprint ultimately causing energy to pass through a node in a neuron circuit, may have a useful effect on the organic body attached to that organic mind. By "useful effect" is meant that the thought may contribute to the survival and/or gene reproduction of the body attached to that organic mind. If this happens, that mind's reaction to the object is evolutionarily adaptive. Humans have evolved to typically and subjectively think that such a mind's reaction to that specific object is "rational, logical and useful," due to a typical human tendency to judge behaviors that improve another human's survival and/or gene reproduction to be "rational, logical and useful."

Humans typically expect that a human who is considered to be "sane" and not "mentally handicapped" would generally have "rational, logical and useful" reactions to objects that a human perceives, with such reactions being those that improve survival and reproduction. For example, if a "sane" human observes an apple, it would be perceived as being "rational, logical and useful," if that human asks itself whether or not that human is hungry and feels like eating the apple, and then eats the apple if the human is hungry and feels like eating the apple. If a "mentally handicapped" human sees the apple, and then only responds to the observation of the apple by clapping his or hands gleefully 25 times in a row, this behavior would generally be perceived as being a "non-rational, non-logical and non-useful" reaction to observing the apple. In the mind of this mentally handicapped individual, the observation of the apple induces thought-conducting particles to travel to a node within a neuron circuit in that individual's mind, such as to trigger a motion or set of motions that results in the individual clapping their hands, seemingly illogically, 25 times in a row. Both the "normal" and the "mentally handicapped" human "are aware of" and "have knowledge of" the apple, in that both can input an energy fingerprint that defines the apple as a specific, differentiated object in their minds. However, their thought reactions to the awareness of the apple are different. The specific thought reaction to the awareness of a specific object has nothing to do with the criteria by which a mind is defined as being aware of or being knowledgable of that specific object.

A subjective perception, by one human mind, of what constitutes a "rational, logical and useful" reaction, by another mind, to the observation of a specific object, is not due to an absolute standard of what is a "rational, logical and useful" reaction to a specific object. Organic minds have evolved to have reactions to specific objects that will improve the ability of the bodies attached to these minds to survive and reproduce, and not necessarily to have reactions that are "rational." The factors that determine which reactions, to which specific objects, improve the ability of a specific kind of organic mind, and the body attached to that mind, to survive and reproduce, are arbitrarily determined by the laws of physics. Human minds have also evolved to think that another organic mind's reaction, to the observation of a specific object, is "rational, logical and useful" if that reaction improves the ability of that mind, and the body attached to that mind, to survive and reproduce. The arbitrary thermodynamic characteristics of an organism arbitrarily determine what kinds of thought reactions to the detection of specific object energy fingerprints would be improve the ability of the organism to survive and reproduce. Consequently, a human perception of what is "rational, logical and useful" in how other minds react to the observations of objects, is itself an arbitrary perception.

Philosophers have asked the question, "how is it possible to know something?" To "possess knowledge of something," a mind must possess an energy-inputting mechanism that can input an energy fingerprint emanating from and differentiating an object. In addition, the mind must be structured molecularly such that the detection of the energy fingerprint pertaining to a specific object eventually results in energy being propagated to a node within a circuit, such that a motion of some kind results when energy passes through that node. A mind possesses knowledge of an object if that mind generates any motion or thought in response to the inputting of an energy fingerprint from a specific object. In typical evolved organic minds, the thought reaction to inputting an object's energy fingerprint is typically considered to be a "logical response to detecting that object," because organic minds generally evolved the ability to have adaptive thought reactions to the detection of specific object energy fingerprints, and what is "adaptive" is generally considered "logical." However, it is not necessary for a thought response to the inputting of an object energy fingerprint to be "logical" or "adaptive" for a mind to by definition "have knowledge of the object." It is only necessary that there be any thought response to the detection of the energy fingerprint of that object, in order for a mind to by definition "have knowledge of the object."

It would seem logical, as an example, that if an E. coli bacterium detects a ribose molecule, that this triggers the E. coli flagella to move the E. coli towards the direction where more ribose molecules may be encountered, based on the logic that the E. coli bacterium can improve its ability to survive and reproduce by absorbing ribose sugar molecules from its local environment and using them for energy (Bell, 2007; Montagnes, 2008). Note that, the E. coli bacterium does not consciously identify that it is detecting a ribose sugar molecule, even though it seems that the E. coli bacterium is both detecting the ribose molecule and is logically using that ribose molecule as a source of energy. Instead, the E. coli ribose-detecting mind is purely a molecular mechanism that has evolved to both detect the ribose molecule and use that molecule in a logical way, according to how the laws of physics make it possible for the E. coli bacterium to benefit energetically by detecting and absorbing the ribose molecule.

An organic mind's thoughts can consist of any "movement" that occurs as a result of thought-conducting particles moving into nodes within organic neuron circuits or pathways, such as a language representation of a thought, a body movement, an emotion, or the consumption of food or the engagement in a reproductory activity. Thoughts generated by organic minds can be broadly fit into three categories. Thoughts can belong to the category of thoughts that contribute to the propagation of genes, such as all varieties of sexual thoughts, and pleasurable emotions that are felt when reproductory activity occurs. Thoughts can also belong to a category of thoughts that contribute to the thermodynamic or energetic stability of an organism's cohesive body form, such as thoughts pertaining to the acquisition of food or shelter. Thoughts pertaining to breathing air or drinking water also fall under the category of thoughts that contribute to the thermodynamic or energy stability of the body.

Breathing air brings oxygen into the body, which is an element that is critical for enabling vast numbers of different bio-chemical reactions to occur in the body, that are necessary for making the body thermodynamically stable. Water is also a molecular matrix that permeates the body and effectively makes organic bodies into water-permeated sponges, where water creates an environment in the body that makes numerous bio-chemical reactions and physical reactions that are necessary to enable the body to be continuously thermodynamically stable. Thoughts pertaining to urination or defecation belong under the category of thoughts that contribute to the thermodynamic or energy stability of an organism's cohesive body form. The elimination of these waste products of body metabolism improves the thermodynamic stability of the organism's body. These waste products were initially generated as a result of the overall food-energy-processing mechanisms of an organism's body, since these waste products are remnants from food-energy-processing mechanisms, from which no further food-energy can be extracted for use by the body. Hence, these waste products result from the overall logical system by which this organism maintains its own thermodynamic stability. Thoughts pertaining to transportation or money-making can contribute to providing an organism access to sources of food, shelter or reproductory activity. Transportation thoughts and money-making thoughts are not separate categories of types of thoughts, but belong under the more general categories of thoughts that improve an organism's thermodynamic stability, or reproductory capabilities. Some thoughts can be platonic, or non-sexual, and may not contribute directly to improving the thermodynamic stability of an organism, such as thoughts pertaining to the playing of a board game, theoretical mathematical thoughts, or thoughts pertaining to walking alone in the woods. These thoughts are genetically evolved in different minds to serve as sources of variations of thought-generating mind activity, just in case by luck some of these thought-generating variations become adaptive.

Object Awareness:
The Basis of Conscious Awareness

A mind can be described by the number of different kinds of sensory inputting mechanisms that send energy fingerprints of different objects to that mind, and the range of objects of which that mind is capable of reacting to by developing a thought in reaction to detecting the object. A single molecular mechanism for detecting and reacting to an object is enough to constitute a "mind," although minds can also consist of multiple such mechanisms, inputting energy from a wide range of different kinds of objects. A mind can also be described by whether that mind contains sensory inputting mechanisms that require that objects be in physical contact with the sensory inputting mechanisms in order for those objects to be detected, or if objects can be detected from a distance. The former kind of mind exists mostly among sessile organisms, while the latter kind of mind exists mostly among motile organisms.

Plants are sessile, or do not move. All of the photons or molecules that are detected by the molecule or photon detection mechanisms within plants must be in physical contact with the mechanisms. A plant would not evolve eyes or ears, that can detect energy fingerprints from objects that are located far from a plant, and which would not necessarily be in physical contact with the sensory inputting mechanism of the plant, because the plant cannot move. Since the plant cannot move, the plant would not gain an evolutionary advantage by being able to detect objects at a distance, or objects that the plant is not physically contacting. This is because the plant would have no way of getting closer to these objects, in situations where directly contacting the object would improve the ability of the plant to survive or reproduce, or getting away from an object, such as if the object was a predatory animal.

Similarly, an E. coli bacterium, such as one that contains a ribose-detecting mind structure, would not evolve eyes or ears. This is because the E. coli's ability to move is extremely limited. The E. coli bacterium can only move slowly, covering microscopic distances per unit of time, and therefore has very limited ability to close the distance between it and useful objects that it detected at a distance. The E. coli bacterium, then, also has sensory inputting mechanisms that require that objects be physically in contact with the sensory inputting mechanisms, for those mechanisms to relay signals through circuits to nodes within the E. coli bacterium.

However, there are animals such as insects, fish, mammals, birds and reptiles that can move large distances in small amounts of time. It would be adaptive for such animals to evolve sensory inputting mechanisms that are capable of inputting energy emanating from objects that are not in physical contact with the sensory inputting mechanism or the animal. Here, the animal can quickly move to be in contact with objects detected from a distance using eyes, ears or smell, and gain a survival or reproduction advantage if being in contact with these objects improves the ability of the animal to survive or reproduce. The evolution of mobility in an animal species, then, is a precursor for it to be theoretically advantageous for that animal species to evolve object-detecting molecular mechanisms like eyes, noses or ears, that are capable of detecting objects located far from the animal. A sessile creature could possess touch and taste sensory inputting mechanisms, but only mobile creatures can possess eyes, noses or ears. The mobility of these animals gives them access to larger numbers of opportunities, provided by the universe generally and the earth locally, to access a wide range of different objects in the environment, and gives them the ability to access larger numbers of objects at a high rate of object access per unit of time. This makes it adaptive for such highly mobile animals to evolve the ability to detect a wide range of objects, particularly if objects may be sources of nutrition or aids in gene reproduction.

Why do only animals have brains, but plants do not have brains? Plants are non-mobile, and therefore have no use of developing strategies for survival and reproduction, and have no use of locating environments suitable for their growth. Plants receive free energy from the sun, and rely on pure luck as the factor determining if their seeds will end up on the ground in an environment that can sustain growth of those seeds. The sprouted plants use the free energy of the sun via photosynthesis to generate the molecules needed for their structures and functions and to prevent their thermodynamically unstable body forms from disintegrating. Plants must disperse vast numbers of seeds, because very few seeds through luck grow into a plant that generates more seed. The reliance on luck, with no mobility that would enable a plant to use mind-calculation to improve survival or reproduction, makes it of no advantage for a plant to posses a complex mind or brain. Animals, however, cannot use the sun's light energy for life support, in general, except for in some cases temperature regulation. Animals generally either consume energy-rich molecules from plants, or consume other animals or both. Animals require mobility to survive, and need a brain to figure out how to move the body attached to that brain to locations where energy-rich food molecules exist. Motility gives an animal the ability to avoid other objects, such as predators or dangerous geological structures like cliffs, that would reduce an animal's ability to survive or reproduce if the animal contacted such objects.

The evolution of hands and fingers, which occurs in the most refined form among homo sapiens, but also exists among primates in general and other animals such as raccoons or squirrels, increases the range of possible ways for manipulating objects and obtaining life support and gene reproduction capabilities from objects. The evolution of hands and fingers creates within a species the theoretical possibility that this species would become more adaptive if its mind evolved such as to possess thinking patterns that induce the species to use its hands in multiple different ways that would all be adaptive. For example, a primate that evolved hands that, theoretically, were physically capable of chiseling stone into hand axes, but which did not possess a cognitive ability to do this, has the potential of improving its ability to survive or reproduce if later, in its evolutionary history, it evolved the cognitive ability to know how to chisel stone into hand axes, because it previously evolved the physical ability to do this via evolution of its hands. The evolution of hands and fingers, then, provides a driver for the forces of natural selection to evolve minds that contain a more expanded library of energy-fingerprint-detecting molecular mechanisms, that permit detection of a wider range of objects, compared to organisms that do not possess hands or fingers. The gradual accumulation of the number of different object-detection abilities in a species' minds, in the timeline that species' evolutionary development, leads to increased complexity of that species' minds over evolutionary time.

Every organic mind contains a library of object-detecting molecular mechanisms, capable of detecting one object, a few objects, or a wide range of objects. Every organic mind also contains a library of axioms pertaining to what can be obtained from, and what can be done with, an object. A mind implements these axioms-pertaining-to-objects while detecting (presumably through mathematical observation of the objects) how objects change over time as things are done to or things are obtained from those objects. Generally, object-detecting capabilities, and understandings of axioms-pertaining-to-objects, is limited, in organic minds, to such capabilities and understandings that improve the ability of those organic minds to survive or reproduce. This is particularly true of organisms that show limited or no learning abilities, such as bacteria, insects or reptiles.

The homo sapiens mind is a potential exception to this generalization that minds within species tend to think homogeneously, since, unlike most non-human organic minds, the genes for the human brain evolved such that, with each subsequent fertilized human zygote, the genes encoding brain function tend to show considerable variations, such that each human zygote, including those of siblings, show variation, often extensive, in thinking and emoting styles. Variations in the cognitive structures of human minds is a trait that seems to have evolved in homo sapiens' minds. The evolutionary purpose of evolving minds with variations in thinking ability between each mind of a species, or minds that can change as more information becomes available in the environment, or minds that have evolved with thinking abilities that previous generations of minds did not possess, and which may or may not add to that mind's ability to occupy a life-support niche and gene-propagation niche on the planet earth, is because variation of mind gives minds access to different life support niches on the planet earth. Whatever mind genes, for example, that gave humans the ability to conceptualize how to sew and make clothes gave humans the ability to live in environments that are too cold for unclothed humans to live in.

If an evolved mind variation gives a mind access to a life support niche or gene-propagation niche that previous generations of minds did not possess, the mind possessing that variation becomes more adaptive and this increased adaptation may add to the genetically-programmed complexity of the mind and open up a new genetic variation of thinking ability that enables occupation of a different kind of life support niche for that species. An eskimo who lives in a small, portable housing unit and subsists on seal meat and fish, a billionaire who manages a skyscraper that he or she owns in a major modern city, a taxi driver who lives on minimum wage, a high school teacher, or a reindeer herdsman who survives on the products of reindeer meat and hide, all require different cognitive skills for each, respectively, to be able to think in terms of the axioms that enable them, respectively, to occupy their respective life support niches. All would be similarly adaptive in their behaviors, if they had a similar number of offspring. A theory of how the mind works should perhaps focus not so much on finding a pattern of thinking that is universal to all members of a mind-possessing species, but focus on explaining how variations of mind functionality within a species enables the species to occupy life support niches that may be different, but which are each, respectively, adaptive to the species, and facilitates gene propagation for the species.

In evolving variations in thinking abilities, human minds have commonly evolved the ability to feel pleasure from platonic (non-sexual) thoughts that do not seem to improve the ability of the body attached to that mind to survive or reproduce. The main evolutionary purpose of a brain is to function as a control center that gives the organism attached to that brain access to a wider range of life support niches on the planet earth, by evolving conceptual abilities to gain life support means in different environments. The genes controlling brain development may mutate such that a homo sapiens brain may find pleasure in an activity that is not directly related to improving survival or reproduction. This would motivate that homo sapiens specimen to frequently think in terms of the concepts related to this activity, and in response to such thinking, feel the release of pleasurable neurotransmitters in his or her brain. This thinking tendency may improve the ability of that homo sapiens specimen to survive or reproduce, which would make that genetic variation survive in later offspring of that homo-sapiens example. Or, the mutation might not do this, and may eventually die out in that homo-sapiens example's subsequent gene pool, or simply co-exist along with other adaptive thinking abilities.

Chess playing is one example of a platonic thinking skill that commonly exists among homo sapiens. Some people love to play chess, others hate playing chess, while different people have a mixture of love and hate, in different proportions, to thinking thoughts related to the playing of chess. An extreme example of this would be chess champion Bobby Fischer, who once said that, "All I want to do, ever, if play chess." This may have been because Bobby Fischer's brain was configured such that, when Fischer was actively concentrating on a chess game, huge amounts of pleasurable neurotransmitters were released in his brain, giving him huge amounts of pleasure, or perhaps a natural high, when playing chess. And, perhaps every other thinking activity in his brain besides chess, such as balancing a checkbook, playing backgammon, driving a car, or watching T.V., may have produced no emotional pleasure whatsoever in his brain, and perhaps produced emotional pain.

Chess-playing may seem like a thinking activity that does not contribute to one's ability to survive or reproduce. However, chess-playing also trains a player to acquire

41

sophisticated strategic thinking, creative thinking, and knowledge-acquisition skills. These skills can improve problem solving in other problem-solving domains that might be useful for improving survival and reproduction. If a person trained in playing chess becomes, as a result, more capable of out-thinking civilian competitors in an industry, and to make more money than the competitors, that person's ability to survive and reproduce could have been improved by being able to play chess, and by feeling emotional pleasure while playing chess, such that chess-playing ability would be passed on to subsequent generations of offspring. Or, perhaps the creative thinking skills generated in a person due to playing chess gives that person a better ability to become a scientific researcher, and could gain access to a life support niche in homo-sapiens civilization as a salaried researcher in a university. In extreme examples, such as with a world-class chess grandmaster, chess-playing at a world-class level can make millions of dollars, which can improve a chess-master's ability to survive and reproduce on the planet earth. This is because homo-sapiens civilization sometimes creates life support opportunities where an extremely competent chess player could make significant amounts of money playing chess, where money is the major facilitator of life support acquisition in homo-sapiens civilizations.

The tendency to think thoughts that improve survival and reproducibility explains why humans are less likely to feel pleasure from studying calculus textbooks than from watching pornography. Or, why it is much more difficult to find someone interested in conceptually comparing the grammatical structures of different languages, compared to trying to find someone who is interested in discussing the pros and cons of various forms of housing or real estate. It is quite remarkable that only a small percentage of humans may gain expert-level knowledge of a non-money-making subject taught in a university, and yet, universally, almost all humans are highly focused on obtaining shelter and sexual opportunities. We are all intellectuals with regard to thinking up strategies for obtaining food, shelter, water, medical care and reproduction opportunities, and yet, it is relatively rare to find a professional anthropologist, political scientist, or meteorologist.

Within a personality, there can exist single specific beliefs and emotional behavior patterns that, by themselves, can greatly influence the ability of a human to occupy specific survival niches and/or gene reproduction niches. Such single beliefs, whether conceptual or emotional, may direct a person's thinking and emoting such that this person can access a vast range of potential life support and/or gene reproduction niches in one way, but be unable to access a vast range of other potential life support and/or gene reproduction niches in another way. The vast importance of such axioms might theoretically cause the brain genes, that determine a tendency to believe in one such axiom and not its opposite, to become important loci of brain gene variation when brain genes are mixed and matched due to sexual fertilization from two different genetic sources. For example, if a person is born who likes solitary activities and avoids interacting with the public, that person may be less likely to occupy a life support niche by taking up occupations that require dealing with the public, such as being a politician or a police officer, and may instead gravitate towards life supporting niches or jobs where solitude is more prevalent, such as working as a truck driver or working as a librarian. If this same person hates reading books, which is a general brain trait that influences if a person tends to input vast amounts of information, or will have a brain that tends to react with great anabolic learning activity when a learning experience is encountered, that reclusive person might be more likely to become a truck driver than a librarian. A male heterosexual who is afraid of women may engage in reproductory activities less often, but as a result, may be less likely to die prematurely from acquiring a sexually transmitted disease, compared to a male heterosexual who has no fear of women. A person whose brain can respond to mathematical ideas by showing great anabolic activity in carrying out bio-chemical reactions within the brain that result in rapid and efficient learning of mathematical ideas, might be able to access the life support niche, provided by civilization, of working as a mathematics teacher or professor, and making money this way. A brain that loves nature and the outdoors, but hates information inputting or learning, may become a reindeer herder or a farmer. Genetic mixing and matching of genes that determine if a person is aware of specific axioms in his or her brain would be analogous to how the human immune system mixes and matches different modular molecular components that determine the molecular characteristics of antibodies. This allows the immune system to custom fabricate a wide range of antibodies to attack a wide range of different pathogens that may try to attack and energetically destabilize the human body.

A personality type may be thought of as a collection of axioms and emotional tendencies, each of which influences where a brain will end up on the "game tree" that contains the possible outcomes of life support and gene reproduction niches. William Shakespeare, and other playwrights, intuitively concatenated axioms and emotional tendencies to form the personality constructs of their characters. Nowadays, psychometricians have developed personality tests designed to determine what kinds of axiomatic and emotional tendencies operate in the minds of the test-takers, and to correlate the result of a personality test to a psychometrically validated diagnosis of a personality type for the test-taker. Since there are so many such potential survival and gene reproduction niches available for homo sapiens on the planet earth, natural selection continuously evolves differentiated human minds, so that the species as a whole can occupy vast numbers of different such niches.

Each organism, whether an earthworm, a bee, a frog, a paramecium, or a human, etc., must input food energy and input molecular water at specified rates of volume per day in order to maintain the thermodynamic stability or the energy equilibrium of the coherent structure of atoms and molecules that form the organism's form. For each organism, there exist a set of different objects in the environment that can be used to obtain energy needed to maintain the thermodynamic stability of the organism's form, and there exist a set of axioms determining how these objects can be identified, captured and ingested. An organism's brain will have evolved a tendency to identify only those objects from which the organism can extract food energy, and in particular, food energy of a quantity commensurate with the organism's energy needs, and objects from which the organism can obtain water, and to be aware of the axioms pertaining to how these objects can be manipulated to extract the energy from them. The organism's senses (touch, taste, sight, hearing, and smell) determine which objects of which size the organism is capable of detecting.

How big are the sizes of the objects in the environment that a particular brain is able to identify, and of which a brain is aware of properties or axioms pertaining such objects? The matter that makes up objects in the environment consists of atoms, molecules and sub-atomic particles, all of which are the same sizes, within statistical ranges. However, these atoms, molecules and sub-atomic particles aggregate into objects of different sizes. What determines which objects, and of which size, tend to be identified and thought about by a particular brain?

An important characteristic of the library of object-detecting molecular mechanisms, and the library of axioms-pertaining-to-objects, that is contained within an organic mind, is the size scale of objects detected, or the atomic-clustering size of the objects that a mind is capable of detecting. For example, in the mind of a honeybee, objects in the form of numerous types of pollen grains, are perhaps the most important objects that are part of the life-support and gene-reproduction paradigm that operates in the honeybee's mind. Honeybees occupy an ultra-specialized life-support niche where they obtain most nutrients from grains of pollen, which are clusters of atoms and molecules smaller than a salt grain. The honeybee locates the pollen grains within flowers, coats its body with the grains, then brings the grains back to the hive, where the pollen functions as the molecular foundation for the nutrition of the hive, the creation of honey, and the creation of the hexagonal cells that are the basis of the honeybee's shelter structure. Objects like pollen, hexagonal wax compartments and honey, are some of the objects associated with the honeybee's life support and gene reproduction paradigm operating within a honeybee's mind. Also, the shelter size of the honeybee's hive, or the volume of the scale of clustering of atoms and molecules that make up the honeybee's hive, is in volume increments of perhaps 1,000 cubic centimeters. Inside this hive macro-enclosure, there exist hexagonal dividing wax shelter compartments, each of a volume comparable to the volume of the honeybee itself, in which honeybee larvae are incubated. These are some of the size scales of atomic and molecular clusters of the objects associated with the life-support niche and gene reproduction niche paradigm operating in the honeybee's mind, in addition to the size scale of the tiny pollen grain (von Uexkull, 1957).

The E. coli's molecular mechanism "mind" reacts to objects the size of molecules, such as molecules of the sugar molecule ribose. The E. coli bacterium is small enough that molecules or ribose, or clusters of small numbers of ribose molecules, provide enough energy to the E. coli bacterium as to significantly improve the E. coli bacterium's energy equilibrium with its environment. Hence, it is adaptive for the E. coli's ribose-molecule-detecting engine to work with objects at the scale level of individual molecules of ribose sugars or small-numbered clusters of ribose sugar molecules. A human would gain minimal nutrition from ribose molecules of such small numbers, so a human mind is not generally interested in detecting such tiny quantities of ribose or other sugar molecules, or in understanding axiomatically how such tiny quantities of sugar can be used for life-supporting nutrition.

The size scale, of the objects that an organic mind has evolved to become capable of detecting, is determined substantially by the physiology of the body attached to that mind. For example, since honeybees are small insects, they require far less energy to maintain the atomic and molecular cohesiveness of their thermodynamically unstable body forms compared to larger animals like raccoons or elephants. One reason for the small sizes of honeybees and other insects is that their bodies do not have an efficient lung or circulatory system, and rely on the slow diffusion of oxygen to get oxygen to their tissues. Since oxygen diffuses relatively inefficiently into small volumes of insect tissue, insects without a circulatory system, that depend on the slow diffusion of oxygen into the tissues, must be limited to small sizes, such as with honeybees. Rarely in evolutionary history, insects have grown to over 30 centimeters in length if the oxygen level in earth's atmosphere was exceptionally high. Hence, pollen grains, even if collected in small quantities, provide a significant enough amount of energy to enable the honeybee's small body and mind to survive and function. It is therefore adaptive for the honeybee's mind to be able to detect edible objects on the atomic and molecular clustering size scale of pollen grains. In addition, the honeybee's physiology allows it to use pollen grains as a raw material for generating beeswax, by metabolizing the pollen grain nutrients such as to convert them into beeswax, and then using the beeswax to create compartments within the hive for raising honeybee offspring. The

46

size of the insect determines the size scale of the shelter and the hexagonal beeswax compartments within the shelter. The pollen grains also provide nutrient raw materials for creating honey and royal jelly, for nourishing the offspring, which also adds to the degree to which it is adaptive for honeybees to define pollen grains as objects in their minds, and to contain knowledge of the axioms by which pollen grains can be used for life support.

The libraries, of collections of memorized objects and axioms-pertaining-to-objects, that exist within the minds of members of the same species of animal, may be homogeneous among the animals of the same species. The insects of a specific species seem to be homogeneous in terms of what objects they can detect and what axioms-pertaining-to-objects they can detect. The highly specialized life support and gene reproduction niches that different insects occupy, and the intrinsic physiological limitations that prevent insects from evolving into larger, more complex animals, presumably lock insects evolutionarily into thinking the same thoughts generation after generation.

The honeybee's gene reproduction niche is highly specialized, in that there is a central queen bee that provides the genes for the hive's inhabitants. The honeybee workers work to propagate the queen's bees, and do so with such precision that if a different queen bee by change happens to begin to grow and develop as a larvae within the hive, the honeybee workers detect and promptly kill the baby queens. This behavior has essentially not altered much in millions of years of bee evolution. The paradigm of life support and gene reproduction that operates in the queen bee's mind is presumably different from that of the worker bees. The queen feeds from nutrients provided by the workers, for example, while the worker bees have to do the work to get the pollen nutrients. The queen lays eggs to reproduce the genes of the colony, while the worker bees do not lay eggs but protect the eggs that the queen has laid.

Mosquitoes are another example of animals that possess highly specialized life support and gene reproduction thought processes. Mosquitoes detect carbon dioxide in the air exhaled from a nearby mammal, then fly closer to the source of the carbon dioxide, knowing that they are approaching the mammal since the carbon dioxide concentration increases as the mosquito gets closer to the animal, and then land on the animal's skin or hide. The mosquito can detect that it is on the surface of the animal probably by detecting distinguishing details like the animal's body heat, surrounding animal hair and fur, and the skin texture of the animal's skin. When the mosquito senses that there is a combination of hair or fur, skin, and animal body heat, and perhaps if the mosquito can detect specific odor molecules emanating from the animal that can identify the animal to the mosquito, the mosquito then pierces the animal's skin with its proboscis, and ingests the animal's blood for nutrients. After ingesting the blood meal, the mosquito flies off to lay its eggs and reproduce. Probably all mosquitos occupy a similar life support and reproduction niche, and limit their awareness to the specific objects and axioms-pertaining-to-objects of these niches. There is probably minimal extra learning outside of the life-support and gene-reproduction paradigms contained within their minds. The nouns or objects that presumably are defined or encoded in the mosquito's mind are such nouns as animal skin, body heat, animal hair, animal fur, proboscis and, of course, the delicious blood they crave. A concept such as, "if I am next to a combination of body heat, animal fur and soft pink skin, then I am probably landed on an animal. If I am on an animal's skin, I can pierce the animal's skin with my proboscis and consume delicious blood," may be encoded somehow in the mosquito's mind, with nouns associated with axioms that make up the "paradigm" of a mosquito's mind. The mosquito is aware of the axiom that an animal's skin can be pierced with its proboscis to obtain blood. Blood is delicious and feels good to consume, a mosquito presumably thinks.

One might assume that the mosquito detects some objects at the scale of molecules or small numbers of molecules, such as when detecting an animal's carbon dioxide emissions. The mosquito may not have visual senses that are powerful enough to enable the mosquito to see an object the size of an animal as a complete object. However, the mosquito presumably can detect millimeter-sized hairs on an animal's skin as complete objects, and can define portions of blood in several cubic millimeter increments, which is presumably the size cluster at which the mosquito ingests and quantifies its ingestion of blood. The mosquito's legs span an area of perhaps half a square centimeter when the mosquito lands on animal skin, which may make the mosquito aware of the noun, "a small area of animal skin." The animal's body heat is a relatively differentiated temperature, that generally is found in nature more with animals than with non-animal objects, so that the specific temperature range of an animal's body may activate specific sensory inputting devices on the mosquito that react specifically to this temperature range.

A mosquito would gain no adaptive advantage by being able to input the energy fingerprint emanated by a human table and chair, so that human tables and chairs are not included in the mosquito mind's library of objects and axioms-pertaining-to-objects. The size scale of the clusters of atoms and molecules that make up human tables and chairs allow human tables and chairs to provide humans with the ability to eat food without being obligated to stand up while eating food. By sitting down when eating, humans use less energy when eating food, such that the activity of eating provides more net energy compared to eating food while standing up. A mosquito can not do anything with a human table or chair besides landing on them. The human-centered or anthropomorphic designs of chairs and tables, which exist partly because of the human physiological ability, unique among mammals and reptiles, to sit on the butt on a chair, with elbows contacting a table surface, and two feet contacting the floor, are not applicable as practical inventions for other non-bipedal animals such as antelopes, raccoons, deer or mosquitos. It would not be adaptive for non-human animals to evolve minds that contain the ability to detect human tables and chairs and to recognize how to use them as humans do.

The scale of atomic and molecular clustering size associated with a few cubic millimeters of blood is of great significance to a mosquito's mind, because the mosquito is small enough and its energy needs small enough that the energy provided by a few cubic millimeters of blood can significantly help a mosquito's ability to survive and reproduce. It is adaptive for a mosquito's mind to define the object of "a few cubic millimeters of blood" and incorporate that into an axiom-pertaining-to-object relative to what can be done with or gained from a few cubic millimeters of blood. Humans, however, would not gain enough nutrients from a few cubic millimeters of blood to significantly improve a human's ability to survive or reproduce. It would not be adaptive for a human mind to be able to identify an object consisting of "a few cubic millimeters of blood" and which would be at the size scale of clusters of atoms and molecules that make up this tiny amount of blood. However, a human can gain a significant life-support calories from a chunk of meat the size of a hamburger patty, so that it is adaptive for the human mind to be able to define an object of the atomic and molecular clustering size associated with a chunk of meat the size of a hamburger patty. A mosquito would have minimal use for the hamburger patty, since the mosquito requires fresh warm animal blood in millimeter-sized increments. The concept of a hamburger patty does not exist in the paradigm of the mosquito's mind, because an energy inputting mechanism that can detect the energy fingerprint of a hamburger patty does not exist within the mosquito. Having knowledge of an object consisting of beef the size of a human-scale hamburger patty, or knowledge of the axioms associated with use of this object, would not be adaptive for a mosquito.

Large mammal predators like tigers or crocodiles would not be able to gain significant amounts of energy from pollen grains, and so they have not evolved a tendency to define pollen grains as objects within their minds. However, they have evolved a tendency to define big and small prey animals as objects within their minds, because catching and eating an animal provides significant amounts of energy to the large mammal predators, for helping to maintain their thermodynamically unstable body forms. The scale of atomic and molecular clustering size of a small animal, that can be used by the predator as a food item, is far larger than that of a pollen grain.

The scale of the atomic and molecular clustering size of the objects that different organic minds have evolved to be able to be aware of is determined by the physiological life-support or energy requirements of the bodies to which those minds are attached. The life support and gene reproduction requirements of an organism prejudices what objects the mind of that organism will have evolved to become aware of. A mind can evolve such that its mind's awareness of objects, and axioms pertaining to objects, is strictly limited to that awareness that improves the life-support and gene-reproduction capabilities of the body to which that mind is attached. This is essentially an arbitrary limit to how "consciously aware" an organic mind can be, and this limit can result in members of the same species being highly homogeneous in terms of how their minds think, and how they feel emotions, which are sensations of physical pain and pleasure felt inside the brain.

A food chain, and the position of a species within a food chain, influences the kinds of objects and axioms-pertaining-to-objects that are generally contained within the concept libraries of the minds of specific species. A species' position in a food chain influences what kinds of thoughts a species' mind will tend to have towards members of its own species, and also towards members of other species. A specific species' position in a food chain influences what kinds of other animals or plants, of a different species than that specific species, will become, as conceptual symbols, parts of the object libraries within the minds of that specific species. Each animal or plant species within a food chain may be thought of as a thermodynamically unstable cohesion of atoms and molecules, and thought of as a kind of energy structure, with different or minimum energy requirements needed to maintain its thermodynamically unstable cohesive body form, compared to other species within that same food chain.

A food chain might then be defined as a multi-faceted, inter-related energy equilibrium structure, where each animal or plant species within the food chain is inter-related with one another in a generalized energy equilibrium structure. By being inter-related energetically, animals may evolve a tendency to have minds that incorporate other animal and plants species as objects defined within their minds, particularly if those other animals or plants become sources of food energy within the food chain, or if other animals are predators, which may deplete energy from prey by partly or completely eating those prey. An animal's position within a food chain helps to explain why animals' minds evolve to possess the libraries of objects and axioms-pertaining-to-objects that they possess. For example, a honeybee uses pollen as a conceptual object, and uses internal mind navigation tools to know how to fly to sources of pollen, and collect the pollen, and use the pollen as a nutrition base for forming beeswax shelter compartments within hives for raising offspring, and for forming honey and propolis nutrients for raising offspring, and integrating this nutrition-acquisition paradigm with the nurturing of a queen bee as the ultimate source of the gene reproduction logic of the species. A bear would not be interested in pollen, which is an insignificant nutrient source for the bear, but is interested in bees as objects, due to the axiom that if the bear follows a bee to a hive, the bear can consume honey from the hive, and perhaps gain nutrients by consuming some of the larvae within the hive.

Suppose a honeybee detects a buckwheat flower. It is assumed that the honeybee's brain intuitively thinks the following thoughts: "Oh! A buckwheat flower. If I enter the flower and make its pollen rub on me, I can take the pollen with me back to my hive, where the pollen can feed my queen's offspring, and also feed myself." Thinking these thoughts facilitates the survival and gene reproduction of the honeybee, partly because the queen bee's genes are similar to that of the honeybee, because the queen made it possible for that honeybee to exist, and because the honeybee is related genetically to the queen's offspring in the hive. The bee's body is small enough to enter into the buckwheat flower to get the pollen, which is digestible by the bee's digestive system. Therefore, thinking these thoughts about the buckwheat flower is evolutionarily adaptive for that honeybee, and facilitates the bee's survival and gene reproduction. The bee also observes the buckwheat flower at the level of the tiny structures that contain the pollen of the flower, and the ability of the honeybee to observe these objects of the buckwheat flower's anatomy are adaptive. A human brain, however, would have minimal use of such thoughts, because the human has difficulty obtaining buckwheat pollen using the human's natural body parts and capabilities, and because the amount of energy in buckwheat pollen is too small to contribute significant amounts of energy to a human body. A human brain, however, would benefit by thinking the thought that the human can raid the honeybee's hive and take the honeybee's honey and honeycombs, which contain energy and nutrients that a human can use.

A frog that flicks its sticky tongue out several inches at super-fast speed to catch the insect, would also have no use for the honeybee's thoughts about the buckwheat flower. The frog might think, intuitively and presumably, if it sees an edible insect, "Oh, I see that insect, it is of a type that is edible. If I flick out my tongue, my tongue can grab that insect flying in the air, and then I can bring that insect into my mouth, and eat it and satisfy my hunger." This kind of thought is not applicable to a honeybee's brain, because the honeybee does not have a tongue with an anatomy that allows the bee to fling out the tongue and grab a flying insect, particularly since the insect would be the same size as the honeybee and would not fit in the honeybee's mouth. A human tongue is also not long, sticky and flexible enough to be able to grab an insect in mid-flight like this, so a human brain would not improve the ability of the organism attached to that brain to survive and reproduce the organism's genes if the human brain thought such a thought as the frog thought. The axiom that flinging out the tongue to grab the insect object is not applicable as a contributor to the ability of a bee or a human to support its life, so the forces of natural selection would not evolve bee or human brains to contain this axiom, and to integrate this axiom as part of the concept library of the human or the honeybee brain, but would evolve frogs' brains to contain this axiom. The structural form of a species and its physical capabilities influence which thoughts, or potential groups of thoughts, will evolve to exist in that species mind.

Each species' minds tend to think about similar types of objects, of similar atomic clustering sizes, depending on what are the general life support and gene reproduction niches of that species. This explains how it is often possible for two different species to co-exist within the same general geographic area, and not be in competition with one another or be concerned with one another's thoughts. Humans, for example, would not compete with honeybees for pollen as a food source, because humans are generally not interested in pollen grains, in general, as sources of nutrition, while honeybees are small enough for pollen grains to be useful for nutrition, and they are physiologically capable of metabolizing pollen grains to produce beeswax and honey. Humans, of course, may compete with honeybees by taking their honey, although humans also farm honeybees to get their honey, which contributes to honeybees' survival.

Cows, which are mainly concerned with eating grass and drinking water, and reproducing with other cows, could rest on a field nonchalantly, while a few miles away, a deadly human military battle rages. Cows would not be interested in human machine guns, tanks, and howitzers. They would not have the hands needed to operate this machinery, which feature anthropomorphic design components like ergonomic shapes that make them operational by those who possess humans' size and physiology, and human hands. Human minds focus on their life support and gene reproduction paradigms, while cows focus on theirs.

Another example of how two different species can co-exist in a non-competitive way is that there is essentially no sexual competition between species, due to the gene reproduction paradigms of each species being generally confined within each respective species, since different species do not by definition mate in a way that produces offspring, so that inter-species mating behavior is generally not adaptive. Each member of a species is only in sexual competition with other members of its own species. Two male walruses violently attacking one other to determine who will be the dominant alpha male would be of minimal or no interest to two seagulls flying nearby. However, female walruses observing the fight might be very interested to see what the outcome would be, since the outcome will activate a thought in their minds that would make them tend to mate with the winner of the encounter, and ignore the loser. The sexual paradigms of thinking are generally isolated within a species community, and do not generally transcend species. One possible exception to this generalization is that homo sapiens contain tiny fractions of neanderthal DNA, suggesting that homo sapiens sometimes mated with neanderthals. Generally, these matings between two different species would not have resulted in offspring, but on rare occasions the physiologies of two different copulating members of either species might have matched up just enough (perhaps due to slight mutations within the genes of the copulators) to allow reproduction to occur. Generally, however, such matings might have been "for entertainment purposes only," and would not have influenced the sexual politics or "alpha-male hierarchy politics" of either species on its own sexual "home turf."

An axiom pertaining to what can be obtained from, or done with, an object is done with or on objects over a period of time, such that, often the object changes over time as a mind is implementing that axiom on that object. It is complex (and impossible using current scientific know-how) to precisely describe how the mind tracks what it is doing with or obtaining from objects over time, or how the mind detects how objects change over time. Nothing can be done with or obtained from an object within the shortest period of time that is posited to exist, or a moment of Planck time, or about 10^{-43} seconds. Vast numbers of units of Planck time must pass before a useful axiom is implemented with respect to an object. How does the mind know, over a period of time, that it is eating an apple? How does the mind know that it is walking towards an object? Perhaps each tiny change in an object, as an axiomatic activity is done with the object, or as something is obtained from the object, is itself an object, detecting by object-detecting molecular mechanisms in the mind. For example, a whole apple is one object, and apple with one bite taken out of it is another object, and an apple that is eaten to the core (which visually signifies the completion of the act of eating an apple) is another object. No two apples, while being eaten, look, feel and taste in exactly the same way, but the mind can accommodate for the lack of an exact pattern of "apple eating" by possessing a concept of what approximately constitutes an apple being eaten over time, within a certain probability range of what approximately would fit the criteria of an apple being eaten over time.

An organic mind can detect that it is eating an apple by observing the reduction in the size of the apple while it is being eaten, which helps the mind monitor the percentage of apple consumption over time. The mind, or at least the cells in the mind's digestive system, can monitor and quantify how much energy is being inputted to the mind's body by the consumption of the apple, which indicates if enough of the apple has been eaten to satisfy hunger and to generally help provide enough energy to maintain the molecular cohesiveness of the thermodynamically unstable body to which that mind is attached.

The mind might also be able to detect that it is eating an apple by detecting the energy fingerprint accompanying each step of eating the apple. Each step of eating an apple can be accompanied by its own energy fingerprint, and this fingerprint consists of a combination of sensations such as the taste of the apple's molecules or mixtures of molecules, the crunching noise of biting into the apple, and the physiological muscle reactions that occur due to swallowing a piece of apple, the visual appearance of an apple being eaten having a new, shallow crater forming with each new bite, and using peristalsis muscle movements to move the apple chunk from the esophagus to the stomach. The particular combination of taste molecules that makes an apple taste like an apple, or like the general category of foods perceived of being apples, is different from that of other fruits like oranges or bananas, and causes different combinations of energy state changes to occur at taste bud receptor molecules compared to those caused by oranges and bananas. Of course, no two apples taste exactly alike, since the proportions of taste-stimulating atoms and molecules are slightly different with each apple. The brain must be able to account for all of the possible ranges of taste variations among apples, to know, in a probability sense, that a particular combination of taste sensations falls within the range of what a brain can classify as being an "apple taste." For example, if two apples have exactly the same proportions of taste-registering atoms and molecules, except that one of the apples has 5% more glucose molecules than the other, the two apple tastes would be close enough to both fall within the range of what the brain would interpret as being an "apple taste," although it is unknown what neurological mechanisms would enable the brain to form this interpretation. The two apple tastes are so different from the combinations of taste molecules that would be found in a typical orange, that these apple tastes would not be within the range of taste molecule combinations that would give them an "orange taste."

A human mind perceives the eating of an apple as a dynamic activity occurring over countless units of Planck time (units of 10^{-43} seconds). Current scientific knowledge does not explain exactly what goes on over time inside a mind as the mind controls and monitors an apple-eating activity. Eating an apple is a highly choreographed process where arms and hands are used to move an apple towards a mouth, and the teeth then bite into the apple, after which the bitten piece is chewed, then muscles are used to swallow the apple, and sensations of hunger satiation are felt as the apple is moved by the esophagus into the stomach, and these apple-biting activities are repeated until the apple is consumed, and the mind must monitor how the apple is being diminished in size while the apple is being eaten, to know at what point the apple has been consumed. There is considerable complexity of sequential behavior performed over time as the mind implements the seemingly simple axiom of "I can prevent myself from starving to death by eating an apple." This implementation of axioms-pertaining-to-objects is a complex and dynamic activity performed over time, and it is now known exactly what is happening in a mind when such implementation occurs. This, of course, makes it simplistic to claim that a mind's sense of conscious awareness consists largely of the range of knowledge of what objects, or parts of objects, exist locally on the planet on which that mind exists, or generally in the universe, and what axioms are pertinent to understanding what can be obtained from or done with a particular object.

The mathematics that animal minds use to track changes of objects per unit of time are likely simple, confined at most in complexity to acceleration and velocity. Animal minds probably also have a mathematical concept of group theory, pertaining to how objects can be grouped into categories. A simple proof of this is that often when an animal is hungry, it thinks, "I am hungry. I need to eat something edible." The animal might not know exactly what it wants to eat or where it can find the food, at the moment when the animal senses that it is hungry, but the animal knows that it wants to eat something that belongs to the general category of "things that to me are edible." Similarly, if a person feels like eating an apple, the person does not think that the person wants to eat a specific apple, such as an apple that is mostly red, but with a tiny splotch of yellow on its underside. The person generally looks for objects that "belong to the category of apple," or that emanate energy fingerprints that describe these objects as "apples in general," and essentially will grab any apple that belongs to the group category of "apple," without necessarily grabbing a specific apple.

One common-sense way of explaining how the mind knows that it is walking towards an object is that the proportion, that the image of the object appears to occupy, of the visual field of that mind, appears to increase at a steady rate while that mind is walking towards the object. How this common-sense notion, if it is actually true, translates into a neurological structure representing this phenomena, is unknown. More sophisticated mathematics, involving velocity (change in distance per unit of time) or acceleration (change in speed per unit of time) might describe more erratic changes in rate of the proportion of the visual field that the image of an object forms in an animal's eye. A predator, for example, would need to track a prey object mathematically with some concept of acceleration and velocity while chasing the prey to try to catch it. The predator's mind might fit the movement of prey during a chase to a mathematical pattern symbolizing a rate of acceleration or velocity that matches the prey's movement during the chase. Minds can represent mathematics presumably through the movement of thought-conducting particles through neural networks that represent plotted equations, similar to how a mathematician might represent equations purely symbolically as number relationships on a cartesian coordinate graph. The movement of an object per unit time could be conceptually matched to an acceleration or velocity equation represented purely by thought-conducting neurotransmitters or electrons moving through neural networks.

Conscious Awareness

There are some "common-sense" notions about what constitutes "conscious awareness." Conscious awareness might be defined as as an awareness of what objects exist on the planet earth, an awareness of what can be done with the objects, an awareness of the causes of events, an awareness of emotions, or family, customers, cars, having logical or reasonable reactions to things or objects, etc. One possible reductionist way of defining conscious awareness is to describe it as a set of thoughts, generated by a mind at various points in time during the life of that mind, in response to energy moving across nodes located on circuits, or across nodes located on relay pathways, within that mind, where such energy can be generated by energy-generating forces located within that mind, but where such energy can also be generated by energy fingerprints emanating from objects located in the planetary environment of that mind, that are detected by energy-fingerprint-detecting molecular mechanisms that relay energy to that mind, where a condition for being "consciously aware" is that a mind must be able to input energy fingerprints emanating from objects within that mind's planetary environment. If energy passes through a node, in a circuit or a molecular relaying mechanism, in an organic mind, this passage of energy through the node can result in a thought. A thought can be a macroscopic movement by the body attached to that mind, or can be some form of communication being generated by the body attached to that mind, or can be another thought triggered by the generation of the first thought, or can be an emotion, or can be an act of desire or an act of questioning, or can be a combination of these, depending on what further nodes become energized after the first node is energized.

Why did conscious awareness evolve (Dennet, 2017; Dawkins, 1987)? "Conscious awareness" is a result or effect of thought-generating minds, consisting of the thoughts that result from the thought-generating mechanisms contained within an organic mind. An organic mind is adaptive if the mind generates thoughts throughout the life of that mind that help that mind, and the body attached to that mind, to survive and reproduce. A more fundamental and precise question to ask, instead of "why did conscious awareness evolve?," is "why did thought-generating minds evolve?" Organic minds, or carbon-based thought-generating sets of molecular sensory inputting mechanisms that generate thoughts typically as a result of inputting energy fingerprints from objects, evolved to provide organic-mind-containing animals with adaptive reactions to objects in their planetary environment.

"Consciously aware" organic minds evolved because organic beings are thermodynamically unstable concatenations of atoms and molecules, and require a continuous input of energy in order to maintain their thermodynamically unstable body forms. An organic being's planetary environment contains energy in the form of food items, and organic minds are adaptive if those organic minds can detect the energy fingerprints of these food items and can then move to and consume the food items. A "consciously aware" organic mind therefore evolved primarily as an interfacing mind that interfaces with the planetary environment on which that mind exists such as to detect the energy fingerprints of objects on in that planetary environment, that can improve the ability of that mind, and the body to which that mind is attached, to survive and reproduce. In the human brain, there is a general, though not complete, separation or isolation between the "consciously aware" mind and other minds within the brain, such as the mind that regulates body metabolism and equilibrium, or the mind that regulates the motion patterns of muscles.

A "consciously aware" mind inputs the energy fingerprints of objects in the planetary environment on which that mind exists, and this inputting of such energy fingerprints gives the consciously aware mind the ability to move the body attached to that mind towards sources of energy and gene-propagation opportunities on the planet on which that mind exists. When the body attached to that mind has received energy fingerprint inputs, emanating from food items detected by the consciously aware mind, or when that body has been energetically altered as a result of reproductive activities, from opportunities to engage in reproductive activities detected by the conscious mind, then other mind systems within the brain, separate from the consciously aware mind, work to regulate the body's equilibrium in response to the resulting changes in the internal energy of the body system. There are other minds in the brain besides the consciously aware mind, such as minds that regulate body equilibrium, or minds that precisely control body muscles or autonomic nervous system reflexes. These minds partially communicate with one another, but the consciously aware mind is not aware of most of what the other minds are doing, because the functions of the other minds are specialized, and there is no adaptive advantage to the consciously aware mind being aware of exactly what the non-consciously aware body-equilibrium-regulating minds are thinking. Somehow, the laws of physics determine under what conditions it is possible for different minds to communicate with one another, and when it is possible for different minds to be isolated from one another, even if they are separate mind-systems within the same organic brain.

Minds evolved to provide animals with the ability to be aware of what life support niches were possible for enabling each mind, respectively, to survive on the planet earth, and to be able to choose at least one of these niches for gaining survival ability on the planet earth. Conscious awareness evolved to provide each organic mind with the ability to know what gene propagation niches existed for each respective mind on the planet earth, and to be able to choose at least one of these niches. Minds might also possess other understandings such as social skills understandings that minds can use to know how to act and communicate such as to prevent members of their

61

surrounding societies from persecuting or killing them, and also to induce such members to provide them with resources that can improve their survival and reproduction. These social skills thinking abilities contribute to the organism's ability to survive and reproduce, and therefore these socials skill thinking abilities are subsets of thinking abilities that contribute to survival or reproduction. The vast majority of organic minds on the planet earth limit their consciousness awareness to awareness of objects that improve their ability to exploit life support niches to survive on the planet earth, or, more generally, to be able to maintain the energy equilibrium of their thermodynamically unstable body forms so that those forms do not disintegrate, and also to detect and exploit gene reproducing niches or options available to each respective organic mind on the planet earth.

When the genes for a mind evolve during the evolutionary history of a species, the forces of natural selection adjust the gene components that determine what sensory mechanisms, that detect what energy-fingerprints emanate from what objects in the environment, will ultimately exist in the organism. Natural selection forces also adjust the gene components that determine what thoughts result when detection of energy-fingerprints by these sensory mechanisms cause energy to pass through specific nodes within neuron circuits or relay pathways within that organic mind. Another variable that is adjusted is what thoughts tend to be internally generated, and at what times or in what environmental contexts, by that mind during the life of that mind. An evolved learning ability also can cause an organism to add or subtract energy-fingerprint sensory detectors, and to change thought reactions that occur when different nodes are energized within the mind, separate from what might exist in the mind purely due to genetic influence.

Is there a "center" of conscious awareness in a human brain? Some studies suggest that a part of the brain called the thalamus is the most important part for conscious awareness, in that if the metabolic activity in this area is depressed due to general anesthesia, then conscious awareness turns off (Baars, 1988). Consciousness then returns when the thalamus is back to normal activity. Also, if the entire thalamus is lost due to brain injury, people tend to no longer show what is considered conscious awareness, but if only half the thalamus is lost, people can still be consciously aware.

However, the thalamus may be only a central integrator of many different brain systems that contribute to conscious awareness, instead of the thalamus being the "true center" of conscious awareness. Functional MRI studies of the brain show that different parts of the brain, besides the thalamus, are activated when a person is thinking of different cognitive or motor tasks. It would seem that different parts of the brain can generate a specific thought reaction to the inputting of an energy fingerprint stimulus from the planetary environment in which an organic mind exists. Many different parts of the brain seem to generate many different thought reactions to the inputting of energy fingerprints, by the five senses, from the planetary environment. If conscious awareness is a system of thought responses to the inputting of energy fingerprints emanating from objects in the environment, where such thoughts are initiated by a wide variety of sensory inputting mechanisms that can detect a wide variety of energy-fingerprints from the planetary environment, then any part of the brain that generates one of those thought responses, at any particular time moment while an organic mind exists on its respective planet, is a component of the conscious awareness of that organic mind.

Does "conscious awareness" consist of "rational," or at least substantially rational, reactions to the detection of objects in the environment? For example, if a human sees a banana, there is a common-sense expectation that the human should want to eat the banana, and not try to stick the banana in his or her ear. If a human is driving a car, the human should drive the car within a pathway on a road, and not drive the car into a river. If a human receives a gift, the human should thank the gift-giver, and not curse out and attack the gift-giver. However, whether or not a mind's response to detecting an object in a planetary environment is "rational" is not relevant to the overall definition of "conscious awareness" as being a system of thoughts that result when energy moves across nodes within circuits or relay pathways within minds, in response to the inputting of energy fingerprints emanating from events or objects occurring in the planetary environment or from internally-generated energies leading to thought generation. This is because natural selection did not necessarily evolve the mind to generate rational thoughts, but evolved the mind to generate thoughts that are adaptive and contribute to the survival and gene reproduction of the thermodynamically unstable organism to which that mind is attached. These thoughts may be "rational," according to some standard of what is rational, or they may not be, or they may be irrational because sometimes irrational mind thoughts can be adaptive, or they may be neither particularly rational or irrational but simply irrelevant to contributing to the survival and gene reproduction of the organism to which that mind is attached.

It is difficult to know exactly which factors induce a consciously aware mind to generate the thoughts that this mind generates at specific time moments in the life of that mind, although certainly one obvious possible thought-generating factor is if the mind's sensory inputting mechanisms detect an energy fingerprint being emanated from an object existing in the present tense in that mind's environment. Not every object in a planetary environment will generate a thought in an organic mind, since each organic mind tends to have a set of sensory inputting mechanisms that input the energy fingerprints emanating from a set of some objects in the environment, but not for all objects that can be found in a planetary environment. For some objects, only an energy fingerprint emanating from a part of an object is detected by an energy-fingerprint-detecting sensory input mechanism, instead of the entire object being detected as a whole. Generally, organic minds have evolved such that these minds only input energy fingerprints from objects that are useful for the survival or reproduction of the body attached to that mind. Some thoughts, such as many thoughts about reproductory activities, are often generated in the mind without an object in the external environment initiating the chain of events that generates the energy that powers the thoughts. The frequent generation of reproductory thoughts can be adaptive by motivating a mind to engage in gene-propagating reproductory activities. Other organic mind thoughts can be triggered by hormones in the body, or by pre-existing memories of objects or other members of a species (which are also objects), or by how an object changes over time, according to some pattern.

Emotions, or feelings of pain or pleasure felt in response to inputting energy fingerprints from objects in the environment, perhaps serve to distinguish mammalian mind "conscious awareness" from the conscious awareness of solar powered calculators, or robots that can, without feeling, input object energy fingerprints from the environment. Emotions are mediated by lifeless matter in the form of thought-conducting molecules. As with the thought-conducting electrons that generate computer thoughts, where it is difficult to define how a "thinking cloud" of large numbers of individual particles moving through conduits to generate thoughts at nodes in the conduits can be "unified" into a cohesive "thinking cloud," it is difficult to see how the thought-conducting particles that generate emotions can be "unified" into a thinking cloud. An emotional feeling can permeate one's sense of self and seem to be a cohesive part of one's self, but, as with a computer "thinking cloud" of electrons, the "unity" of this feeling is difficult or impossible to define in atomic or molecular terms.

Are some minds more "consciously aware" than other minds? This question is similar to asking if some minds have "more complex or better" systems of thought reactions, resulting from their mind structures, compared to other minds, when those minds input sensory information from the planet earth's environment. For example, if a fly detects a banana by homing in on the scent molecules emanating from the banana, and reacts to that landing with the thought of sucking on the banana with its sucking mouth, is that fly less consciously aware than a human who sees a banana as a "complete object, shaped like a yellow crescent moon," and has a thought to peel the banana and bite of pieces of the banana until the entire banana is eaten? Both of the thought reactions, respectively, of the fly and the human, in response to detecting the banana, represent reasonably optimal ways of either animal to use the banana for improving the energy stability of the thermodynamically unstable body forms of either animal. If both responses are appropriate given the energy requirements and the food energy inputting styles, respectively, of flies and humans, in what way does one thought of how to eat the banana represent a more "consciously aware" thought than the other?

Many humans have used a magnifying glass to observe a honeybee in the wild moving

65

from flower to flower while gathering pollen for the hive. The honeybee seems oblivious to the fact that it is being observed by the human, and the honeybee seems like a machine that is myopically focused on carrying out its mind-program of gathering pollen from flowers to take to its hive. The observing human might amuse himself or herself with the thought that this dumb honeybee is too lacking in intelligence and knowledge to know that it is being observed by a higher order human mind. Indeed, many humans have the intellectual ability to understand everything about the thinking style and lifestyle of honeybees, and can, at least in theory, detect, at least in general, every type of particle, structure, nutrient, atom and molecule that is part of the life support and gene reproduction paradigms that operate in a honeybee's mind, and understand how each of these objects fits into the mind paradigm of a particular species of honeybee. In addition to this, of course, humans are aware of a much wider range of objects and axioms-pertaining-to-objects compared to honeybees. The entire thought process of the honeybee mind seems to be only a subset of the thought process of a human mind (at least for a human who takes the time to study and analyze the lifestyle elements of honeybees). But, does this mean that humans are more "consciously aware" than honeybees?

Suppose there existed in the universe a "supreme mind," that contained energy inputting receptors capable of inputting the energy fingerprint projected from any possible definable object that could exist in the universe, and could generate every possible "rational" thought reaction to the inputting of such energy fingerprints, and was capable of mass-scale number-crunching, to the point of being able to track all sub-atomic particle movements in real time in any simulation of any phenomena existing in the universe, whether this consisted of a sugar cube dissolving into a glass of water, or two galaxies colliding. Compared to this "supreme mind," the typical human mind is an extremely limited thinking device. Even if, compared to the typical honeybee mind, a typical human mind was 100,000 times more sophisticated (perhaps a reasonable assumption, given that a honeybee mind has approximately 1 million neurons, while a human mind has approximately 100 billion neurons), both minds would be vastly more limited compared to that hypothetical "supreme mind." It would be trivial to claim that, relatively speaking, the human mind was 100,000 times more sophisticated than the mind of a honeybee, when both minds are, in absolute terms, as dumb as a rock compared to this hypothetical "supreme mind."

Any object that a mind encounters on the planet on which that mind exists consists of a cohesion of atoms, molecules, or sub-atomic particles. The laws of physics dictate arbitrarily how sub-atomic, atomic and molecular particles can cohere to form various different objects. There are a practically infinite variety of ways by which these particles can be concatenated into objects, in accordance with the rules of physics. All objects formed will eventually disintegrate. Some objects, like rocks, may take millions of years to disintegrate, while other objects, like tomatoes, disintegrate very soon after formation. Objects can be thought of as constructs of matter, in that objects are arbitrary concatenations of atomic, molecular and sub-atomic particles, and that the atoms and molecules making up an object can be arranged in a practically infinite number of other ways into other objects besides that one existing object, with these atoms and molecules cohering according to arbitrary laws of physics. In addition, all the forms of energy that emanate from objects, whether sound energy, light energy, touch, taste or smell energy, are also energy constructs because they emanate from matter constructs. Matter coheres into objects when vast numbers of individual particles, scattered in the infinity background of the universe, cohere into objects, and eventually, these particles disintegrate and become scattered once again into the infinity background of the universe, in an endless cycle of concatenation and scattering. The present tense environment in which a mind exists, with its various objects, and with the present tense environmental context (weather patterns, temperature, air composition, colorations, etc.) of the planet on which these objects exist, consists of temporary groupings of concatenated objects, that eventually will become disintegrated. These concatenations are temporary concatenations that will be replaced soon by any one of an infinite number of other matter concatenations.

So if, for example, a person is sitting in their kitchen, and is "consciously aware" of the kitchen floor, the microwave, trees and grass seen outside the kitchen window, and a nearby cat coming into the kitchen to eat cat food in a bowl, the person is only aware of a temporary concatenation of matter. All of these objects that make up the person's awareness of the kitchen environment will eventually disintegrate, and will be replaced entirely by other constructs of matter that will in the future occupy the position point on the planet earth where that kitchen is presently located. There will be an infinite number of cycles of object concatenation and object disintegration, and an infinite number of different combinations of objects clustering together to form "scenery" of which a mind can be "consciously aware" if that mind is observing that scenery at that position point on the planet earth, and then later de-clustering, to be replaced by another clustering of different objects. The person who is "consciously aware" of the specific objects making up that person's kitchen environment is actually being aware of one of a theoretically infinite number of object-clustering realities that can make up that position point on the planet earth. Also, given that the earth is rotating on its axis approximately 1,700 kilometers per hour, and moving around the sun approximately 107,000 km. per hour, the position point in the universe of that kitchen scenario is continuously changing at a rapid pace. Also, the quantum energy states of the kitchen objects of which that person is aware are constantly changing at an ultra-rapid pace, which leads to the internal energy and matter of those objects changing at a rapid state, even though the objects appear to be essentially the same to that mind's observation. One's sense of reality is ultra-dynamic. The kitchen scene of which that person is "consciously aware" exists only temporarily, prior to its total disintegration. Any fond memories that this person will remember, on his or her deathbed, of fun times in that kitchen, such as memorable and warm-hearted meals with friends and family, would have been of object-clustering events that either did or will catastrophically disintegrate. The minds that remember these memories will disintegrate as well.

One might argue that the homo sapiens mind is more consciously aware than the mind of a honeybee because the homo sapiens mind is capable of understanding the causes of origins of the objects that the homo sapiens mind can perceive. For example, the honeybee mind knows that pollen grain objects exist, but the honeybee mind does not know something that the homo sapiens mind knows: why pollen grain objects exist. However, many people are not aware of why pollen grains exist. And, even if a person could trace the complete chain of causal events explaining why a pollen grain exists, even to the point of explaining how the Big Bang, which is the presumed origin of the universe (notwithstanding the possibility that an infinite number of universes may exist, which would be a phenomenon associated with an infinite number of Big Bang events occurring), initiated a chain of causal events leading up to the existence of that specific pollen grain, the ultimate causal origin of that pollen grain would consist of an arbitrary original cause, that was caused by arbitrary laws of physics. How can one be consciously aware if one can only trace the ultimate causes of things to arbitrary causal elements? Adding further complexity to this question is that there is no proof that the human mind is rational enough to rationally understand the causality of things, or of how things came into existence.

Most people do not have the cognitive ability or education to trace the origin of objects to the Big Bang event of the universe, assuming that the Big Bang is the ultimate initiating causal event of all components that constitute mind paradigms of conscious awareness on the planet earth, and that the human brain's understanding of the Big Bang is rational to begin with. Even if a person had such education, that person would not remotely be capable of the scale of computational number crunching required to precisely simulate how the Big Bang could have resulted in any particular present tense earth environment that combines multiple objects and a background environment in which those objects exist. Most people have a superficial knowledge of how objects can exist, a superficial knowledge which would not be considered a definitive form of conscious awareness. A small child, for example, might think that apples come from a fruit bowl on the kitchen table. With more education, the child might think that apples come from a pile of apple fruits in a supermarket, from which mommy buys a few apples using money, takes them home, and puts them in the kitchen table fruit bowl. A more educated child might know that apples come from apple trees. A smarter child than that would realize that apple trees come from apple tree seeds. From there, a biologist would know that apple tree seeds come from previous apple trees, which also came from previous apple trees, which, after going back enough generations, came from a tree that was an evolutionary precursor to apple trees, which, going back enough generations, ultimately came from the first single-celled organisms. The first single-celled organisms were originally created by God, or seeded onto planet earth by space aliens, or spontaneously came into existence due to an extremely improbable event whereby the atoms and molecules forming those first reproducing cells spontaneously concatenated into that original cell, an event that perhaps could have occurred at least once in hundreds of millions of years of random chance events on the planet earth, and then the planet earth itself originated, directly or indirectly, from countless quintillions of events that occurred after the Big Bang about 13 billion years ago.

What mechanisms determine which thoughts a mind thinks about in a particular present-tense moment? With an inorganic mind, such as a computer, humans, who designed the computer, determine which thoughts the computer thinks at which present tense moments. Clicking on an icon on a desktop for a chess-playing computer program makes the computer play chess and generate chess thoughts. Running an executable file also generates the thoughts pertaining to that executive file. Inputting characters onto a computer screen in a word processor makes the computer think thoughts pertaining to how to arrange the words in a formatted way for printing into a document.

With an organic mind, the question of what mechanisms determine which thought or thoughts an organic mind generates at a particular present-tense moment is complex to answer, particularly since the thoughts that an organic mind generates have evolved to be "customized" to facilitate achieving the particular life-support requirements and gene-reproduction requirements of the body to which that mind is attached. Unlike with a computer, organic minds do not have a human pressing digital buttons that make them think certain thoughts at certain times, or have human-programmed background processing thoughts that they implement on a timed basis. Ultimately, the universe generally and the earth locally provide the physical and chemical energy inputs that make different organic minds think different thoughts at different present tense moments.

Which memories will be retrieved from the total storage of memories in the person's mind, and when such specific memories will be retrieved, such as to become one of the present-tense thought of the moment, is mysterious and difficult to explain in a reductionist way. Conscious awareness in part consists of the thoughts generated from the storehouse of memories of objects, axioms-pertaining-to-objects, perceived descriptors of one's sense of identity, and perceived understandings of the informational environment of the planet on which one's mind exists, and the mechanisms that determine which ideas, existing in the memorized storehouse of ideas, will become one of the thoughts of a present tense moment (James, 1890). The present tense thought of the moment can be determined by what objects exist in reality nearby a mind, such as to project energy to sensory receptors capable of detecting energy fingerprints emanating from specific objects in reality, and relaying the information from such detection to the mind. The present tense thought of the moment is also determined by the specific mechanisms that determine which ideas from the stored memory bank of ideas will be retrieved to accompany the ideas associated with the real life object or objects nearby that mind that are also stimulating that mind in the present tense. The rather unpredictable appearance of different ideas at different present tense moments throughout the lifetime of a mind as a total constitutes the total amount of conscious awareness of that mind. Conscious awareness at any particular present-tense moment in the lifetime of a mind is strictly limited to whatever thought or thoughts is being thought at the present tense moment. In addition, however, the emotional reaction or reactions to the thoughts being thought at the present tense, or that specific mixture palette of pain and pleasure feelings existing inside the brain at a particular present-tense moment, combines with the thoughts of the present-tense moment to constitute the "package" or "synthesis" of conscious awareness at a particular present tense moment.

If a person is eating an apple, while eating the apple, the person might reach a present tense moment when the person is only thinking of the taste of the apple, and then a moment later, the person might be thinking of what color is the apple, and the next moment, of the sound that the apple makes when bit into, and the next moment, a thought of how nice and warm the room feels in which the person is eating the apple, and another moment of how much that person liked his or her deceased grandfather. Then, suddenly, the person may ask, "where am I and who am I and why am I eating this apple?" An instant later, his or her mind reaches into the mind's memory banks and comes up with an answer. "I am named so-and-so, I am of such-and-such gender, I am in my kitchen, on the planet earth with trees, blue skies and where objects fall down and not up, and I am eating this apple because I am bored and hungry." Then, a moment later, these thoughts, which make the person aware of the background context in which the person is eating the apple, are no longer the present tense thoughts, and instead may be replaced by another thought, such as how pretty the wallpaper in the kitchen looks (Dennet, 2017; Hobson, 1999; Treisman, 1996; Baars, 1988). This example shows how the stored memory of the background context (the components of the person's perception of his or her own identity, and the background environment of the planet on which that person exists and performs various activities) through which the person eats an apple, exists in the stored memories of that person's mind, but these stored memories do not constitute that person's conscious awareness. Instead, the mind uses these stored memories as is needed, to retrieve some of these stored memories as is needed, to remind the person in the present tense of where and when that person's mind exists in the universe or on the planet on which that person's mind exists, by retrieving some of these stored memories such that they become one of the present tense thoughts of the moment.

Superficially Mathematical Organic Minds

Objects that an organic mind can detect are associated in that mind with axiomatic properties, or with axioms about what can be done with or obtained from the object. A human can eat a banana and gain enough energy to prevent starvation for a day or so, for example. The banana can also be painted and be made part of a painting still life. A rotten or expired banana can be dumped into a compost bin and fermented to help produce fertilizer, which can be used to grow crops for food. A hundred ants can be fed for several days off of one banana, while a single human can be fed for a few hours or a day from the banana. A banana can be put in a blender with water and vanilla ice cream to produce a banana milkshake. A fruit fly can lay its eggs on a banana, and when the eggs hatch, the baby fruit flies can eat off the banana and grow into reproducing adult fruit flies.

Some axiomatic uses of an object are not relevant to the mind that is perceiving the object. A fruit fly's mind would have no use for the axiom that a banana can be composted to produce fertilizer, or for the axiom that a banana can be blended with other ingredients to produce a milkshake. However, a human mind can access a food blender machine, a cup of water and a scooper to scoop vanilla ice cream into the blender to create the milkshake.   The resulting volume of milkshake would, axiomatically, feed one or two humans, but would, axiomatically, feed hundreds of fruit flies if the fruit flies decided to consume the milkshake. The type of mind that is perceiving the object determines what axioms, pertaining to that object, are relevant to that mind. A human mind would have no use for the axiom that eggs can be laid on the banana, since humans do not reproduce via eggs, and because a banana would not provide sufficient nutrition to feed a developing human zygote. A human would think to eat the banana by biting off chunks about 6-7 cubic centimeters at a time, but if a fly landed on a peeled banana, the fly thinks to eat the banana in volume increments of a fraction of a cubic millimeter, or to suck microscopic amounts of fluids and nutrients from the banana.   Axioms pertaining to how to eat a banana (or fruits in general) evolved to be different in the minds of humans and flies based on their different respective energy needs and physical mouth traits.

In general, minds perceive objects in terms of what axioms are associated with the objects, but these same minds, in general, are aware of only a tiny fraction of all of the information that, at the sub-atomic level, characterizes the object. The amount of information contained in a banana is colossal, given that a banana consists of countless quintillions of sub-atomic elements, each of which is interacting with multiple other sub-atomic elements, as the countless electrons within the banana orbit around the countless protons in the banana, and the countless sub-atomic particles in the banana move in and out of countless quantum energy states, as the banana undergoes countless internal chemical reactions, and constantly is exchanging heat energy with the sub-atomic particles and atomic and molecular particles of its surrounding environment.   Almost all of this incredibly vast amount of information is not consciously perceived by the typical organic mind observing the banana. Instead, this vast information is mostly ignored, and the mind thinks of the banana largely in terms of the axioms associated with the banana. A child sees the banana as a "cute moon-shaped yellow thing on the kitchen table, that can be conveniently peeled and eaten for a tasty treat" while not being capable of computationally simulating in its mind all of the sub-atomic activity taking place within the banana. A human, with more abstract thinking abilities than a child, is aware of the connection between a rotting banana and an opportunity to enrich a compost bin. The compost bin would be another ultra-complex system of dynamic sub-atomic activity and quantum energy state exchanges, to which the banana thrown into it would add vastly more computational complexity. But, the human mind that throws the banana into the compost bin thinks, crudely and non-scientifically, "this rotten banana is disgusting. I'll just dump it into the compost bin and later use that to feed my tomato plants." Of course, a growing tomato plant is also an ultra-complex whirl of sub-atomic activity, which is not computationally simulated by the mind that just dumped the rotten banana into the compost heap "to later be used to feed the tomato plant."

In perceiving objects only in terms of non-scientific axioms of what can be done with or obtained from the objects, the organic mind ignores vast amounts of information associated with the object. However, the possession of such computationally dumbed-down axiomatic understanding can be adaptive, or can aid in the survival and reproducibility of the mind possessing the axiomatic understanding. To evolve a mind that is able to learn and remember the axiom that a banana can be used for food is adaptive. However, this adaptive understanding is a very crude, unscientific way of understanding the true nature of the banana, which would require ultra-sophisticated number crunching ability to comprehend the banana's activity at the sub-atomic level in real time. This axiomatic way of interpreting objects is a very dumbed down way by which the forces of evolution have provided the human mind with the ability to think in a way that is adaptive. A mind does not have to be able to understand reality completely to be able to survive and reproduce, but needs only to be aware of a small number of non-scientifically or non-mathematically sophisticated axioms about objects, and can gain survival and reproductory capabilities by perceiving objects in conceptually superficial, but adaptive ways, that ignore the scientific and mathematical essences of the objects.

In the universe, objects can exist that consist of aggregations of sub-atomic particles, such that enormous computational power is required to compute how all of these sub-atomic particles interact with one another at the sub-atomic level within these objects. Yet, these objects can be associated with axiomatic properties, in that there can be axioms concerning what can be obtained from the objects, and what can be done with the objects. These axioms can be understood by organic minds, without those minds needing to understand the computational complexity of the objects at the sub-atomic level. The axioms themselves can be simple for the organic minds to understand. If understanding different axioms pertaining to different objects can improve the survival and reproduction of a species, it will be adaptive for that species to evolve to be able to identify these objects and to identify the life-supporting and reproduction-supporting axioms associated with those objects.

Different organic minds within the same species, and among different species, contain different sets of capabilities concerning objects and axioms pertaining to objects. The sizes of the objects that different minds tend to be able to identify is determined essentially by if the organic body contains the physical apparatus needed to implement the axiom pertaining to that object, if such an axiom improves the survival and reproduction of that body. This helps to determine the contents of the conceptual library of objects and axioms pertaining to objects that organic minds tend to posses similarly within the same species, and differently between different species. Variations in these libraries within and between species provide a mechanism by which different specimens of different species might be able, by luck, to access new life support and reproduction-facilitating niches on the planet earth, that might not be available without a specific variation developing in that specimen's genes through a mutation.

The fact that human minds ignore vast amounts of information when they think of objects in terms of the axioms associated with the objects implies that the human mind may not be capable of understanding reality, simply because the human mind cannot perform the colossal quantities of floating point operations per second that are needed to understand reality at the sub-atomic level. This fact must make one question what is education, or what does it mean to be educated, in the human sense of the term "educated?" Does not all education consist of teaching students of the non-scientific or crudely scientific axioms associated with objects, while ignoring the true nature of objects at the sub-atomic level? And, even if a student learns about sub-atomic physics, the student still will never be able to simulate in the student's mind the mathematics of sub-atomic activity of an object in real time. A student might, for example, become slightly more educated by learning that George Washington was the first president of the United States. However, the United States is, at the sub-atomic level, an ultra-complex interaction of people, places, things and activity. George Washington's being was also ultra-complex computationally, if one were to simulate on a computer how all of the atoms, molecules and sub-atomic particles inside George Washington's body interacted with one another in real time. All of this ultra-complex activity is distilled into a computationally simplified fact, that George Washington was the first president of the United States. This fact contains only an astronomically tiny fraction of all of the information associated with the sub-atomic particles that made up George Washington or the United States, and yet, an American who does not know this fact is said to become more educated by eventually learning this fact.

William Shakespeare, hailed as one of the greatest, ultra-high-IQ geniuses of the homo sapiens species of animal, wrote two thousand pages of plays that are widely viewed to be the most sophisticated literary works of homo sapiens civilization (Shakespeare, 2005 edition). Vast numbers of people who read his plays believe that they became more sophisticated and educated as a result of reading his plays. Yet, Shakespeare is guilty, in every line he wrote, of describing objects, and axioms associated with the objects, in a way that is extremely computationally simplistic. Shakespeare's insights seem to be scientifically plausible, because most people agree that his perception of reality, as put forth in his plays, seems to make sense, and that there is some truth to the idea that if vast numbers of intelligent people agree with an idea, then the idea is probably true. However, Shakespeare ignores vast amounts of the computationally complex mathematical relationships existing among the sub-atomic particles that theoretically exist within his theoretical characters and all of the theoretical things these characters talk about in Shakespeare's theoretical, instructively metaphorical literary scenarios. Take the opening lines from Shakespeare's famous 18th sonnet:

> Shall I compare thee to a summer's day?
>
> Thou art more lovely and more temperate.
>
> Rough winds do shake the darling buds of May,
>
> And summer's lease hath all too short a date.

These lines are commonly perceived by english speakers to be poetically beautiful. Yet, from a number-crunching standpoint, they are a dumbed-down conceptual disaster. The narrator is a human, consisting of approximately seven billion billion billion atoms. Colossal amounts of computational power are required to simulate, to sub-atomic precision, the world pathways of every sub-atomic particle in that human per unit of Planck time, to fully understand this ultra-complex molecular machine. This narrator arbitrarily compares another human, thee, who also has a body form that is similarly ultra-complex computationally, to a summer's day. A summer day consists of an area of the environment on the planet earth that consists of colossal numbers of sub-atomic particles, atoms and molecules moving in computationally ultra-complex ways per unit of Planck time. Juxtaposing "thee" with a "summer's day" implies an extremely computationally crude way of associating one colossally complex dynamic sub-atomic/atomic/molecular system with another.

The line "thou art more lovely and more temperate," implies that the narrator is comparing his emotional reaction to his perception of a "warm summer's day" with his emotional reaction to "thee," presumably in the context of love, by fondly looking at "thee," or engaging in reproductory activities with "thee." The narrator presumably experiences less of a rush of pleasurable neurotransmitters like dopamine or norepinephrine in response to the narrator's perception or inputting of the informational stimuli of the "warm summer's day," compared to the bigger rush of pleasurable neurotransmitters that the narrator feels when contemplating "thee" or engaging in reproductory activities with thee. No one knows what the exact quantity is of the pleasurable neurotransmitters released during either act of perception.

Essentially, the first two lines of this sonnet are comparisons of the release of pleasurable neurotransmitters between the two perceptual activities, with no scientific or mathematical details quantifying these releases. The perceptual activities are also perceived by the narrator in a computationally dumbed-down way, in that there is no way that the narrator, or Shakespeare, could have had the ability to track in his mind in real time the world pathways of every sub-atomic particle associated with I, thee, or the warm summer's day, per unit of Planck time, in any particular timeframe when I, thee or the warm summer's day were being conceptually tracked by the narrator.

The lines "rough winds do shake the darling buds of May," describe wind, which is an extremely computationally complex phenomenon to simulate, given the vast numbers of sub-atomic particles that move, in statistically complex ways, when the wind blows. The narrator simplistically describes the effect of wind as "shaking" flower buds. The sub-atomic particles of any flower will move in extremely complex ways computationally in response to winds, so describing this movement using a non-quantified, non-qualified crude term like "shaking" represents an extremely information-omitting way of summarizing reality.

These buds also appear in the month of May. The use of the word "May" also represents a vastly detail-omitting way of describing the time when these buds appear. The word "May" implies that the buds are appearing at the beginning of the summer season. Seasons are computationally ultra-complex phenomena that occur when the earth's axis tilts, changing the solar energy watt-power magnitude shining on different parts of the earth, resulting in ultra-complex changes in the temperature ranges of different parts of the earth, which cause ultra-complex changes in the types of organic chemical reactions that can occur in different parts of the earth, making photosynthesis, and the plant-based greening of the environment, occur in some parts of the earth, but not in others.

The names of the months are ways of dividing the earth year by labeling 30-day increments of the earth-year with twelve words representing months. It would require incredible amounts of computational complexity to track all of the world pathways of all of the sub-atomic particles moving on the planet earth in a single month, in order to be able to understand what exactly happens during a month on the planet earth. Yet, all of this computational complexity is represented in one single word, "May," and Shakespeare is simplistically associating the word "May," and the vast amount of computational complexity that the word "May" represents, with "buds."

The buds themselves induce release of pleasurable neurotransmitters in the mind of the narrator, making the narrator perceive these buds as "darlings." This imagery provokes the idea that there is some kind of ranking or hierarchy in terms of how three elements, "thee," the "buds of May" and the "summer day" induce different degrees of release of pleasurable neurotransmitters in the mind of the narrator, when the narrator's mind inputs energy fingerprint information about these elements. Which is more pleasurable in the narrator's mind, that is, which perception releases more pleasurable neurotransmitters in the narrator's mind, "the buds of May" or the "summer's day," or "thee?"

The line "and summer's lease hath all too short a date," is a tremendously computationally crude simplification. The colossal computational complexity of tracking all of the world pathways of all of the sub-atomic particles that are needed to understand what happens during an entire summer in a geographic area is associated with a simplistic feeling of emotional pain that summer is too short in duration.

Given that vast amounts of mathematical and scientific information are omitted in Shakespeare's way of implying relationships between different objects, how can it be justified to think that one becomes more educated by reading Shakespeare? Could Shakespeare simulate in his mind a waterfall flowing down a mountain in real time, down to sub-atomic detail, or a category 4 hurricane occurring in Bermuda? Doubtful, and because of that, we must think of Shakespeare as an unscientific, and perhaps ignorant, thinker who was unable to understand reality because his mind was incapable of performing the mass-scale number-crunching that would be required to mentally simulate reality with precision down to the sub-atomic level.

Such lack of computational, number-crunching detail results in presumptuous writing, where the reader must make vast amounts of implicit assumptions about what the writer means, because the text itself is not exactly scientific enough, in its descriptions, for all of the information needed to interpret the text to be included in the text. Yet, we cannot only blame Shakespeare for creating writing that lacked detail about what world pathways the sub-atomic particles that are presumed to exist in his theoretical scenarios follow per unit of Planck time. In reality, all literary authors wrote in this computationally crude way that presumes relationships among ultra-computationally-complex objects, while omitting vast numbers of computationally-complex details about the world pathways of the sub-atomic particles that make up their theoretical literary scenarios. Some of these writers are hailed as geniuses, because their writing generally stimulates the human mind in such a way as to make many critics consider these writings to be poetic or spiritual or instructive. However, these writers only "discovered" axioms or word combinations that the human mind typically and arbitrarily interprets as being "instructive axiomatic ways of understanding society and the universe," while being too naive to be aware of how computationally simplistic these axioms are. In other words, these writers are only discovering patterns, or "house of cards" structures, of ignorant thinking, that juxtapose objects with axioms, or objects with posited relationships with other objects, in computationally simplistic ways, but in ways that paradoxically and naively seem to be thought-provoking, analytical and instructive.

How can computationally crude descriptions of reality be nonetheless perceived as being beautiful, poetic, spiritual or instructive by significantly large numbers of human critics? The answer is that the writers recognized as being great have discovered specifically what arbitrary kinds of computationally dumbed-down thoughts "resonate" with the human mind's perception of specifically which arbitrary kinds of computationally dumbed-down thoughts are intellectually stimulating. When people, significant enough in their numbers to make the idea true that "Shakespeare is generally considered a literary genius," read the opening lines of Shakespeare's 18th sonnet, pleasurable neurotransmitters are released arbitrarily in their minds. Somehow, those words stimulate thought, speculation, metaphorical thinking, or, to describe this in a more reductionist way, simulate the anabolic organic chemical reactions that generate memories of concepts and of conceptual relationships, in the minds of the readers.

It is possible to re-phrase those lines from Shakespeare's 18th sonnet, to say the same basic thing but in a way that does not stimulate neurotransmitter release or anabolic brain-learning bio-chemical reactions occurring in the brain, such as to be considered "poetic," or "spiritual" or "thought-provoking," at least to the extent to which Shakespeare's words are widely thought to be. For example:

> With respect to summer days,
>
> Which feel good to me because they are warm,
>
> You make me feel to me as those days do,
>
> But you make me feel better than I feel
>
> When I bask in the warmth of a summer's day.
>
> The wind of May blows through,
>
> And pretty flowers dance in it,
>
> Sad--it is indeed crappy--that summer is so short.

A poet I ain't. However, the point is, that it is arbitrary and unknown why certain computationally-simplistic word combinations, such as the words of Shakespeare, when combined into sentences and paragraphs of poetic speech, can induce anabolic brain activity, accompanied with release of pleasurable neurotransmitters, while other such word combinations do not, such as the aforementioned paraphrasing of Shakespeare's 18th sonnet. A human mind can cognitively fixate on literary descriptions of reality that omit vast amounts of the computational complexity that is needed to precisely understand, in sub-atomic terms, these posited literary metaphor descriptions of reality. Such descriptions are so simplistic that we must rationally think of them as being conceptually misleading. Yet, if a literary author conceives of the right kind of concatenation of words, this concatenation will somehow "hit the buttons" and induce pleasurable neurotransmitter release and anabolic learning behavior in human minds, making humans perceive these words as "interesting," or "thought-provoking" or "spiritual," and then hail the author as a genius.

If the brain has 100 billion neurons, as has been estimated, and an estimated 16 billion neurons in the "intelligent" part of the brain, the cerebral cortex, and yet is incapable of conscious mass-scale number-crunching, this makes one ask a couple of rhetorical questions. How can it be justified to think of the human brain as a "computer" if the conscious human mind is not capable of the mass-scale number-crunching that is needed to simulate natural phenomena in the mind, down to sub-atomic level precision, as is needed to truly understand reality? If the brain did not evolve to such that the consciously aware part of the brain was capable of mass-scale number-crunching and computation, then to what extent is the consciously aware part of the brain rational in its understanding of reality? What is the consciously aware part of the brain actually thinking, if it did not evolve to be capable of precise, mass-scale number-crunching such as a man-made computer is capable of performing?

The brain seems to become damaged from molecular free radicals generated during acts of concentration or thinking. This would imply that if a brain performed ultra-high-level computational number-crunching tasks, such as simulating a category 4 hurricane in the mind, the brain would become severely damaged via free radicals generated from the thinking process. No homo sapiens brain computer has come remotely close to beginning to begin to begin to achieve a super-computer's level of number-crunching ability. The average person is barely competent enough, or brain-energetic enough, to add up twenty numbers in a row when balancing a checkbook, let alone simulate the fractal growth of a snowflake crystal in his or her mind. Even Albert Einstein, hailed as the poster boy of scientific genius, nowhere near possessed this level of number-crunching ability. In fact, comparing Einstein's number-crunching capability to that of a super-computer would be like comparing a caterpillar's mind to

83

the mind of the dean of a world-class university, and even this comparison may excessively flatter Einstein.

Many philosophers, who seek a scientific explanation of what a mind is, think of the human brain as a "computer," but the "brain is a computer" idea may be a misconception. Most of the brain's thoughts are limited to axiomatic understandings of how specific objects can be used to prevent the thermodynamically unstable cohesion of atoms and molecules that make up the body attached to that brain from disintegrating, due to what is common sensically thought of as "starvation," without having a rational computation-based understanding of how those objects exist at the sub-atomic level. Other thoughts consist of axioms related to how the brain can reproduce its genes, by thinking axioms about how other humans can be convinced to engage in sexual reproduction activities that will increase the probability of propagating the genes, again without having an ability to compute precisely what is happening at the sub-atomic level in the mind and body of another human when that human becomes convinced to engage in a reproductory activity.

Actually, Shakespeare's insights into human nature are rational, in that these insights inform human readers of ways to improve the ability to obtain life support and gene reproduction assets on the planet earth. However, these insights are only useful in that specific, parameterized way, that is itself computationally simplistic, by which these insights posit a description of reality within homo sapiens societies. The human brain has evolved such that the consciously aware part of the brain fixates on computationally imprecise axioms for understanding how to obtain food energy and gene reproduction assets within homo sapiens societies. These computationally imprecise axioms are in fact applicable for obtaining food energy and gene reproduction assets within homo sapiens societies on the planet earth, because humans evolved such as to arbitrarily think in terms of these computationally imprecise axioms. Each species of animal, whether a reptile, insect or mammal, etc., contains computationally simplistic axiomatic understandings of how to obtain food energy and gene reproduction assets within the respective life support and gene reproduction niches of their species, and it is these computationally simplistic axiomatic understandings that form the backbones of thinking within the minds of these animals. In contrast, a super-rational, mathematics-based mass-scale number-crunching ability to precisely understand reality by being able to track all of the sub-atomic particles as they move in real-time in the context of a specific phenomenon on the planet earth is not an ability that has evolved to exist within the consciously aware minds of animals on the planet earth.

If the approximately 16 billion neurons in the cerebral cortex, combined with the vast numbers of synapses that inter-connect the neurons, do not give rise to a powerful and conscious number-crunching computer, this suggests that the human cerebral cortex is computationally inefficient, in that there is minimal number-crunching ability per unit of thinking element or neuron. A computer central processing unit has tens of millions of transistors, but the silicon microchip easily outperforms the 16 billion neurons of the consciously aware human brain when performing number-crunching tasks. It would seem that a large number of neurons in the cerebral cortex are required just to give the human brain the ability to possess an understanding consisting of a large collection of minimally mathematical axiomatic understandings of how identified objects on the planet earth can be used for survival and reproduction. Perhaps vast numbers of neurons are required for the sole purpose of being able to identify objects, and another vast number of neurons needed to form concepts of the axioms associated with uses of the objects. The human brain is often viewed by scientists as a "complex parallel computational device," due to the vast numbers of inter-related synapse connections among vast numbers of neurons, but this parallel computation seems to be used for memorizing large amounts of computationally simplistic axiomatic understandings of what can be gained from or done with numerous specific objects on the planet. The "parallel computational architecture" of the consciously aware human brain is obviously not capable of simulating computationally complex phenomena inside the mind, which makes this "parallel computational architecture" to be highly underwhelming.

One demonstration that the computational ability of the conscious human brain is minimal, is that when two people are talking with one another in a conversation that results in them becoming mutually convinced to engage in a reproductory act, they are exchanging ideas that are not mathematically or computationally complex. Each partner has a slightly different axiomatic understanding of what will convince the other to engage in reproductory behavior, but these different understandings complement each other, in a way that is mutually intuitively understandable, such as to convince the two to engage in the reproductory act. Both understandings are non-computationally-complex axiomatic understandings of how to convince the other partner to engage in reproductory actions, without any concept of the mathematical and physical sub-atomic forces that are actually driving the motivation to reproduce. However, these understandings are convincing, though dumbed-down, because the forces of natural selection have evolved people to intuitively understand these different axiomatic communication styles that lead up to mutually convincing two people to engage in a reproductive act. In other words, different minds with different, and arbitrarily dumbed-down axiomatic understandings, of how to convince one another to engage in reproductory acts, have somehow been programmed by the forces of evolution to understand each other's axiomatic understanding intuitively.

This simplified, axiomatic, non-mathematical or non-computationally-complex way of understanding the universe extends to many domains of human thought. The concept of war is one example of this. If, in a battle, general A kills enough of enemy general B's soldiers, general A will have more killing power on the battlefield compared to general B, so general A can force general B to surrender, or to retreat from the battlefield. If enough battles are won, the total killing power of one warring party will exceed the other, which will force the other warring party to either surrender or retreat. In addition, vast numbers of civilians, monitoring the outcome of the battles and, more generally, the war, will become convinced to surrender to the more powerful warring party, or to run away from it. That, simply encapsulated, is the logic of how war convinces people to obey certain political organizations.

Yet, the number of floating point number-crunching calculations that are required to understand precisely what is happening on a battlefield, and a war in general, are so astronomically colossal in scale that no human brain can begin to begin to begin to understand battles and wars precisely. To carry out these calculations, a brain would have to simulate in real time exactly what a soldier's body is doing, at the sub-atomic level, during the battle, which by itself is a computationally colossal task. A brain would also have to simultaneously simulate how the bodies of all of the other battlefield soldiers are operating during that battle. In addition, the brain would have to simulate weather patterns, military machine operations, and anything else that could influence the battle. No human mind is remotely capable of carrying out this calculating task. Instead, civilians simply think, "Okay, there is a battle going on. Who will win it? Okay, if that side won, that side may also later win the war. If that side wins the war, I will obey the politics of that side, to prevent being accused of rebellion and then imprisoned or killed." Both the warriors and the monitoring civilians understand the war in an extremely crude, non-mathematically computational way, and then are influence by it via the simple axiom that the side with the highest killing power after the war is finished is the one whose politics will be obeyed.

How could Napoleon Bonaparte, Douglas McArthur, Alexander the Great, or any other top-ranked military general, rationally understand how to wage a battle or a war, if their human brains were incapable of the ultra-colossal scale of number crunching that would have been required to precisely understand the battles and wars they waged to sub-atomic precision? The answer is that they understood war in terms of superficially scientific or mathematical generalizations that, nonetheless, gave them enough understanding to know how to win the war, without precisely simulating in their minds what, computationally, was happening on the battlefield. A simple example of this is if general A has ten tanks with a missile range of 5,050 feet, and the enemy general B has ten tanks in that battle with a missile range of 5,000 feet, general A can win the battle by carefully ensuring that his tanks never get closer than 5,000 feet from general B's tanks, and never get farther than 5,050 feet from general B's tanks, while shooting missiles at those tanks. General A would be following a conceptually simplistic axiom, that victory will occur in this skirmish if General A's tanks are between 5,000-5,050 feet from General B's tanks while shooting missiles at the enemy tanks. General A can win the battle while being blissfully unaware of the colossal amounts of number-crunching power that are required to exactly simulate how twenty tanks and their missiles are moving in this battle, with such precision as to be able to track the world-pathways of each sub-atomic particle of each tank, soldier, missile, explosion and other battlefield-relevant elements on the battlefield in real time.

In order to track the progress of the battle, general A has to track, to some extent, the progress of the battle in real time. This requires some concept in general A's mind of how the tanks, missiles, soldiers, explosions, and other battlefield-relevant elements are moving in real time, or, in other words, the general must have a concept of the verbs pertaining to how these objects are moving. Questions like, which tanks are being blown up when? Which tanks are moving where? Which soldiers are being killed where, and which soldiers are doing the killing? Is the rate at which general B's tanks are being blown up less than the rate at which general A's tanks are being blown up, per unit time? In theory, answering these questions in a strictly reductionist sense, by tracking the progress (or at least simulating in the mind the progress) of every sub-atomic particle that is relevant to influencing the battlefield outcome, for each unit of Planck time (or for each 1×10^{-43} second time unit) of the battle, requires incredible amounts of computational number-crunching power. Since it is impossible for the human brain to begin to begin to begin such a colossal computational task, there must be some way of the brain to represent or encode verbs, which are the grammatical representations of the movements of objects per unit time, in a computationally simplistic or dumbed-down way. This computationally simplistic way of representing how objects change or move over time necessarily must delete colossal amounts of information regarding the world pathways of all of the sub-atomic particles involved in any object-verb relationship. This computational reality forces the human mind to be trapped in a perpetually dumbed-down state of existence, where vast amounts of information must be truncated from any human mind's perception of reality, due to it being impossible for the consciously aware brain to perform number-crunching on a colossal scale.

And yet, amazingly, the dumbed-down, necessarily rather arbitrary, colossal-amounts-of-information-truncating way by which any organic mind perceives reality has evolved to be adaptive for that organic mind. Not only do organic minds tend to have a limited conceptual library of objects or nouns that their minds are capable of identifying, and associating with axioms of what can be done with or obtained from the object, and not only are those organic minds unable to track all of the world pathways of all of the sub-atomic particles per unit of Planck time associated with these objects and the objects' respective axioms, but these minds' evolved ways of thinking are adaptive. How can a dumbed-down way of perceiving reality be adaptive, for any particular organic mind, whether it be a bumble bee's mind, a mouse's mind, or a human mind? If one was to genetically engineer an organic mind, how would this bio-engineer design a dumbed-down way for that organic mind to perceive its reality, such that that mind's way of perceiving its own reality added to its life support and gene reproduction abilities? Would this bio-engineer know enough about the laws of physics to determine that an insect of a honeybee's physiology could use objects in the forms of pollen grains, containing the collection of protein, fat and carbohydrate molecules that pollen grains contain, as a central object in the life support and gene-reproduction paradigm of the honeybee's mind, and be able to use its own physiology to use the atomic and molecular materials from pollen grains as a basis for creating edible honey and propolis, and beeswax to create honeycombs, for purposes of propagating the genes of the queen at the head of the hive, while having enough food energy to maintain the thermodynamically unstable atomic and molecular cohesive body forms of the honeybees in the hive? How would this bio-engineer choose the size of atomic and molecular clusters of the objects that the engineered organic mind is able to conceptually define, and conceptually incorporate into an axiom-based understanding of how objects can be used to add to its own life support and gene reproduction?

The human brain also has a concept of axiomatic cause-and-effect that also is dumbed down in terms of its lack of mathematical detail. One example of this is the common cause-and-effect axiom that, "if a person has an electric bill to pay, the person can mail a check to the electric company to pay for the bill today, and within a few days the electric company will receive the check, deposit it, credit the account, and the bill will be paid." Vast numbers of events occur at the sub-atomic and molecular level from the time the check is put in the mailbox, to the time that the account will be credited. None of those events are noticed, simulated or calculated by the mind carrying out the axiom. How do the forces of natural selection or evolution cause evolved minds to settle on the specific, computationally dumbed-down, computational-detail-omitting axioms that evolved minds use in their everyday perceptions of reality? How did a dungbeetle's mind evolve to contain the computationally simplistic axiom that, "If I see a piece of dung, I can roll it up into a ball, and roll it into my home hole in the ground to use as a food supply later."

Driving to work is also another example of a computationally dumbed-down axiom-guided behavior. While driving to work, a person passes by incredible amounts of information, in the form of the informational characteristics and mathematics of all of the sub-atomic particles contained within the large numbers of objects that the person's car passes during the commute to work. The commuter does not think about this vast amount of information, or engage in any computational number-crunching attempt to understand how each sub-atomic particle, of every object that the commuter passes on the way to work, moves along its respective X,Y,Z and T world-pathways through space and time. Instead, the commuter is mostly consciously aware of a computationally dumbed-down axiomatic principle that if the commuter drives from home to the place of work, and the commuter performs the work-related tasks that are needed to generate professional-quality services or products, then the commuter can get money, which the commuter can use for life-support and support of any offspring of the commuter.

And yet, there is evidence that the body is capable of mass-scale number-crunching computation. The process by which food is digested suggests this. When a piece of food is eaten, essentially every atom and molecule within the food is intelligently sorted by the body so that each respective molecule or atom winds up in a location within the body where the atom or molecule can become a useful addition to the body, or if the molecule or atom is useless or poisonous, processed as such and (hopefully) excreted by the body.

90

Suppose that a single grain of table salt (NaCl or Sodium Chloride) contains approximately 1×10^{18} atoms of sodium and chlorine (a reasonable assumption based on known ideas of stoichiometry). When the salt grain is consumed, it is dissolved into separate ions of sodium and chloride. Each of these individual ions is absorbed by the body's cells and is intelligently allocated by the body to various locations in the body where these atoms are needed for the body's equilibrium processes. Suppose that every time one of those salt ions crosses a molecular membrane within the body, or every time one of those salt atoms is contacted by a molecular-scale ion channel within a body cell, that one bit of computerized processing occurs. Suppose that 5 bytes of processing occur per salt ion, and all of these processing bytes occur over approximately 10,000 seconds as the salt grain is completely digested. The total amount of bytes involved in the digestion of just this one salt grain would be 5×10^{18} bytes or floating point operations, occurring over 10,000 seconds, giving a processing power in this simplified hypothetical example of $5/10,000 \times 10^{18}$ or approximately 5×10^{14} floating point operations per second, just to process a single grain of salt. This is comparable to the fastest super-computers, which currently process information at approximately 1×10^{15} (1 petaflop) floating point operations per second. Many billions of separate human cells and many quintillions of separate body molecules are involved in the processing and sorting of the atoms of this salt grain, with each separate processing entity contributing a bit or so to the process, which would make the digestion of this salt grain essentially a parallel processing computation process. The digestion of a larger piece of food, such as a hamburger patty, would process far larger numbers of atoms and molecules than a salt grain, and blast the super-computing capabilities of the human food-molecule-processing digestion system apparatus to well beyond the petaflop computational level of today's fastest super-computers.

Of course, none of the mass-scale parallel computational processing of the body's molecule-sorting and atom-sorting digestive system is available as number-crunching activity that can be used to inform the conscious part of the human brain. It is not as if each of the many trillions of body cells or molecular processes involved in digestion could each contribute a floating point operation or two to a larger computational simulation problem that a thinking center in the conscious human brain was trying to figure out. This is not how natural selection evolved the body and brain. The parallel computational power is there in the body's digestive system, but it is not harnessed for the power of conscious awareness. Actually, the amount of heat energy, and quantity of free radicals, that would be generated to send one petaflop per second of computed information from myriad body cells, through myriad nerve pathways, all the way up to the brain would probably be enough to severely damage the body and brain.

There is great intelligence operating in the body with respect to a knowledge of the different atoms and molecules of nature, but little of this is available to the consciously aware mind. In addition to the body's intelligent sorting of atoms and molecules via the digestive system, the body's immune system uses ultra-intelligent ways of identifying different pathogens, and custom-tailoring an immune response to intelligently target and attack different pathogens in the body, using a molecular precision of disease-identification and disease-targeting that human doctors can barely imagine or implement. The body is a great intellectual of the science of atoms and molecules. Yet, most peoples' conscious human minds struggle to memorize the most basic concepts of chemistry and atomic physics. In this respect, the body evolved to be far more sophisticated at understanding atoms and molecules, and in utilizing mass-scale computation to process mass numbers of atoms and molecules, compared to the conscious mind. The forces of evolution dumbed down the conscious human mind in favor of making the body's cells computationally intelligent and savvy in their knowledge of the chemistry and physics of atoms and molecules.

The Sexual Over-brain:
The Ultimate Slave Driver

A homo-sapiens body is thermodynamically unstable and its molecular structures will eventually disintegrate completely. This requires that a homo-sapiens individual reproduces in order to generate new molecularly concatenated body forms to replace the parental body forms that will eventually disintegrate. The genes of a person who has a behavioral tendency to not reproduce are more likely to be wiped out of the gene pool.

Many people find reproductory pursuits to be extremely pleasurable. Ironically, however, sexual behavior is generally harmful to a person's personal survival. The offspring that may be generated from sexual behavior will generally subtract energy and resources from the human parents of the offspring, so that energy and resources that can be used for the parents' personal survival is instead directed to facilitate the offspring's survival. Pregnancy diverts large amounts of nutrition, that could have gone into nurturing the pregnant mother's body, into nurturing the body of the pregnant mother's fetus. Large amounts of food and clean water, expensive to acquire, are required to feed the offspring that are born. Sexual behavior can also result in acquiring sexually transmitted diseases, including potentially fatal diseases like AIDS, which can shorten the lifespan of the people engaging in the behavior. If a person feels a desperate emotional need to have sex, the person may consider using, or actually use, fraud, coercion, rape, or date-rape drugs to obtain sexual pleasure, potentially causing physical and emotional harm to a victim of such activity. Only by subtracting large amounts of energy from oneself, and risking catching an STD, can a person generate offspring.

Although reproductory activity can harm the ability of participants to survive, sexual activity can be emotionally beneficial. Natural selection has shaped the homo-sapiens brain such that individuals may feel large amounts of emotional pleasure from engaging in reproductive activities. Natural selection has probably also shaped the brain such that if a person does not engage in any reproductive activities, the person may experience disturbing mental illness and may even go crazy. These powerful emotional mechanisms motivate people to engage in reproductory activities even though, from a cost/benefit standpoint, the offspring benefit far more from these acts than do the parents. The propagation of the gene is at the expense of the welfare of the propagators, but powerful emotional mechanisms propel the propagators to create offspring in spite of the harm these activities may cause the propagators. The gene is "selfish" in this regard (Dawkins, 1976).

The great pleasure that animals may feel from sexual reproduction is a "consolation prize," given to the animal by the brain's evolved pleasure centers, that offsets the cost that sexually reproducing animals accrue due to having fewer resources to use for personal survival, because the animal must spend large amounts of resources on gestating and/or raising the offspring resulting from reproductory activities. The forces of evolution are almost duping animals, by evolving animal brains to give animals huge amounts of emotional pleasure as a reward for engaging in sexual activity, and also perhaps by evolving animal minds such that animals feel like crap emotionally, and may even go crazy, if they do not engage in any sexual activity. These emotional forces compel or force animals to engage in reproductory activities, but animals harm their own personal survival and welfare due to having to devote large amounts of time, energy and resources to the raising of the offspring. This may have been what the poet William Blake had in mind when he wrote, "Joys impregnate, sorrows bring forth." (Blake, 1793). However, from an evolutionary standpoint, this duping is an excellent idea.

Those who gain large amounts of pleasure from sexual activity are presumably more likely to engage in this activity, and are presumably more likely to have offspring, and to generate a greater number of offspring, which in turn propagates the genes of this horny individual in the gene pool. People who do not like sexual activity may be less likely to have offspring, or will have fewer offspring, such that there is a higher chance of their genes being wiped out of the gene pool. One exception to these generalizations would be that if dangerous sexually transmitted diseases are rampant in a society or an epoch, those who have sex less may live longer lives, so that they may have greater numbers of offspring compared to hornier individuals who live shorter lives due to acquiring sexually transmitted diseases at younger ages.

There are other exceptions to the generalization that minds generally find sex to be extremely pleasurable. Females pay the highest price for sexual pleasure because their bodies lose large amounts of nutrients when gestating a fetus, so females tend to be choosier when choosing mates, and more hesitant to engage in reproductive activity, simply because they do not want to invest energy in gestating a fetus unless the male contributing the genes for that fetus meets their standards of desirability in a male partner. Significant numbers of females find sex to be not particularly pleasurable, which can be an adaptive tendency, if delaying sexual activity until a more "optimal" male partner is found can result in offspring that have better access to resources. Such offspring of more "optimal" males may also have genes of physically stronger males who are more resistant to disease and disability. In homo sapiens civilization, despite its advanced medical care, doctors cannot cure all diseases and sometimes doctors actually injure or kill patients via misdiagnosis of disease or incorrect treatment procedures. Hence, civilization has not obviated the need for, and the adaptability of, having an intrinsically disease-resistant body, that can resist disease in the absence of modern medical care.

Compared to females, males generally invest less time and effort and energy in the rearing of offspring, and are punished less, from a resource-loss standpoint, for engaging in sexual activity. This helps to explain why, in general, males may feel more pleasure from sexual activity, since males incur fewer costs per sexual act compared to a female who must gestate the baby. Of course, if homo sapiens civilization structure forces men to spend large amounts of money on rearing offspring, the men incur a large resource-losing cost for having sex. Males can also be seriously injured in fights with other males to determine alpha male status within a species' sexual dominance hierarchy.

The evolution of people who do not find sexual behavior particularly pleasurable can be adaptive. In some historical epochs, in some human societies, frequent sexual behavior could reduce the ability to propagate genes, if there was a high prevalence of dangerous or deadly sexually transmitted diseases within those societies within those epochs. Pregnancy during times of famine also might not be useful for gene propagation, if there was a high chance of offspring starving to death before those offspring could reproduce. Evolution has therefore evolved humans with a wide variety of intensities of libido. A high libido is adaptive with societies and epochs where there is plenty of food and minimal prevalence of sexually transmitted diseases. A low libido is adaptive with societies and epochs where the opposite may occur. Other variables impact the affect of libido intensity on the ultimate evolutionary goal of gene reproduction.

The fundamental evolutionary measure of sexual success is not how much sex an organism has, but instead how many offspring the organism generates. An organism is an evolutionary success if the organism generates enough offspring to offset the loss of the parents' genes caused by the eventual death of the offspring's parents or, more ideally than that, that the parents generate greater numbers of offspring than the quantitative loss of the parents that would occur from the eventual deaths of the parents. There are a wide variety of styles of sexual behavior that are adaptive, with a wide range in the amount of pleasure a mind gains from sexual activity, or for how many years a mind is sexually active. For example, if two parents both hate sex, and have very little sex, but have more offspring than is required to replenish their numbers upon their deaths, then these parents' reproductory behavior is adaptive. Theoretically, only one sex act is required to generate one new offspring, so even if a parental pair has sex a total of four times in their lives, because they both hate sex, if they generate four offspring from those four sex acts, their sexual tendencies in hindsight are very much adaptive, more than a pair of parents who have sex hundreds of times a year, but only generate two offspring between them.

If the fundamental evolutionary measure of sexual success is how much offspring a parent has, the "morally good or bad" or "rational versus irrational" traits of the parents is of secondary relevance to the propagation of their genes as a measure of their sexual success, even if the personalities of the parents harm the parents' own survival. Suppose a woman prefers a male partner who is low in intelligence, very macho and very aggressive, even if the male is aggressive to the point of being physically abusive. Yes, such women do exist among the homo sapiens species, political correctness aside. Suppose this woman meets such a male, and this male's qualities arouse powerful impulses in that female, such that this female continuously engages in reproductive activity with this male, and generates four children as a result. Then, the male turns out to be a bit too aggressive, and murders someone over a drug deal gone bad, after which, that male is also violently murdered in revenge, dying at the age of 35 and leaving behind four children and a mother with no income. Many in society would be judgmental towards this male, calling him a kind of irresponsible thug, who made his living through drugs instead of through legitimate work, and who irresponsibly lived a dangerous life that resulted in him dying young and no longer being able to care for his children, while physically harming his wife while alive. Society might also be judgmental towards the wife for choosing such a partner and now, after losing the partner and having no income, being potentially obligated to accept public welfare

97

indefinitely, while raising four children in a resource-deprived environment. And yet, putting value judgements aside, this male's behavior was quite adaptive from an evolutionary standpoint. He generated four offspring, which is above the replacement level of approximately two, or the numbers of the parents' gene pool who would be lost once the parents died. Actually, these parents are more adaptive than two other, more educated parents, who only had one child because they performed an intelligent calculation, thinking ahead twenty years to consider twenty years of budgeting, that they could only provide an excellent amount of resources for raising one child, and not more than one.

If a bio-engineer could design an organism from scratch, by forming the organism's DNA from scratch, and the bio-engineer was faced with the question of how to design the organism such that this organism would be aggressively motivated to reproduce, would the bio-engineer also incorporate "questionably ethical" components into the mind-function of this organism, that are similar to those that the forces of natural selection install in mammalian mind-function? There are insects where females kill and eat their male mates shortly after having sex. This is bad for the male, but great for the male's genes, and is also an ethical disaster resulting from the forces of natural selection that evolved this behavior in such insects.

The pleasure of having sex may be so extreme, that many people see having sex as one of life's central goals, and may constantly be thinking up elaborate strategies to gain sexual pleasure. This is because evolutionary selection pressures generally favor evolving mammals that feel ever more pleasure from sexual activity, because the feeling of such pleasure is generally extremely adaptive for the purposes of gene propagation. In addition, a mind's sense of well-being, or day-to-day sense of feeling good about life, is in many minds linked to a realization or assessment of how well that mind's sex life is or was. Not only is plentiful sex rewarded with the release of large amounts of pleasurable neurotransmitters, but long after the completion of the sexual acts, a steady flow of pleasurable neurotransmitters may continue in the brain, even during platonic activities, due to the continuous realization that, in the past, a mind had a good quality sex life and a good supply of pleasurable sex. The forces of evolution have evolved brains such as to reward brains that engage in sex not only with extreme pleasure from the act, but also with a continued steady supply of pleasure from the improved sense of well-being resulting from having had a good sex life in one's personal history.

With human sexual reproduction, two people must both come together and engage in reproductory activities in order for an offspring to be generated. A single, sexually frustrated homo sapiens individual cannot generate offspring by masturbating to porn. Masturbation, however, is safe, with no sexually transmitted diseases being exchanged, and does not harm a person's personal ability to survive on the planet earth, because no offspring result from masturbation, so that a person does not have to expend resources, that could be used to improve that person's own survival, on the survival of offspring. Since masturbation is better than two-person sex in these two regards, why don't people avoid sex entirely, and just spend their time masturbating alone? Certainly, the advent of high-definition internet porn, often freely given when it is a form of advertising, makes masturbation much more fun than it ever has been. The simple answer is that masturbation behavior is not adaptive from an evolutionary standpoint, and does not result in offspring generation and gene propagation. This would imply that natural selection tends to evolve people such that people feel emotionally bad if they engage alone in imaginary masturbatory pursuits, or, if they do feel pleasure from masturbation, that they feel much less pleasure than if they engage in a real-life reproductive act. Presumably, then, there must exist cognitive structures in the brain that somehow motivate a person to seek out an actual sexual encounter with another person, instead of exclusively engaging in imaginary sexual activities like masturbation.

Given that imaginary sexual activities like masturbation, or watching porn, are not as exciting or fulfilling for most people as are real-life sexual encounters, there presumably exists a part of the brain, that humans cannot control, that monitors a person's sexual behavior to determine if that sexual behavior is imaginary or real. If the behavior is imaginary, and this sexuality monitoring part of the mind detects the behavior as imaginary, then the emotion-inducing neurons that will be activated as a

99

result of this imaginary behavior will not release as many pleasurable neurotransmitters in response to such behavior compared to a real-life sexual act. Also, these neurotransmitters may be released in a part of the brain where there are large amounts of neurotransmitter re-uptake mechanisms, such that any released pleasurable neurotransmitters may be rapidly re-uptaken and broken down. Here, a masturbation high would be like a dysfunctional cocaine high that is quickly followed by a depression-inducing crash.

In contrast, a real-life reproductory encounter may result in release of neurotransmitters in an area of the brain where there are few neurotransmitter re-uptake mechanisms, resulting in a more prolonged high in response to the sexual activity. If the sexual behavior is real, and if this behavior may result in propagation of a person's genes, then the sexual monitoring part of the mind will detect that the behavior is real, and as a result of this behavior, different emotion-inducing neurons will be activated, that will provide more intense pleasure compared to those emotion-inducing neurons that are activated in response to an imaginary sexual event. Having frequent good-quality real-life reproductory encounters may also physically change the brain such as to create in participants a long-term feeling of increased well-being and optimism that participants continue to feel throughout their lives long after the real-life reproductory episodes have ended. Masturbation and other imagined reproductory activities may not create this sense of long-term well-being, which would manifest as an increased release of pleasurable neurotransmitters that occurs throughout the person's life, in response to the general act of existing, like a release of pleasurable neurotransmitters happening in the background of the person's mind-function.

How can this sexual monitoring part of the brain detect if a sexual encounter is real or imaginary? The simple answer is that different combinations of sensory inputs, or energy fingerprint inputs, are received by the brain in a real-life sexual encounter compared to an imaginary sexual encounter. Different sensory neurons on the skin, inputting different combinations of touch and temperature energy fingerprints, are activated in a real life reproductory encounter compared to an imaginary encounter.

Different combinations of energy fingerprint inputs from sounds, tastes and smells are inputted, by sensory inputting mechanisms that send signals to the mind, in a real-life sexual encounter compared to an imaginary sexual encounter. The different combinations of sensory stimuli experienced during a real-life reproductory encounter, compared to an imaginary masturbatory experience, serve as a set of energy fingerprints that enables the sexual monitoring part of the brain to detect the difference between a real-life and an imaginary reproductory act. The sexual monitoring part of the brain can then induce a person to feel different degrees of pleasurable emotions, and different senses of well-being, temporary or permanent, in response to imaginary versus real-life sexual encounters. The sexual monitoring cortex forces people to feel greater amounts of emotional pain in response to imaginary sexual encounters, and greater amounts of emotional pleasure in response to real-life sexual encounters. The inability of people in general to "fool" this sexual monitoring cortex forces people to seek out real-life sexual encounters, to avoid the emotional pain that the sexual monitoring cortex may impose on a person if a person spends too much time in life experiencing imaginary sexual encounters.

Those minds that do not engage in reproductory pursuits may experience repeated jabs of emotional pain from the lack of reproductory pursuits. From time to time, an intense feeling of emotional pain may be felt, along with a thought experienced by this mind that this mind needs to engage in a reproductory activity. This may be due to frequent firing of neurons in a part of the mind that registers a sensation of emotional pain, in response to a detection, by the sexual over-brain, that the mind is not stimulating frequently enough, if at all, those sensory inputting mechanisms that receive sensory inputs during real-life reproductory activities. The mind knows instinctively and consciously that only by engaging in a real-life reproductory encounter can this repeated feeling of stabbing emotional pain be eliminated. A mind may try to distract itself from these negative feelings by engaging in pleasurable platonic thinking activities, such as physical exercise, playing chess, listening to music, or reading, but an attempt to distract the frustrated mind may not prevent a continuous firing of those neurons that generate great emotional pain when a mind fails to engage in a reproductory activity. Each time those neurons fire, it is as if a miniature knife is stabbed into the brain, and the desire to avoid this pain provides a strong motivation for that mind to seek out reproductory activity. Only the energizing of the various energy fingerprint inputting mechanisms that are activated during a real-life reproductory encounter will trigger a reflexive cessation of the emotional pinpricks that keep occurring while that mind is in a period of extended celibacy. The neuron pathways that are activated while engaging in a pleasurable platonic activity may themselves be connected to nodes that send energy through a neurological conduit directly to those neurons that generate a stab of emotional pain in reaction to extended periods of celibacy. This kind of recurring emotional torture is, of course, adaptive from an evolutionary standpoint, and is a cruel, but understandably practical, result of the mechanisms of natural selection that evolved this neuron reflex. One wonders how beta males within gorilla societies feel after they have been defeated by alpha males and have been deprived of any access to female gorillas.

In an attempt to satisfy a sexual yearning, what an organic mind is really trying to do is to put that organic mind in a situation where energy is flowing across the neuron pathways that generate the most intense sexual pleasure emotions in that mind. This, in the most reductionist sense, is the ultimate goal of implementing the activities that are attempts to satisfy sexual yearnings. In theory, these neuron pathways can be energized by directly touching those pathways with an electrode probe to send an electric voltage through that neuron pathway. This is generally impractical, since this would probably require brain surgery, assuming that these neuron pathways could be safely accessed through brain surgery.

The other way to send energy flowing across these high-pleasure neuron pathways is the hard way, by doing what is necessary in life, according to an evolved program dictating what is necessary in any particular mind, to induce the sexual over-brain monitoring system to permit energy to flow across these pathways. For a gorilla, this might require earning the status of alpha male, by risking physical and emotional injury by violently and laboriously beating up any rival male gorillas, such as to convince those rival male gorillas that the alpha male has the right to control a certain territory and the harem of females living in that territory, convince the female gorillas that that alpha male has the right to mate with them, and then engage in real-life reproductory activities with the females. For a human, a wide array of strategies are used for attracting mates, all of which require effort and probably money, to obtain access to environmental contexts that would induce energy to flow across those pleasure-inducing neuron pathways.

The things that must be done by a specimen of a species before energy will flow across those pleasurable neuron pathways are essentially arbitrary thinking constructs within the minds of that specimen, arbitrarily installed in the mind via natural selection over the evolutionary history of that species' genes. But without these things being done, the filtering mechanisms of the sexual over-brain will not permit energy to flow across these neuron pathways. There are "layers" of other neuron pathways that must be energized first, often as a result highly procedural or step-by-step behavioral activities, before energy will flow across the neuron pathways that generate the most pleasurable sexual emotions. In this way, the sexual over-brain structure is a kind of neurological gate-keeper, that will only permit energy to flow across those neuron pathways if an organic mind is experiencing energy fingerprints that are projected from a real-life reproductory activity involving at least one real-life mating partner.

Physical beauty and ugliness are remarkable phenomena of evolution. These traits seem to exist for no other reason but to function as variables that arbitrarily reduce or enhance a person's sexual attractiveness, without any regard to other physical attributes that are relevant to fitness for reproducing one's genes, such as physical strength, resistance to disease, or access to life-support resources. The common sense notion, that homo sapiens exist in a world where homo sapiens are of varying degrees of physical beauty and ugliness, is part of the "that's just how it is" awareness, that people tend to have, of what exists on the planet earth, along with such "automatically clear and present things" like rocks, trees, blue skies (on a clear day), and water rivers. The homo sapiens mind seems unable to not notice physical beauty and ugliness, and the homo sapiens mind seems to possess mechanisms for judging the sexual attractiveness of a person based partly on their physical appearance.

Why did physical beauty and ugliness, and the associated mind mechanisms that detect and rate physical beauty and ugliness, evolve? It is possible that, in human history, there have been many epochs and societies where frequent sexual behavior was, at one time point, not dangerous, but which suddenly and unpredictably became dangerous. Epidemics of dangerous sexually transmitted diseases may have suddenly and unpredictably occurred. Crop failures or wars may have suddenly occurred, that would be destined to kill off large numbers of newly procreated offspring. The people who might be most likely to survive these disasters, and/or to later propagate their genes, are the ugly ones who arbitrarily had sex less often. The ugly ones might have sulked in a corner while the beautiful ones had vibrant sex lives, but then, if the beautiful ones suddenly died en masse due to a sudden and unpredictable epidemic of deadly sexually transmitted diseases, the ugly ones would take over and begin to dominate the gene pool. Or, if the offspring of the beautiful ones suddenly died en masse due to a sudden famine or sudden war, the ugly ones, who had saved their energies and resources because they did not have enough sex to have offspring, find themselves more robust and energetic than the beautiful ones who depleted their energies and resources raising now-deceased offspring. These events would give the ugly ones a reproducing advantage over the beautiful ones. The persistence of physical beauty and ugliness in the human gene pool, and the associated mind mechanisms for rating and responding to these phenomena, shows that the existence in the gene pool, of this arbitrary variable that arbitrarily influences sexual attractiveness, can be evolutionarily adaptive. The physically ugly may be viewed as evolutionary "sacrificial lambs" who are statistically destined to sulk in the corner and experience less exciting sexual lives than the beautiful people, but who will become the "hero saviors" of the homo sapiens gene pool in those epochs and societies where the beautiful people die like flies due to sexually transmitted diseases.

In any species, the thinking that motivates sexual behavior might evolve into a "free-for-all" mentality, where both males and females rush to engage in as much reproductory activity as is possible. Or, instead, the thinking that motivates sexual behavior can evolve into a "parameterized" sexual mentality, where a species' minds have evolved such there is some kind of tacit agreement among minds of the same species that reproductory behaviors will only occur under certain circumstances.

A "free-for-all" reproductory behavior might be evolutionarily adaptive if the specimens of that species were generally equal in mind functionality and physical attributes. Such equality might exist, to some extent, among insects, which have somewhat homogeneous mind and body functionalities that are locked into highly parameterized life-support and gene-reproduction niches. However, most animals are not equal in strength, immune system robustness, or other traits. This has resulted in the evolution of minds that parameterize sexual activity, to steer such activity towards activity that results in more "fit" genetics being installed in the gene pool of that animal species. Often, females do not mate with a male unless that male wins some kind of dominance fight, where that male fights with another male, wins the fight over the weaker male, and thereby convinces the female to mate with the winner of the fight. Here, there is a kind of tacit "cooperation" or "agreement" among multiple minds that the winner of the fight convinces the female to mate with that winner, while the loser is marginalized on the sidelines.

Homo sapiens have elevated the phenomenon of "parameterized sexual behavior" to a level that far eclipses non-human animals in its complexity. Payment of dowries as a pre-requisite for permitting a marriage, obligating people to show monogamous loyalty to their married spouses, marriages contingent on the approval of family authorities, the wearing of clothes to block visual information about genitalia, discouraging public discussion of sexuality, rating sexual the attractiveness of males to be higher if the males are physically strong, rating the sexual attractiveness of females to be higher if the females are are thin, or having legal systems that regulate sexual issues such as divorce, rape or adultery, are all examples of how humans have created complex parameterizations of human reproductory behavior. The obligation imposed by society that people should not have children unless they are married, with the money to support the children, is another parameter. Home mortgages, and their parameters, are probably influenced by sexuality, in that the demand for houses is linked to the demand to have a private shelter for engaging in reproductory activities in private, so that information about such activity is not leaked to the public. Signing onto a home mortgage is harmful to a person's psychological and financial welfare, but doing so is adaptive behavior, if this enables a marital couples to gain access to a house, as an organized meeting place for raising offspring, which then satisfies societal parameters, imposed on the couple, to limit sexual activity and offspring generation to those activities occurring in the context of possessing a house. Remarkably, it is often little more than "mind-thought" that enforces these sexual parameters. The simple observation by a female that a male does not have a steady job, that can generate money that can pay for raising offspring, or that may be used to convince a bank to loan a home mortgage to that male, may be enough to convince that female not to marry that male.

The Qualia Question

In philosophy, there exists what is known as the qualia problem. A qualia is defined as a subjective experience (Dennet, 1990, 1991, 2017; Pinker, 1997; Jackson, 1982). For example, one may speak of the qualia of eating a banana. How or what do I feel when I eat a banana? How does another person or a chimpanzee feel when they eat a banana? Does each person feel different feelings, and at different times, when eating a banana? A similar qualia question might also be: what does a frog feel like if it eats a bug, and how does that differ from what a human might feel like if the human eats the same bug? How is it possible to describe in reductionist terms these subjective feelings (Nagel, 1974)? The difficulty or impossibility of doing so is posited to be proof that it is impossible to describe the human brain, or any other organic brain, in reductionist terms.

However, the qualia question, or the problem of how to explain subjective experiences, is scientifically imprecise. Although we do not understand why we feel pain or pleasure, and perhaps never will, it is not necessary to describe why we feel anything to be able to understand how an organic mind works in reductionist terms. The reason is that all feelings, that a particular organism feels, at a particular moment of Planck time, are felt as a result of the specific types and proportions of atoms and molecules making up that organism at that moment of Planck time, and the specific inter-molecular and intra-molecular atomic bonding forces that make those atoms and molecules cohere with one another into that coherent organism, and also the individual quantum energy states of all of the atoms and molecules within that system. All of these atoms, bonding forces, and quantum energy states elements are strictly parameterized, in that they cohere in a strictly parameterized way to make up that organism at that moment of Planck time. Therefore, whatever feelings that organism feels at that specific moment of Planck time, those feelings result from a strictly parameterized arrangement of atoms and molecules, bonding situations, and quantum energy states within that organism.

It is impossible for an organism to feel a particular feeling at a specified moment of Planck time, unless the precise matter parameters that make up that organism, and that organism's aggregate of quantum energy states, exist exactly such as to make the feeling of those feelings possible, at that moment of Planck time. This would make it impossible for a being to exist that was physically identical to another person, but was not consciously aware (Chalmers, 1996, Kirk, 2005). In order for that person to be consciously aware, that person must be consciously aware within a range of units of Planck time, and that person's specific state of conscious awareness must result from a strictly parameterized arrangement of matter of strictly parameterized quantum states. If another person could be generated who was physically like that person, but not consciously aware, by definition the unconscious person cannot be of the same parameterized aggregation of matter as the consciously aware person. The two people would consist of two entirely different states of matter and therefore could not be identical. In short, zombies, if they can exist, cannot be identical copies of the consciously aware counterpart to that zombie.

The experience of eating a banana projects energy fingerprints to the five senses. These energy fingerprints alter the quantum energy states of the atoms and molecules in the organism's system. However, this banana-eating experience can only change the quantum energy states of the organism system in strictly parameterized ways, dictated by the laws of physics. Therefore, it is scientifically imprecise to describe eating a banana in terms of the "qualia" or "subjective experience" of eating a banana. Instead, one can, in theory, describe the experience of eating a banana in a strictly reductionist, scientific way, by calculating how the consumption of the banana alters the quantum energy states of all of the atoms and molecules that make up the organism, for each unit of Planck time during which the organism is consuming the banana. Of course, practically, this is not possible because there does not exist a super-computer that has enough number-crunching power to perform this calculation in real-time.

An interesting consequence, of the idea that feelings result from strictly parameterized matter states within organisms, is that moods and feelings are, in theory, infinitely reproducible. The atoms and molecules, and their individual proportions, that make up an organism at a particular moment of Planck time, can be thought of as a set of atoms and molecules in various proportions, quantum states and atomic bonding relationships with one another. The same set of atoms and molecules, and their proportions, that make up an organism at a particular moment of Planck time, exists on the planet earth in billions of potential copies of these sets of atoms and molecules, and in the universe in a practically infinite number of set copies. It is theoretically possible, for example, for 1 billion copies to exist, on the planet earth, of Albert Einstein, at any particular moment of Planck time in Albert Einstein's life, that duplicates the exact mood felt by Einstein at that specified Planck time moment. There are enough sets of atoms and molecules on the planet earth to make over 1 billion copies of Albert Einstein at any particular moment of Planck time in Albert Einstein's life. Any mood or feeling felt by any organism at any particular moment of Planck time in that organism's life, and the parameterized set of atoms and molecules of the body and mind at that moment of Planck time, the arrangement of which makes it possible for the mind attached to that body to feel that mood or feeling, is essentially infinitely reproducible. The specific elements that make up an organism at any particular moment of Planck time in that organisms's life, namely the sub-atomic particles, atoms, molecules, bonding force structures, and quantum energy states, are immortal elements that form states of matter when interacting with one another, in ways that are always strictly parameterized by the laws of physics.

Of course, practically, homo-sapiens do not have the technology to make an exact atomic copy of any human down to the exact quantum energy states of all the atoms and molecules that make up that human at any particular moment in Planck time, as the laws of physics permit in theory. Humans can, practically speaking, create a genetic clone of a human by putting that human's genome in a zygote, implanting the zygote in a female womb (which is a molecular machine, the only one that we know of, with the capability of concatenating atoms and molecules into a homo-sapiens body form by following a DNA information script contained within a zygote), and waiting about 18 years for the human to gestate, be born and grow up into an adult. However, this adult clone would not be an exact copy of its human predecessor, because the quantum energy states of the predecessor's mind were altered by the energy fingerprints emanating from that predecessor's relatives, people met, environments lived in, and contemporary historical times. The clone would not have access to these energy fingerprints. The energy fingerprints from the environment that the predecessor was exposed to would have altered the aggregate quantum energy states of all of the atoms and molecules of the predecessor, at various moments of Planck time in the life of the predecessor, in ways that would not occur with the predecessor's clone. The clone would be exposed to a different variety of energy fingerprint stimuli, that would alter the quantum energy states of the clone's being in ways that would not occur with the predecessor.

The fact that all feelings felt by a mind at a specific moment in Planck time result from a mind being composed of a strictly parameterized concatenation of sub-atomic particles and their respective quantum energy states, implies that there must exist a theory of physics that specifies under what circumstances organic minds that can feel emotions can exist. A theory of physics can exist that specifies parameters of coherent sub-atomic particles of various kinds, that are arranged in specified positions in three dimensions space due to specified bonding forces, such that the arrangement results in minds existing that are attached to bodies, such that the minds can feel emotional feelings. Physicists have not yet developed such a theory, and even if they did, it may forever be unknowable or arbitrary why specified parameterized three dimensional arrangements of sub-atomic particles could give rise to emotion-feeling organic minds. The natural world implements such a hypothetical physics theory whenever a biological gestating machine such as a womb follows a DNA information guide to direct the arrangement of lifeless atoms and molecules into sub-atomically parameterized, three dimensional organisms that can feel feelings. However, to paraphrase Winston Churchill, it is a mystery, wrapped inside an enigma, wrapped inside a puzzle, wrapped inside a burrito, as to why such an arrangement of lifeless matter would result in feelings, or why a state of matter is capable of feeling anything.

Presently, physicists do not have explanations or theoretical frameworks for predicting when matter will give rise to feelings in minds attached to the matter. However, if a biologist sequences the DNA of an organism that is known to feel pain or pleasure, the biologist knows that if this DNA is incorporated into a zygote, and the protein synthesis instructions in the DNA are followed to produce a clone of this organism, then the resulting organism will have feelings. That organism will be made up of lifeless atoms and molecules, but the arrangement of these atoms and molecules, dictated by the DNA, such that all of the information of the DNA is precisely knowable to scientists, will give rise to a feeling organism. So, the biologist is aware of specific situations where lifeless matter can be structured into a state of matter that consists of feeling organisms, but the biologist does not have a physics theory to explain why these situations result in the existence of the feeling organisms. Therefore, the scientific ability to "make feeling creatures out of lifeless matter" exists among scientists, and this skill is implemented every time a scientist edits DNA that will eventually be used to generate a zygote that matures into a feeling organism.

A question sometimes asked by philosophers is, if a teleportation device (like in the TV show Start Trek) could disintegrate a person and then re-integrate the person at another teleportation device located a distance away from the first teleportation device, would the person at the distant teleportation device be the same as the person who entered the first teleportation device? The answer is that they would both be the same, because a specific human body at a specific moment in Planck time is defined by what sub-atomic particles make up that body, and the locations in three-dimensional space of these sub-atomic particles, said location being determined by the energy states of each sub-atomic particle at that moment in Planck time, where said energy states also determine how those sub-atomic particles are bonded together. It does not matter if different physical examples, of the same types of sub-atomic particles, are used to form the body duplicate at the second teleportation device. The second body will be the same as the first body, because the same types of sub-atomic particles, in the same proportions, and bonded together to be positioned in the same way in three-dimensional space, were used to form the second body, as initially constituted the first body. The state of matter that generates a human at any moment of Planck time during that human's life is, in principle, infinitely reproducible.

Scientists have determined that all of the atoms and molecules in a body at one point in time become completely changed out and replaced by the same atoms and molecules, approximately every 7-10 years. 98% of the atoms and molecules in the body are changed out completely within 1 year. Yet, the person remains essentially the same person, although a person containing altered quantum energy states due to the energy fingerprints that emanated from the person's added experiences over those years. The atoms and molecules can change, while the person remains mostly the same, showing how the person's body is defined by how the atoms and molecules in that person's body are arranged in 3-dimensional space, and not by which specific specimens of those atoms and molecules exist in that person's body. The automatic, natural change-out of the atoms and molecules that make up a person every 7-10 years, which occurs while the person remains that same person, within a range of statistical tolerance, is practically a natural version of the hypothetical Star Trek teleportation device, and serves as a kind of proof that the effect of the natural atom changeout and the Star Trek teleportation device are the same. That is, the specific examples of the specific atoms are different, but the person is the same, because the basic arrangement and proportions of the atoms that make up the person are essentially the same.

A question similar to the teleportation question is, if a person smashes a computer with a sledgehammer, what happens to the computer's mind? The specific atoms and molecules and sub-atomic particles that made up that computer's mind no longer cohere in the sledgehammered computer to make that computer's mind possible. However, that same model of computer can be reproduced exactly, within a range of statistical tolerance, by assembling other combinations of the same types of atoms, molecules and sub-atomic particles, by following the original design of that computer. The specific atoms, molecules, and sub-atomic particles that make up the new computer mind are different, but the computer's mind functions exactly like the previous computer. It is not the specific atoms, molecules and sub-atomic particles that determine the characteristics of that computer's mind, but the specific types and proportions of these particles, and how they are arranged together and inter-related with one another via inter- and intra-molecular bonding forces.

A slightly different question would be, if a computer mind is thinking or processing something, and while the computer was doing this, the computer was smashed with a sledgehammer, what would happen to the computer's thought process? Smashing the computer scatters the electrons, that were somehow "unified together" into a "cohesive thinking cloud or entity." However, what was destroyed here was only an inter-relationship between the electrons, and not a non-reproducible thinking computer mind. Duplicating the computer by manufacturing another of the same model can result in duplication of essentially the same inter-relationships between the electrons that caused the computer's thinking process at the moment when that computer was smashed with the sledgehammer.

A computer cannot, in practice, be duplicated exactly, down to the exact sub-atomic details, and down to the exact quantum energy states, of all of the sub-atomic particles of the computer being duplicated. The duplicate computer will, at the sub-atomic level, show vast variations in differences between it and the previous computer of the same make and model. Each microscopic silicon transistor will be an approximation of the shape of the corresponding silicon transistor of the previous example of the same model, and perhaps be inaccurate by a few thousand or million silicon atoms in each dimension. However, within a reasonable probabilistic range, the two computers will be identical, and will be probabilistically identical enough to have the same mind functionality.

Suppose a person is swimming in the ocean and is suddenly attacked by a saltwater crocodile. Feelings of horror may overtake the person for each moment of Planck time while the person is being eaten alive. With each moment of Planck time, the aggregate quantum state of the person's body varies in total energy-level. The total energy level at a particular moment of Planck time results from the proportion of atoms and molecules in that person's body, the quantum energy state of each atom and molecule, and the specific intra-molecular and inter-molecular forces that bind or cohere these atoms and molecules into a coherent body form. The total quantum energy of the entire body system at each moment of Planck time is strictly parameterized, and in theory practically infinite numbers of copies of that body's aggregate of quantum states can be made in the universe. Each specific feeling of horror felt by the person, at each Planck time moment while the person is being eaten alive, is associated with a strictly parameterized description of the aggregate quantum energy state of all of the atoms and molecules that make up that person. This implies that a feeling that is felt at a particular moment of Planck time cannot be felt, unless the corresponding precisely parameterized quantum energy states of that person's body, that are associated with that particular feeling, exist as energy states within that person at that moment of Planck time. Since the quantum energy state of a body is strictly describable by the laws of physics, it follows that all feelings are strictly parameterized, in that specific feelings can only arise from strictly parametrizable states of matter.

Some Philosophy of Mind

Not Feeling Like Doing Something

A common phenomena among humans, that most people feel at some point during every day of their lives, occurs when a human is obligated to perform a task, but does not feel like performing the task. The person thinks to himself or herself, "I have to clean the bathroom, but I don't feel like it," or, "I have to pump gas for this customer now, but I don't feel like it." If that human then proceeds to perform this task that the human "does not feel like doing," then the human may feel considerable emotional discomfort, and perhaps a tiny amount of lasting emotional trauma, while performing the task, even if the task is a seemingly simple task like sweeping the floor or pumping gas. The American writer Herman Melville wrote a famous short story, called "Bartleby the Scrivener," that expands on this concept with absurd and lurid satire

(Melville, 1853). A human brain is not like a computer. A computer is not limited by by a feeling of "not feeling like doing something," since the computer does everything that a human directs the computer to do, without resistance, instantly upon command, with absolute precision of analytical and algorithmic thinking, driven by unlimited electrical energy.

Why does this phenomenon of "not feeling like doing something" exist, and how does this phenomenon occur at the neurological level? This question cannot be precisely answered using existing scientific knowledge. The existence of this "I don't feel like it" phenomena probably represents a defect or weakness of the human brain, because this phenomena shows that the human brain is not willing or able to perform all useful tasks that it should ideally perform at all times when the tasks require performance. One might speculate at some reasons why this phenomenon exists. A task may be emotionally painful to perform, such as cleaning out a septic tank for free, or as part of a job requirement performed for a minimal compensation. A task may be intellectually complex, such as to rapidly deplete neurotransmitters like dopamine in the brain, or generate large amounts of damaging free radicals, or rapidly deplete the brain's resources that the brain uses to perform anabolic learning tasks that are needed to perform the intellectually complex activity. A person may start performing the intellectual activity with some enthusiasm, with this feeling of enthusiasm being caused by pleasurable neurotransmitters being released within the brain in response to performing this activity, but soon after beginning the activity, the activity rapidly depletes the brain's neurotransmitter and nutrient resources to perform this activity, making the person feel "tired" from the activity.

The depletion of neurotransmitters causes the brain to be incapable of performing a task efficiently, or at all. At this point, further attempts to continue the activity would be like trying to push at a stubborn horse to make the horse perform more work. The brain may rebel at performance of a complex intellectual task that the brain is too depleted of resources to perform, by making a person feel painful emotional feelings as a result of attempts to perform this task. This is the brain's way of saying that the person should take a break from this task, and rest or eat a nutritious meal, so that the

116

brain has time to re-synthesize the neurotransmitters that are needed to continue performing this task. A task can also be psychologically unpleasant, such as being tasked with killing people in war. Also, peoples' brains, as they age, may become less capable of performing the anabolic bio-chemical reactions that are needed to perform an activity that involves learning, such as learning a new job. The inability to learn may cause a brain to incur powerful emotional feelings of resistance, if that learning-incapable mind attempts to perform a task that requires extensive learning, and this resistance results in a thought that one does not feel like doing that task.

Tasks that are highly mathematical or scientific, or that require multiple steps, each requiring precise timing, are perhaps more likely to rapidly deplete the brain's nutritional resources compared to tasks that require less such thought. However, even a simple task like pumping gas can be emotionally painful to perform if the brain is depleted of the nutrients or neurotransmitter chemicals that are needed to perform this simple task. Free radicals, that build up in the brain while performing a task, can also cause temporary brain damage to the neurons that are involved in performing this task, leading to a person resisting the obligation to perform the task and thinking that they do not feel like performing this task at this time. After taking a rest, the brain may, during the rest period or nap, engage in anabolic and neurotransmitter synthesizing activities that restore to optimal functionality the neuron networks involved in performing these tasks, leading a person to feel like their minds have become "refreshed" and are now able to perform those tasks again, and now feel like performing these tasks. However, the brain usually performs any one task in bursts of activity, and not continuously, like a computer, because unlike the computer, the brain must constantly stop to repair the free-radical-damaged brain circuits involved in the activity, or to replenish those brain circuits by re-synthesizing neurotransmitters to replace those that have been consumed. A computer has an unlimited supply of thought-conducting electrons to power its thinking tasks, and this energy moves along relatively inert and indestructible silicon logic gates, so that the computer can generally think non-stop, such as by playing 500 expert-level chess games in a row.

Unlike a computer, an organic mind has a finite supply of thought-conducting particles to use for carrying out any one particular thought. Consequently, organic brains might have evolved to have mechanisms for conserving neurotransmitters. Brains may have evolved with a compromise solution for solving the problem of relatively low levels of neurotransmitters, by requiring that a brain, depleted of neurotransmitters, pauses the performance of a thinking task, and instead spends considerable amounts of time napping or sleeping so that bio-chemical synthesizing activities can replenish the supply of neurotransmitters. Brains may have evolved such that the same thought is not thought multiple times within a short time period, to prevent rapid depletion of neurotransmitters along the neuron pathways that generate that specific thought. The "I don't feel like it" reaction to engaging in specific thinking activities is a mechanism for not thinking using neuron pathways that are depleted of thought-conducting particles. Another possible way of preventing neurotransmitter depletion along a specific neuron pathway is to have multiple copies of that same neuron pathway that conducts a specific kind of thought or thinking process. If a neuron pathway, that thinks that same kind of thought, is used many times per day, having multiple copies of that same pathway enables the mind to switch to a different copy of that pathway, one that contains a fresh, unused supply of neurotransmitters, if another copy of that pathway was previously used and was previously depleted of its neurotransmitters. Then, later, after all of the neuron pathways that carry out for that same thinking process are depleted, the mind stops thinking those kinds of thoughts, and the mind can nap or sleep to provide an opportunity for replenishing the neurotransmitters of all of those redundant neuron pathways.

Sometimes, a feeling that one does not like to do something results from physiological discomfort, that causes emotional discomfort from performing a task. For example, if a task involves use of muscles, then as the task is being performed, lactic acid may build up in the muscles, which fatigues the muscles. The brain may react to this lactic acid buildup by activating neuron pathways that make a person feel emotionally fatigued from performing the activity. The person would then need to take a break to allow the muscles to metabolize and neutralize the lactic acid buildup, which then would remove the emotional feeling of discomfort at performing the task, and make the person feel "refreshed" again and "motivated" again to continue performing the task. Tasks that involve bending the back may also cause back pain, which also may trigger the brain to activate neuron pathways that generate unpleasant emotions in the mind, and obligate the worker to take a break and let the back recover from the activity. Certainly, if a person is physically sick, that person may not feel like doing anything but resting.

Why Humans Compose Music or Create Art

The human mind contains systems of yearnings, consisting of numerous examples of emotional pains that are consistently felt by a mind until that mind performs some activity, or achieves some achievement, which causes replacement of the emotional pain by more pleasurable emotions. A proposed molecular mechanism of "yearnings" is explained in the section of this book on questions and desires. Yearnings evolved in humans to induce humans to focus their actions and thoughts towards behaviors that improve the thermodynamic stability of their body forms, and that improve their abilities to survive and reproduce. Without these yearnings, humans might simply not do anything in life, and instead could, in theory, stand in one place perpetually until they starved to death. The various systems of yearnings existing in human minds are therefore adaptive. Some yearnings, however, may not be adaptive, but exist in some minds as part of the tendency of the forces of evolution to evolve minds with variations of mind-thought, because this variation might with luck enable that mind to access different, but profitable, life support and gene reproduction niches.

If large numbers of humans have similar yearnings, there will be great competition among humans to achieve the goals that will eliminate the emotional pain of these similar yearnings, resulting in some humans not fulfilling their yearnings because they could not compete against other humans trying to gain the things that are yearned for. Not being able to fulfill a yearning could result in a human continuously feeling a quantity and quality of emotional pain, that follows that human around throughout his or her life, wherever they are or whenever they are. Each example of a fully or partially frustrated yearning can feel like an "emotional pinprick" of pain in the mind.

A small number of such psychological pinpricks may not be very troublesome emotionally, but large numbers of these psychological pinpricks can induce the mind to feel an on-going lack of emotional well-being. Since systems of yearnings exist in human minds because these systems are adaptive as systems that motivate humans to improve their ability to survive or reproduce, systems of yearnings are unavoidable evolved traits in human minds. Since the yearning systems are unavoidable traits of the mind, the existence of people who feel continuous emotional pain due to not being able to satisfy their yearnings is also unavoidable, since the competition that causes some people to be pushed aside and not be able to achieve their yearnings is also unavoidable.

One philosophy of living, Buddhism, is based on the idea that the main source of on-going emotional pain is caused by desiring things in life that are manifestly non-permanent, and failing to satisfy those desires. One may, for example, desire to own a sports car, and feel emotionally upset throughout life if one's desire is not fulfilled, and yet the desired sports car will eventually become obsolete and break down completely due to wear and tear and the passage of time. The Buddhist solution to the emotional pain of having desires is for the Buddhist practitioner to try to convince himself or herself not to have desires. The motivation to create the Buddhist philosophy stems from the adaptive evolution of systems of yearnings in organic minds, and the corresponding systems of emotional pain that (generally unavoidably) accompany the inability to satisfy all natural yearnings existing in any one person's mind. Systems of emotional pain, in response to not achieving yearnings, are ways to punish organisms for failing to achieve naturally pre-programmed yearnings, and therefore serve to motivate organisms minds to satisfy these yearnings. To avoid that incessant emotional pinpricks of unsatisfied yearnings, a Buddhist tries to use meditation to convince himself of herself to not have desires. Some peoples' organic minds are cognitively structured such that such Buddhist meditation can work. Perhaps such meditation results in re-organizing the node structures around peoples' neurons, such that neuron pathways that are associated with the communication or encoding of the fact that a particular desire is unfulfilled will not induce energy to pass through a node in a neuron circuit or relaying mechanism such as to cause a painful emotional feelings to be generated. It is not necessarily non-adaptive for some people to have the ability to use Buddhist mind tricks to convince themselves not to be interested in fulfilling yearnings for things that do not directly improve the ability to survive or reproduce. For example, the incremental survival or reproduction advantage of owning a luxury sports car may be minimal compared to owning an old, but functional car that gets one from point A to point B. Although, it is possible that owning a luxury sports car may make the owner appear to have higher socio-economic status, that may result in an increased probability of the owner generating an increased number of offspring for the owner. It would not be adaptive, however, for a Buddhist to convince him or herself that reproductory activities are undesirable, although an ability to do so may be compatible with that Buddhist having an evolutionarily optimal ability to reproduce if, in spite of having such conviction, that Buddhist nonetheless engaged in enough reproductory activities, however minimal, to generate enough offspring to carry on that Buddhist's genes.

A human can sometimes avoid feeling the continuous emotional pain of an unfulfilled yearning by distracting the mind. This may be done by thinking a thought, such that this thought results in energy flowing across a node within a neuron circuit, such that the flow of energy across that node results in a pleasant emotional feeling that may temporarily eliminate the emotional pain of the unfulfilled yearning. Engaging in activities like exercise, reading, exposure to art, or listening to music, might result in pleasurable emotions being felt, due to these activities causing energy to flow across various nodes in various circuits, such as to generate these pleasant emotional feelings, that can reduce or temporarily eliminate the emotional pain of unfulfilled yearnings. The motivation to create art or music or religion is driven by a motivation to create mathematically and/or logically structured patterns such that, when the mind is exposed to these patterns, these patterns induce energy or thought-conducting particles to flow across nodes, such as to result in pleasurable emotions that can reduce the emotional pain of unfulfilled yearnings. Although the motivation to create art, music or religion may not, in and of themselves, seem adaptive, the emotional pain

121

that these creations seek to alleviate result from something that is adaptive, namely the adaptive system of yearnings that has evolved in humans. (Actually, all animals have yearnings. The yearning to reproduce is one obvious example of a yearning that evolved to exist universally among all animals.)

The motivation to create art, music or religion may not itself be particularly adaptive for the creators, since the creators generally have a low chance of gaining money or resources from the creations. However, if the creators feel great emotional pain in their lives due to their own unfulfilled yearnings, the creators may have a motivation to create their creations if only to make their own selves feel emotionally better as a result of exposing their minds to their own creations. The creators also may simply have evolved with mutations for mind functionality that enables them to create their creations, where such mind functionality is not adaptive, but is simply a useless mutation.

However, the motivation to learn about art, music and religion, that is, to cognitively consume the creations of the creators, can be adaptive. The ideas and insights learned from these creations can improve the ability of individuals to survive or reproduce. Learning about a religion can also be adaptive if such learning gives an individual access to mates who will only marry and reproduce with people who believe in and are competent at practicing that particular religion. Religious learning can also be adaptive in societies and epochs where not being competent in the religion can subject a person to exclusion, persecution or execution.

Music has a well-defined mathematical structure. Musical notes consist of sounds with frequency values. In the Western musical scale, each note differs from the note that is chromatically one note away from it by a factor of the 12th square root of two. That is, when the frequency of a specific note in a musical scale is mathematically raised to the exponent of the 12th square root of two, the resulting new frequency value is the frequency value of the next chromatic note up from the first note. After twelve such exponential iterations, the resulting frequency value is exactly double the first frequency value, and this doubled frequency is the octave note of that scale. In other words, all of the twelve notes of a twelve-tone Western musical scale are part of a group of notes that is related to one another by the exponential factor of the 12th square root of two. A twelve-tone Western musical scale may be described mathematically as a geometric series, with the multiplier "r" being the 12th square root of two. Mathematically, when a number is exponentially raised to the 12th square root of two for a total of twelve iterations, the value of the number exactly doubles after the twelve iterations.

When a piece of Western music is heard, the mind is hearing frequency values that are all related to one another by an exponential factor of the 12th square root of two. The notes of a key signature consist of a mathematical group of twelve notes of twelve different frequency values, related to one another by the exponent of the 12th square root of two. A different key signature will consist of a different set of such notes. Modulation, or the movement of a music piece from one key signature to the next, is a kind of mathematical operation that somehow bridges one group of note frequency values with another group.

The mathematical structure of music makes music "graspable" as a structured concept by the mind. Somehow, listening to music generates emotions in the mind (emotions which, presumably, help to reduce the emotional pain of unfulfilled yearnings). No one knows how music generates emotions in the mind. However, it is likely that, because musical notes belong to well-defined mathematical groups, an intuition for understanding music requires an intuitive understanding of group theory in mathematics. It is possible that the mind, when listening to music, intuitively analyzes how the different frequency values heard in the piece of music are mathematically related to one another. The mind may detect many patterns and sub-patterns in how different groups of notes in the music are related to one another, and, with each detection, may react to the act of such detection by feeling an emotion of pain or pleasure, or a mixture of pain or pleasure, as a result. While listening to music, energy or thought-conducting particles flow across large numbers of nodes in neuron circuits, resulting in an emotional reaction with each different example of energy or particles flowing across nodes. This is essentially a kind of emotional reaction to inputting the mathematical patterns perceived in the stream of notes, of various sound frequency values, emanating from the music. It seems arbitrary why the human brain is neurologically wired to feel emotions from streams of sound frequency pixels.

The emotions that may be felt, as reactions to inputting the mathematical patterns emanating from musical works, can be highly differentiated combinations of pleasurable and painful emotions. There are emotions that music can elicit that cannot be elicited by any other emotion-inducing stimulus. Music can invoke ideas if the highly differentiated combinations of pleasurable and painful emotions induced by music can be conceptually matched to an idea that could induce similarly differentiated emotions if that idea was thought. A simple example is that music that makes one feel a feeling of triumph can invoke ideas associated with triumphant behavior, such as discovering a cure for a major disease, or militarily conquering a country. A piece of music can be instructive if the differentiated emotions induced by the inputting of the music induces a listener to become aware of differentiated ideas.

Other art forms such as painting or sculpture also derive their analytical "grip" on the mind by containing patterns that the mind can detect as being mathematical or logical. The detection of these patterns also results in energy or thought-conducting particles moving across nodes within neuron circuits, such as to generate emotions, such that these emotions lessen the emotional pain of unfulfilled yearnings.

The motivation to create artworks or music works can also result from the artist's desire to teach or instruct the public, by creating for the public a pedagogical tool in the form of the artwork that projects a concept, or a posited mathematical or logical relationship between two or more objects. Here, the artist feels upset emotionally that people are not aware of an idea, and wants to teach the idea through the artwork. This kind of teaching behavior may be a form of altruism, that may or may not be adaptive, and the motivation to engage in such behavior may have resulted from a non-adaptive mutation in the genes of the mind of that artist. The artist may think that the public is poorer because the public does not have access to the artist's idea, so the artist wants to increase the wealth of the public by giving them access to the idea.

The Perception of Life Stages

Broadly speaking, humans often divide up their lives into general stages, such as birth, development into adulthood, young adulthood, older adulthood, decline and death. These general stages and the logic of progressing through these stages serves as a kind of general conceptual framework for generally predicting the expected progression of humans and also of societies. Often, people think of other people in terms of where those people are in different stages of their lives. Common human conversation is filled with stage-of-life statements such as these: "Well, my sister recently graduated from college and got married, and now has a 1 year-old" or "My parents worked for thirty years in the restaurant business, but eventually retired and now live in a group home" or "We lived in a small house for a few years, but as our family grew, we decided to buy a bigger house" or "My grandfather was in a group home for a few years, but them developed Alzheimers, and things went downhill from there. We had to change his diapers for a couple years before he died. It was devastating to see this happen to someone who was once a lawyer and a bank chairman." Stage-of-life statements about friends, family and acquaintances tend to be thoughts of the moment for many people, and the logic of people progressing through stages of life is part of what seems to make humans "complex" and "spiritual." Inanimate objects such as rocks and rivers do not seem to go through stages of life, after all. Other living creatures, such as bacteria or squirrels, do go through stages of life, but not with the "spirituality" and "complex, goal-oriented behavior" of humans.

However, the seemingly complex progressions that humans go through in their stage-of-life progressions are dictated largely by the mechanics of the physiological development of the human body and brain over time, as the body follows a growth and development program that progresses the body physically from a baby to toddler to young adult to a less energetic adult, to an old adult, to an adult in declining health and finally a dead adult, disintegrated into the infinity background of the universe. The initial formation of a baby occurs in the female womb, which is a molecule-concatenating machine that obtains individual atoms from the universe and concatenates them into a thermodynamically unstable baby body form. A DNA "program" is followed while this gestation period occurs whereby this baby is concatenated. The baby is born with a set of molecular and mechanical machinery for obtaining more atoms and molecules from the environment, and using these to increase, form, develop and concatenate other body parts outside of the womb. Babies tend to develop in rather predictable, generalizable patterns of growth and development, from age zero to age eighteen, towards young adulthood. These relatively predictable patterns of growth and development have led humans to create time milestones that correspond approximately to these growth and development stages, such as "sweet-sixteen" parties, or the common trend of timing graduation from high-school at around the age of eighteen.

The minds of children go through growth and development phases. Some generalization of this concept might be that at an earlier phase of mind development, a child and the child's peers may find it entertaining if the child wears a super-hero costume, but after a few years the child and the child's peers may be more interested in playing video games than in wearing super-hero costumes, and a few years later sexual maturity kicks in and the child has become a young adult that may find the opposite sex more interesting than video games or super-hero costumes.

The bottom line is that the physiological progression of the human body over the lifespan of the human, a progression driven by the laws of physics and the tendency of the universe to evolve towards thermodynamic equilibrium, is the origin of the conceptual expectation among humans that life is structured in stages. This is also the origin of many conversational topics and thoughts that humans have that fall under the general category of discussing the various life stages that various people are in, and having various emotional reactions to such thoughts.

The Anabolically Youthful Brain

One of the major determinants of the growth and development of the mind is the extent to which the brain tissue itself is metabolically and anabolically active. A brain that is capable of anabolic (or molecule-synthesizing) activity at a fast rate is also capable of learning at a fast rate. An organism that is in the youthful phase of its life

126

tends to have a brain that is at peak anabolic activity. The brain at its anabolic peak can rapidly carry out bio-chemical reactions that lead to formation of molecular structures that encode memories, knowledge and ideas, and that enable the brain to think fast enough to implement these ideas quickly and efficiently when needed for problem-solving. A brain in this phase is most capable of high-order learning activities such as studying at a university, earning a graduate degree, becoming a chess expert, or plotting a complex plan for creating and managing a corporation or earning a position as a government leader. Typically, younger minds are most capable of these kinds of activities.

It is said that creativity in humans peaks before the age of 35, and that mathematics geniuses produce their best work before the age of 35. This generalization would be due to the human brain's anabolic activity peaking before the age of 35. After age 35, anabolic activity begins to decline, and as adults age past the age of 35, they may become less capable of inputting information and forming new knowledge structures as a result, or learning new job skills or changing entirely into a different job. A political leader in his or her 30s may seem to be more lively, creative, progressive and dynamic compared to that same political leader in their 60s. Some politicians have crafted complex statements of their personal philosophies while in their 20s and 30s, when their brain's anabolic activity was at the highest, then applied these philosophies after getting political power, but as they aged, they became less creative, due to less brain anabolic activity, but continued to apply their previous political philosophy without much progressive or imaginative alteration.

Much of what makes people divide human lives into stages is determined by the typical rates of anabolic activity of brains during different times of a brain's lifespan. People in their 20s and 30s are more likely to be able to learn complex job skills, or change their jobs entirely. Their energy levels are higher, giving them increased tolerance of extreme environments and extreme emotional pressure, and increased ability to form conceptual work-arounds to deal with unusual stresses and environments. If someone in their 20s is fired from a job, a fierce determination may ensue to change careers entirely, due to the brain's still-functioning ability to learn new skills by being anabolically active, such as to be able to form new neuron structures that encode for these skills. If that same someone was fired from their job while in their 60s, he or she might be at a stage of their life where the brain is not very anabolically active, and rather than try to re-tool for a new job, that person may simply drop out of the workforce, too unmotivated to get a new job or "start over."

A young person starting a career might feel a desire to achieve success, and think that as a new career person, this person is young and energetic, and wants to build a life, obtain a job, a house, kids, and other paraphernalia associated with a classical "nuclear family lifestyle." This young entry into a career might see him or herself as part of a "new generation" of young people, replacing the positions in life of older people who once had these positions but have since grown old, retired, and died. An interesting question to ask is, "from where does this cycle of the young replacing the old in the workplace originate, and why does this cycle seem perpetual across human history?" This is an important question to ask because the motivation to perpetuate this infinite cycle repeats itself with each new young person. Is there some force of physics creating this infinite cycle and generating new generations of young people with the motivation to perpetuate this cycle, like perpetual hamsters on a treadmill? It is likely that the thermodynamically unstable human body unavoidably progresses towards disintegration and death, requiring the replacement with a "fresher" young human that is in the earlier stages of thermodynamic breakdown. The laws of thermodynamics, and the tendency of the universe to move towards thermodynamic equilibrium, seem to be the ultimate drivers of this phenomenon.

One reason why U.S. president John F. Kennedy was such an exciting speaker, and often tried to point the U.S. towards progressive societal goals such as putting a man on the moon, is that he was a young man in his early 40s, and his mind was at a relatively peak level of competence at generating new, anabolically synthesized learning structures. The public's perception of how "exciting" or "dynamic" a politician is, is largely influenced by the rate of anabolic activity in those politicians' minds. Fidel Castro grabbed power when he was in his early 30s, at the same peak age of brain anabolic activity that would make creative people produce their best work. Castro in his 30s was an emotional, dynamic speaker, and was (in his own autocratic and rather dangerous way) a highly adaptive, competent political leader, excellent at taking charge and maintaining control. That same Castro forty years later was more of a placid, gentlemanly politician, repeating the same mantra he was speaking of when he was in his 30s, and repeating the same tried-and-true methods of selectively neutralizing or "pruning" anyone who challenged his rule as the gentleman autocrat. There was something quite emotional and exciting about the 1961 Cuban missile crisis, since the brains of the two major political competitors, Kennedy and Castro, were in prime health, capable of robust anabolic neuron-structure-forming activities.

The emotional systems of the brains of Kennedy and Castro worked at peak capacity at those relatively young ages of their lives during which the Cuban Missile Crisis was happening. Their minds were synthesizing dopamine and other emotion-inducing neurotransmitters at a peak rate, which is expected of youthful brains, and their brains had not yet experienced significant loss of, or death of, dopamine receptors or dopamine-producing neurons in their brains, phenomena that accompany the aging of the brain. Hence, not only were their adversarial reactions strategic and interesting, but so were their vibrant emotional expressions at the time. The public was no doubt gripped by the spirit of this adversarial conflict between two brains at peak anabolic activity. Things would be less exciting later on in the 1980s, and more peaceful in a gentlemanly way, from interactions between older politicians like US president Ronald Reagan and Mikhail Gorbachev, with older minds that were still sharp and competent, but (presumably) with slower rates of anabolic activity for both learning and dopamine-formation compared to their respective younger minds.

A common generalization among humans is that love is most exciting among young lovers, or that a marriage is most exciting among young newlyweds. This general phenomenon is also explainable from the standpoint that young brains are most competent at anabolic neuron-structure-forming activity, and are most competent at synthesizing emotion-inducing neurotransmitters, and contain the largest numbers of neurotransmitter-synthesizing neurons, compared to older brains. The higher learning capabilities of younger brains, due to their having higher anabolic activity, leads to phenomenon where young lovers and newlyweds tend to tolerate or seek out changes in environment or geographic location, finding new and exciting environments in which to engage in romantic activities. The higher neurotransmitter synthesizing activity of younger brains results in young lovers having more emotional and "magical" experiences as lovers. Younger lovers' brains can feel more emotional excitement from experiencing new environments compared to older lovers' brains, due to higher releases of pleasurable neurotransmitters in their younger brains.

As lovers' brains age, fewer neurotransmitters may be synthesized, due to aging that causes death of neurotransmitter-synthesizing neurons, and because less anabolic activity occurs in the mind due to aging, which reduces the initiative to seek out new environments or to adapt to new environments. Free-radical damage to the brain's neurons, over the years, causes these general losses. These losses may lead to later years of marriage feeling less emotional and more routine, to the point of the marriages becoming boring, and possibly so boring as to lead to divorce, or to a continued existence of the marriage as a somewhat pleasant but perhaps also unexciting relationship. Eventually, the aging damage to the brain may be so extensive that dementia may set in, where the brain's built-up anabolic structures and memories break down, leading to net simplification of a brain's cognitive structure, and loss of the memories of a once-vibrant marital experience in the early years of marriage.

A mind can become completely erased from dementia, and such incompetence of brain function may develop that the brain may no longer be able to regulate functions important for basic body chemistry equilibrium. Death, or the disintegration of a body into the infinity background of the universe, may soon follow, and the magic of a life lived with love and excitement, due to a mind continuously flooded with pleasurable neurotransmitters, comes to a depressing end. Again, this illustrates one example of how the anabolic competence of the brain at various ages of a brain's life, and the neurotransmitter-synthesizing competence of the brain at various ages of a brain's life, combined with physiological development rates of the body, creates the perception of a human's life moving in stages. A person is born, develops, reaches sexual maturity, marries and hopefully enjoys magical youthful years of marriage, then the marriage becomes a bit boring, dementia sets in, death occurs, and the cycle repeats, ad infinitum, as the married peoples' offspring repeat the pattern, or repeat some variation of this pattern within a statistically possible range of variations of this pattern.

The "I-ness" of "I"

It is a mystery from where the concept of "I" comes from. This mystery can only be solved through a molecular or sub-atomic level understanding of how the brain works. How can a computer be programmed to possess a concept of "I?" Where does the "I-ness" of "I" come from? Rene Descarte's expression, "I think, therefore I am" is perhaps a reasonable encapsulation of what the concept of "I" means. People express their sense of "I" in terms of the sum total of ideas and emotions contained within their minds, in terms of what ideas they tend to think on a daily basis, and in terms of the emotions they feel. A computer's sense of "I," if it existed, might be defined in terms of what thinking calculations are generated by the cloud of electrons that makes up the computer's mind, said electron cloud being guided by the silicon logic gates of the central processing unit through which the electron cloud moves. However, if it is difficult to determine how a cloud of individual electrons within a computer's silicon logic gates can be "unified" into a thinking cloud, it may be difficult to determine how a computer can have a sense of "I."

The object "I" might be differentiated from other members of a species who are not the I-object, by an energy fingerprint projected by "I" to the mind of "I," such that non-I members of the same species cannot project that energy fingerprint. For example, "I" is that object that feels its body pulsate in exact synchronization with I's heartbeat, but not in synchronization with the heartbeat of any other member of its species. Another example would be that "I" feels a pinprick stuck into its body, but does not feel a pinprick stuck into the body of another member of its species. Another example is that "I" can taste an apple in its mouth, but cannot taste an apple in the mouth of other members of its species.

Some scientists believe that an organism only contains a concept of "I" within its mind if that organism can recognize its reflection in a mirror.   However, this mirror-recognition ability is an abstract cognitive skill that a mind needs not possess in order to have a concept of "I."   Probably most or all animals have a concept of "I," simply because animals display behavior that is designed to make their own selves survive. An animal would not behave such as to improve its survival and gene reproducing ability if it was not able to distinguish the self object from non-self objects.   Probably all animals with a heartbeat intuitively define themselves as a self-object by thinking that only they can feel their own heartbeat.   There are various conceptually simple ways of distinguishing self from non-self, by distinguishing the energy fingerprint emanated by a self-object versus a non-self object, that make the abstract ability to recognize oneself in a mirror unnecessary for being able to recognize one's self.

Is a person's sense of identity important?   This question is important because most members of the homo sapiens species of animal on the planet earth are profoundly affected emotionally and intellectually by their concept of their own identity, and this concept greatly influences individual behavior.   One intellectual problem with having a sense of identity is that matter, and by implications the objects that are made of matter (such as humans), are mostly empty space, and the sub-atomic particles that make up a specific object also make up all other objects, but in different proportions and with different quantum energy states.   If one magnifies an apple or a human or a termite to the sub-atomic level, one only sees the same thing, sub-atomic particles, each one being one of the few dozen elementary particles that make up the Standard Model of sub-atomic particle principles that physicists use to describe matter. How, then, can a human be "solid" enough as an entity or an object for the human to have an absolute definition?   How can one claim to be a human, or a member of the homo sapiens species of animal on the planet earth, as a fundamental component of a human's sense of identity?   Are all objects, living and non-living, the same thing, namely clusters of energy, of various degrees of thermodynamic instability?   Also, how can a human claim to belong to a nationality, ethnic group, or culture, given that if there is anything material about these things, or any material representations of these things, such as flags, unique decorative symbols, distinctive clothes, or foods, etc., unique to the culture, nationality or ethnic group, those material objects are also made mostly of empty space, and of the same sub-atomic particles as any other object?

A sense of identity is also temporary, in that once a person dies, the atoms, molecules and sub-atomic particles that once made up that person's cohesive body form disintegrate into the infinity background of the universe, and this disintegration is so comprehensive that it completely destroys any component of the person's sense of identity, including the most basic component, namely that the person was once a specimen of the homo sapiens species of animal on the planet earth, and belonged to a certain physical gender of either male or female, and was associated with and sensorily integrated with all of the arbitrary information constructs generated by the physical and chemical environment of the planet earth, and powered primarily by the arbitrary quantity of watt power that the earth receives from the arbitrarily existing earth's sun located an arbitrary 93 million miles away from the earth. Given that this disintegration process is so comprehensive, and that it erases all component's of the person's identity on the planet earth, the person, by disintegrating via death, becomes identical to all people who have ever existed and died on the planet earth, in that all such dead people have zero identity. How can one claim to possess an identity while alive, when that person was predictably destined to develop into a zero identity via unavoidable death, and this zero identity will be the same as the identities of all people who have died on the planet earth? A parallel question might be, to what extent are humans justified intellectually in remembering deceased people in terms of the identities these people supposedly possessed while alive, if in dying the life-identities of these people catastrophically and completely disintegrate into a state of zero identity? Why remember an identity that becomes instantly destroyed and irrelevant instantaneously upon the death of the person having that identity? Here, this identity construct, that became instantly obsolete with the death of the person identifying with the identity construct, becomes after the death of that person nothing more than an abstract information construct, that humans may remember but which no longer is of relevance to contemporary real-life actual human interactions. A human who is completely molecularly fractured by the disintegration process of death, becomes no more a representation of his or her identity while alive as would a clump of dirt of a rock. In recollecting the memory of this person, we are talking about someone who is in the present tense as relevant and differentiable as a human as would be a pile of sand.

In possessing a sense of identity, whether in a national, ethnic, racial, or religious sense, a person belongs to a crowd of people sharing that identity construct. All the members of this crowd of people existing in that person's contemporary times will eventually disintegrate and die, so that the crowd of people with whom a person relates his or her identity construct exists only temporarily. Once that group dies, the person's identity construct becomes irrelevant, replaced by other slight variations of this identity construct maintained by a new generation of offspring of those who once held the construct. The construct, then, essentially acts as a temporary body of people that can be considered as a kind of "team," to which each member belongs. This team can function like an asset distribution mechanism, with some teams having access to greater amounts of assets to distribute among themselves compared to other teams. Racial, ethnic, national or religious groups are all essentially asset distribution mechanisms, accessing and distributing various monetary, physical, political, sexual and emotional assets. Belonging to a specified group is like temporarily belonging to a team while alive on the planet earth, and being subject to the asset gains and losses of belonging to that team, with that sense of belonging instantly disintegrating upon the death of an individual holding the identity construct associated with that belonging. Upon dying, an individual is no longer a member of that identity construct "team" any more than a rock or a clump of dirt is a member of that team. The person's life might be summarized as a caption in an obituary page, perhaps proudly mentioning that person's belonging to a specified ethnic, religious, or racial "team." However, any reader of this obituary caption summary will be reading about what is now an irrelevant construct of matter or energy, or a variation of one of a practically infinite number of possible three-dimensional matter or energy clusters allowable by the laws of physics, that once existed in the past, but has now completely disintegrated.

Multiple humans can contribute to helping any one person gain life support resources or gene reproduction resources within the life support and gene reproduction niches occupied by that person. One's parents provide one with his or her most valuable asset, namely one's life, body and mind, both by initiating the existence of this asset, and by providing large amounts of resources to develop the initial baby human into an adult, and perhaps by later providing assets to facilitate the growth and development of the grandchildren, or their offsprings' offspring. This makes it highly adaptive for a human, in the early developmental years of his or her existence, to be instinctively motivated to identify who his or her biological parents are, or at least to identify surrogate or step parents if the biological parents have died. It is also adaptive for that human to want to prolong the survival of asset-providing parents, and to feel pleasurable feelings from knowing that those parents survive and thrive, and feel painful feelings knowing that the parents became injured or die. A person instinctively may feel pleasure at the survival and prosperity of their siblings, because these siblings also carry that person's genes.

One's employer or customers provide money. Money is a construct that represents the purest distillation of life-support assets in homo sapiens civilizations, because money is inter-changeable with valuable goods and services. People can develop strong emotional reactions to their employers, potentially liking employers who provide a steady source of money, and fearing or hating those who withdraw the money or withdraw the job that generates the money. Job training experts can also be a source of affection, if they provide job training that leads to acquiring a job that results in money gain. Farmers can be loved for providing food energy, which supports life and gene propagation. Customers can also be loved and respected as sources of money. Although these examples may be simplistic generalizations, with many potential exceptions or gradations, it seems that the human mind has evolved such that humans instinctively look for which other humans are sources of life support, and to arrange these humans in the mind as objects in a kind of conceptual matrix or hierarchy that maps out from where a person's life support assets originate.

For each human mind, there is a different combination of peoples who are involved in helping that human occupy the life support and gene propagation niche that this human occupies on the planet earth. This combination of "other people involved in a person's life support and gene reproduction niches" is essentially unique with all people. It is like a "fingerprint" that helps differentiate one person from another, and is a central component of a person's sense of identity. For example, a person's parents are exclusively that person's parents, except for possibly a few brothers and sisters. A person's in-laws are exclusively that person's in-laws, unless there is close inter-marriage among families. The combination of different employers (or employees) that a person has had is generally uniquely his or her own, as is the combination of large numbers of people a person has encountered in everyday activities such as shopping, meeting classmates in schools or religious meetings, at the beach, as lovers, etc., and of course, a person's offspring are exclusively their own. In addition, even if two people share the same "combination" or "fingerprint" of humans with whom they interacted in their lives, which would be an astronomically improbable event, the two people would not interact with this combination in exactly the same way.

This combination of people, with whom a particular person interacts in the course of his or her life, helps define the identity of that person. Yet, this combination is temporary, since this combination is made up of people, with whom a person interacts in their life, who will all eventually die, and disintegrate into the infinity background of the universe. The interacting person will also eventually disintegrate as well, which wipes out the vast majority of the information and memories, rational or irrational, that described in that interacting mind the facts and feelings involved in these interactions. The factors that determine this combination are arbitrary and unpredictable. It is pure luck who one's parents and siblings are, and one cannot predict who one will meet in their life on the planet earth. If free will does not exist, one cannot control whether or not one will interact with any one particular person in the course of their life. Hence, there is something trivial about being on a deathbed and being visited by people from one's past, or about having a feeling of having accomplished something in life, while a person mulls over what they did in their life while on their deathbed. A funeral can be an emotional experience for those whose minds contain memories of the dead individual, but eventually those who had emotional memories of the object of the funeral will die and disintegrate as well, which renders the emotional memories of the dead funeral object obsolete, irrelevant and inapplicable. A gravestone may occupy space on the planet earth long after the emotional pain felt by those grieving the dead person became obsolete and inapplicable with the death and disintegration of the initial graveside grievers.

How any particular combination of people, with whom a person interacts with in life, becomes installed as energy fingerprints pertaining to those specific humans, in a person's mind, during the course of that person's life, is too complex a question to answer with current scientific knowledge. This combination changes with time for each human, since the people that a person knows in that person's life change and die, in ways that affect the extent to which a particular human adds to the life support or gene reproduction niche of another human. A simple example is that of a person who works at a gas station owned by an employer, and is able to support his or her life and propagate his or her genes using the income from that gas station. One day, the employer dies, and the gas station is bought and demolished to make way for a new restaurant. It is now no longer applicable, in that ex-gas station employee's mind, that the gas station employee can depend on that now-deceased human employer as a source of life support and gene propagation by pumping gas for a living in that employer's gas station. Instead, that employee must now look for another job, under another employer, where that new employer becomes the "employer-object" that occupies an employer/employee money-earning concept in that employee's mind.

A person's employment forms a component of their identity. People can be farmers, gas station attendants, doctors, etc. In what sense, however, can a person be identified as a specific kind of worker? A doctor is a doctor because the doctor thinks doctor thoughts, and is recognized by societal legal systems as a doctor. A gas pumper is such because that person works in a gas station pumping gas. Yet, a person spends a relatively small proportion of their day engaging in the actual working or thinking activities associated with work. A person spends hours sleeping, eating, or doing other non-work-related activities, and only a fraction of the day working. A person is defined as being a particular kind of worker because, for a substantial amount of hours

137

during the week, that person is thinking thoughts related to carrying out the problem-solving tasks of that kind of worker. However, a worker, when working, only pays attention to an extremely tiny fraction of all of the sub-atomic particles that exist in that worker's workplace environment while that worker is working, and tracks only an ultra-tiny fraction of the total number of world-pathways taken by these sub-atomic particles. In this sense, the actual working activity represents an ultra-parameterized focus on only an ultra-tiny fraction of the sub-atomic particles in that worker's workplace, and in that worker's life in general. How can a worker be defined as being of a certain kind of job or career, when such an incredibly tiny fraction of the sub-atomic particles in the worker's environment are directly influenced by that worker's work?

Suppose one has ten computers, all of the same model, and the computers were each labelled with a number from one to ten, and then each computer was programmed to answer the question, "Who are you?" with the answer "I am computer number X," where X would be whatever number was labelled on that particular computer. The computer would not be consciously aware of its own identity, because it was simply outputting an automated answer to the question typed into it. It is said, in contrast, that when humans answer the question "who are you," the answering human is consciously aware of their answer. But, in what sense if the human consciously aware of his or her own identity?

Imagine a person named Sam is asked to explain his identity. Sam might say something like this:

> "My name is Sam Jones. I was born on April 4, 1957, in Wichita, Kansas, to Wilma and Robert Jones. I am a male, married to my wife with two children. I live in the country of the United States, in the state of Illinois, in the city of Chicago, in a two-bedroom apartment. I am a schoolteacher by trade. I am generally a nice guy, but sometimes I can be selfish, and I pride myself on being law-abiding. My favorite food is pizza, but I avoid eating it since I have a history of heart disease."

Ultimately, all components of Sam's sense of identity are arbitrary. "Sam Jones" is a sound energy fingerprint, one of a practically infinite number of possible sound energy fingerprints, that is arbitrarily assigned to label the cohesion of atoms, molecules and sub-atomic particles that Sam is. Sam's date of birth occurred 1,956 years after the arbitrary year 1 of the Gregorian calendar system, a system that arbitrarily assigns a year 1 to the posited birth of Jesus Christ, a lord in the Christianity god paradigm. Sam might be more scientifically precise by saying that he was born approximately 13.8 billion years after the Big Bang, or the explosion of the singularity that resulted in the birth of the human-observable universe. However, the date of the Big Bang, if the Big Bang actually occurred, was set arbitrarily by the laws of physics, which also arbitrarily made possible phenomena such as Big Bangs, and the birth of this universe may be one of an infinite number of universes, according to string theory. Not only is Sam's date of birth arbitrary, but if there are an infinite number of universes, neither Sam nor anyone else knows exactly when or where Sam is in reality. Sam's parents are arbitrary cohesions of atoms, molecules and sub-atomic particles, whose existence was arbitrary and unpredictable, and made possible by the laws of physics. Sam also makes references to various arbitrary political constructs such as the United States, Illinois, Chicago, and Wichita, Kansas, which are arbitrarily perimiterized macro-land-areas where the threat of military force causes people to respect these physically invisible geographic boundaries. These political constructs are only applicable to the planet earth, and would not be applicable to any other hypothetical planets in the universe with hypothetical intelligent beings that form hypothetical political systems. Sam's self-described personality traits, such as being generally nice, sometimes selfish, and law-abiding, arbitrarily were instilled in his mind due to his genes, and due to personality-forming learning traits programmed by his genes. These personality traits influence what specific assets, and how many of each, Sam will own in life, the extent to which Sam is at risk of being imprisoned or executed by his government, and Sam's ability to survive (i.e. maintain the thermodynamic stability of his body and mind) and reproduce on the planet earth, and what life support and gene reproduction niches Sam occupies on the planet earth. Natural selection evolves people such that each person has a different personality, to prevent each person from having the same exact personality type, which may result in extinction of the species if that one personality type eventually become non-adaptive. It is due to luck how genes mix and match to form a specific personality type in a specific person. "Pizza" is an arbitrary sound-energy-fingerprint assigned to a food object consisting primarily of the molecules found in bread, cheese and tomatoes, that is digestible by the human body for arbitrary reasons dictated by the arbitrary laws of physics. Sam's heart, which is necessary for nutrients to circulate in Sam's body, so that Sam can have the energy needed for his body to be thermodynamically stable, is itself thermodynamically unstable, causing Sam to have heart disease. The laws of physics arbitrarily dictate that the fats in pizza cheese might clog Sam's arteries, increasing the amount of force that his heart would have to put forth to pump blood in Sam's body. The common perception of what makes a human "consciously aware" of his or her identity is a result of the awareness of things that are arbitrary.

If one wanted to program a computer to possess a sense of identity that was "consciously aware" in the way that a human sense of identity was "consciously aware," the computer would have to be programmed to simulate the arbitrary physics patterns of the arbitrary sub-atomic particles that create the body and mind forms of humans. The computer would need to simulate a universe in which there existed the automated patterns of behavior that the many different atoms, molecules and sub-atomic particles show in the real universe, given environmental conditions of temperatures, atmospheres, pressures, etc. The computer would need to simulate and quantify the thermodynamic stability of its simulated human body form, and relate this to the thermodynamic characteristics of the simulated planet or environment on which the simulated human body form exists. The computer would also have to quantify when time began in this simulated universe, which presumably means that a computer must count in its simulated universe how many years after the posited Big Bang did its own simulated human existence come about. The computer would probably also need to evolve a simulated emotional need to form a sense of its own identity. Ideally, the computer would use ultra-simplified simulated cellular automata that would be undergo simulated permutations in a simulated environment in which simulated natural selection mechanisms occurred, in the context of a simulated thermodynamically unstable universe, such that these cellular automata, driven by simulated laws of physics, would undergo vast numbers of simulated natural selection evolutionary events, and increase their complexity in a simulated way, until they evolved into simulated human body and mind structures, in the context of a simulated food chain, such that these simulated human body and mind structures possesses a simulated sense of identity similar to that of real-life humans. Here, the development of the human mind would be simulated starting from scratch, using ultra-simple simulated automata driven by simulated laws of physics to evolve into simulated human bodies and minds. This would be the most realistic simulation of how the human mind, and the "soulful" sense of human identity, would have evolved in nature, after millions of generations of evolutionary natural selection iterations.

Why Do Humans Work for Money?

Working for money is often a complex activity, involving transportation logistics to travel from home to work, the actual work activities, interfacing with employers, fellow employees and customers, etc. All of these activities, and the thoughts pertaining to them, are motivated by arbitrary thermodynamic laws, that obligate people to make money to buy food and shelter to prevent the thermodynamically unstable body forms of the workers and their families from disintegrating. Money is an arbitrarily recognized medium of exchange or way of exchanging assets, which enables more precise and efficient asset transfers compared to barter exchange transactions that involve two or more trades of real-life goods or services delivered at the time of the transactions. The need for money to fund reproduction activities, and the shelter and bedding needed for such activities, and to pay for offspring resulting from such activities, motivate the formation of a wide variety of present tense thoughts. These thoughts originate in the mind due to the evolved tendency of minds to perform activities and behaviors that improve the thermodynamic stability of the bodies attached to those minds, or that result in the propagation of their genes. The specific reasons for why each individual mind, initially born with minimal or no

141

knowledge, grows into possessing specific money-making habits, are too complex and mysterious to understand here. Whatever working activities a person performs during their life, no matter how complex the activity, essentially all of these thoughts pertaining to the activity belong to a larger category of thoughts pertaining to thoughts that add to a mind's ability to survive or reproduce on the planet earth. The need to improve the thermodynamic stability of the body attached to a mind, and to maximize the amount of propagation of the genes of that body, is the cause of thoughts pertaining to working, which operate in many humans' minds.

Why do Animals Sleep and Dream?

The urge to sleep tends to occur in organic minds at least once per day. The origin of the thought that one wants to sleep presumably is that brains are susceptible to extensive damage from the act of concentration and thinking. Concentration and thinking generate free radicals and other toxins, that damage the brain, as a result of daily thinking activities, and thinking activities also deplete the brain of the neurotransmitters that are needed to conduct thoughts. The main purpose of sleeping is presumably to shut down many of the brain's neurons temporarily, so that there is minimal activity among many neurons, so that the brain's brain-repair mechanisms can repair damage to those neurons caused by the previous day's thinking activities. Temporarily shutting down neurons also seems to be necessary to allow the brain's neurotransmitter-synthesizing molecular pathways to become active, so that the neurotransmitters needed to conduct thoughts can be re-synthesized, to replenish neurons that have been depleted of the neurotransmitters due to daily thought-generating activities.

Dreaming, a seemingly arbitrary and often irrational activity, perhaps is triggered by the mind-repair mechanisms of the brain in order to "test-run" the recently repaired brain circuits, to make sure that they are performing as well as the repair is designed to make them perform. Dreams are typically irrational presumably because only some cognitive centers of the brain are activated during the "test-runs," and the thoughts generated at these cognitive centers are not balanced, refined or filtered as concepts by other cognitive centers that would be active if the person was awake.

The Genetic Persistence of the Soldier's Mentality

A political conflict between countries can arouse powerful patriotic feelings among many people, and if a war occurs, many men become very emotional in feeling angered and agitated by such a war, and voluntarily go to enlist as soldiers to fight the war. This soldier mentality might at first glance seem to not be adaptive, because wars technically provide a bad deal for the soldier who fights in the war. The soldier can suffer physical injury or death, abandon a civilian career or business, and suffer long-lasting psychological scars from post-traumatic stress (PTSD) disorder, which occurs if continuous exposure to traumatic episodes or violence causes relatively permanent, negative emotional changes in the brain. These costs are potentially incurred by an individual soldier while fighting a war that may only help a group of oligarchs or a group of politicians. Although there are ways to justify some altruistic behaviors in the context of the evolution of a "selfish gene," it would seem that a soldier's sacrifices are too altruistic or are too "anti-egotistical" in behavior to be adaptive.

(It is difficult to explain in molecular terms why PTSD occurs. Perhaps exposure to trauma increase the number of nodes among neuron pathways in the mind that connect to parts of the brain that generate painful emotions such as fear or anxiety, or that connect to parts of the mind that generate flashbacks of traumatic incidents. So, for example, a node in a neuron pathway, such that energy passing through that node would normally send energy further on to another node that would normally generate an emotion of boredom, such as might happen if a person detects of the sound of a civilian helicopter flying overhead, instead in the PTSD victim might send energy to a node that triggers an emotion of great fear, as if the civilian helicopter was an enemy attack helicopter hovering overhead.)

There are some possible reasons why the soldier's mentality, or the patriotic mentality that induces people to enlist as fighting soldiers in wars, can be adaptive. The gene pool within a specific country may be more similar to itself than the gene pool in the enemy country, such that a soldier fighting a war fights to defend the gene pool of his or her own country. Such behavior is more adaptive the more that soldier shares common genes with the people in his or her own country, and the less the soldier shares genetic similarity with the people in the enemy country. Historically, however, governments have also provided selection pressures in favor of the evolution of a soldierly mentality, because governments throughout history have at times had mandatory forced conscription of civilians into the armed services, and any civilian who balked at conscription or avoided conscription often faced severe penalties, possibly including severe persecution or physical death through execution. The mentality that makes a soldier submit to the draft probably shares similarities to the mentality that makes a soldier volunteer to fight in a war.

Many civilians who want to enlist in a war have a powerful, emotionally-driven motivation to enlist, and may communicate the desire to enlist with a strongly emotional sense of conviction. The common prevalence of large numbers of civilians who have such strong positive feelings to enlist when wars threaten, throughout history, in numerous epochs and societies, suggests that the evolutionary selection pressures, that evolve men or women who believe ardently in enlistment, must have been very strong throughout human history. The frequency of forced military conscription, and the threat of execution for draft-dodgers, must have been so common throughout thousands of years of homo sapiens history, as to result in the evolution of entire cognitive structures in the homo sapiens brain that become activated with pro-enlistment ideas when the concept of the threat of war by an enemy power becomes a present tense reality within a country.

These selection pressures also could have evolved people who derive various strong pleasures from war, such as having a strong feeling of emotional pleasure from being a "comrade-in-arms" or being part of a group of fighters fighting for a common cause, or having a fondness for dogs and other predators, or liking to kill, or having feelings of pleasure from the excitement of war. It would also be adaptive for a civilian to feel a pleasurable emotional feeling of profound satisfaction from realizing that this civilian was on the way to participate in war, despite the possibility that this feeling would rapidly go away and convert to emotional pain when the soldier experienced the potentially harsh realities of war. What would be adaptive here would be that the soldier cannot predict or conceptualize how harsh would be the actuality of war, up to the point of actually experiencing the war, but instead feels great emotional pleasure and a sense of satisfying conviction, due to a continued release of pleasurable neurotransmitters in the soldier's brain, from the time of deciding to enlist, up to the point of experiencing the war. It might not be adaptive for minds to evolve that had a tendency to analyze, in a deeply reductionist way, what exactly the cause was that was being fought for, for any particular war, in any particular epoch or human society or nation-state. Any such mind-thinking patterns would increase the probability of a civilian having an inclination to dodge the draft, along with the risk of being caught and executed.

Since many drafted civilians throughout history have been young in age before being drafted, they had not yet had children, such that their summary execution for draft dodging would not be palliated, from an evolutionary standpoint, by the fact that they had already generated offspring to carry on their genes, prior to being executed for avoiding the draft. This reality would help to wipe those with a draft-dodging mentality out of the gene pool. It would also be adaptive for those who had a draft-dodging inclination to feel a sense of paranoid fear that somehow this draft-dodging behavior, even if limited only to the thought of draft-dodging, would result in capture and execution.

Also, however, the physical traits that make a good male soldier, such as physical strength, tallness and body bulk, masculinity, and lack of fear, also correlate with that soldier being a good alpha male. A male primate with these traits would be more likely to successfully fight off male rival primates to become the alpha male with exclusive access to a harem. A male soldier will become a much stronger, more physically fit man as a result of spending months or years in a war zone. It is said that soldiers in a battlefield, and people who routinely chop wood, probably do not have much need for membership in a workout gym. The technically bad deal that male soldiers pay by being soldiers, from potentially paying a huge personal price to serve a collectivist group interest, or a temporary, specialized political interest, may be made up for, from an evolutionary standpoint, by gaining from their participation in the war the physical and emotional traits that are valued by heterosexual females, which may give the surviving soldiers a higher probability of propagating their genes after they come home from war.

Countless stories of romances, that occurred after females grabbed heart-throbbing male soldiers returning from war, have been recorded in history and in romance novels. A famous American all-female singing group, the Chordettes, recorded a song in 1954 called "Lay Down Your Arms," that shows the popularity and perpetual durability of this concept. One of the lines in the song, directed at the hypothetical returning male soldier, who is praised highly in the song, is "lay down your arms, and surrender to mine." The theme of this song is that females find soldiers to be macho and sexy, and will reward them sexually if they successfully return from the war, presumably with their gonads intact. There is a correlation between the physical fitness of the male soldier and his perceived sexual desirability to heterosexual females, which helps make the soldier's mentality to be adaptive. Having a tendency to rationally analyze the potential self-damaging payoff of participation in war, using a strictly rational cost/benefit analysis, might not be adaptive, particularly if that tendency results in a draft-dodger who will be perceived as being less sexually macho compared to a soldier, and who may later be caught and summarily executed by a firing squad.

Calendar Systems and The Perception of Time

The universe in which humans exist is colossal in scale, both in time and space, is aged approximately 13.8 billion years and is so huge that light, which moves at 186,000 miles per second, would take billions of years to move from one end of the universe to the other (Sagan, 1980, 1994, 1997). Human thoughts and feelings may be rendered infinitely insignificant in the context of this practically infinite universe. String theorists in the field of physics suggest that there are infinite numbers of universes, and that every possible event that can occur in the universe, according to physical laws, will occur, and repeatedly occur, for an infinity of time. The universe in which we exist seems to have originated, according to scientists, from a "Big Bang," or a fast-moving expansion from a single point or "singularity" from which all of the matter and energy of the universe originated. In a multi-universe or multi-verse concept, Big Bang events happen an infinite number of times, giving rise to an infinite number of universes.

Do humans know where, or when, they are in this universe, to say nothing of a multi-verse? Technically, the planet Earth exists on an outer arm of a galaxy that humans call the Milky Way galaxy, which is one of trillions of galaxies in the universe. But does this technical statement explain where or when the homo sapiens species exists, when the universe is so vast in time and space? Where or when does the earth's sun exist? The sun, which powers life on planet earth and powers the minds on the planet, essentially appeared arbitrarily within a practically infinite expanse of time and space. It seems that, to be able to understand humans' own thoughts processes rationally, humans must relate their thought processes to the overall context of the infinity of the universe.

There are a practically infinite number of things that humans can do, and a practically infinite number of thoughts that human minds can generate, while existing on the planet earth, but only a small fraction of these actions or thoughts contribute to the human ability to survive and reproduce on the planet earth. For example, a human may be surrounded by thousands of potential mates, but generally is forced to focus on choosing only one or a few of these mates for reproducing the human's genes. A human can in theory spend years performing an activity that does not aid in survival or reproduction, such as playing with a beachball or staring at a wall, but this behavior would not be a practical way of surviving or reproducing, and would quickly result in the disintegration of the thermodynamically unstable body form of the human. The human mind evolved to think of time and space in finite terms. Concepts of finite time and finite space so thoroughly permeate human thinking that it is difficult for humans to grasp the concept of an infinite universe. Finite concepts of space and time distort the human ability to comprehend the infinite nature of the universe, but these concepts induce human minds to focus their thoughts, and focus the way they use their time, on a narrow range of behaviors that improve the their ability to survive and reproduce.

Human calendar systems are an example of how humans attempt to make time seem finite. The internationally adopted, standardized calendar system is the Gregorian Calendar, introduced by Pope Gregory XIII in 1582, which modified the Julian calendar to incorporate the need for leap years. In this calendar, there is a year one, chosen because this was the posited year that Jesus Christ, a lord in the Christianity god paradigm, was born. This calendar creates two ways of making humans think that time is finite: of the 13 billion years that have existed since the posited day that the universe was created via the Big Bang, a single year is arbitrarily chosen as the first year, as if conceptually humans anchor their concept of time to this year. Also, this calendar connects following the calendar system with the following of concepts related to the Christianity god paradigm. The Christianity god paradigm conceptualizes the universe as being a finite entity, centered around the homo-sapiens species, and a single main God and a single lord Jesus Christ, governing an earth created in seven days that, through analysis of the Christian bible by various religious scholars, was posited to be only a few thousand years old in age.

Some people are surprised to learn that there are multiple different calendar systems besides the Gregorian calendar, and that each calendar has a different starting date, with a different rationale for selecting that date as the start date. The universal, global adoption of the Gregorian calendar system can be controversial intellectually, because it will always be controversial which religion is best. Also, many god paradigms tend to intellectually bundle all ideas into frameworks of finiteness, which denies the possibility of an infinite universe. Also, setting the zero date of any calendar system is potentially controversial, because the zero date of a calendar can make humans assume that the zero date of the calendar is the beginning of time itself, rather than believing the scientific fact that time is either extremely long, because the universe is about 13.8 billion years old, or that time may be infinite, if there are infinite universes, according to string theorists.

Also, god paradigms can be political, which adds to their controversial nature. For example, the ancient Egyptian pharaohs promoted a centralized religion based on the sun god Ra, a god that was supportive of the pharaoh gods, according to the ancient pharaoh religion. The ancient pharaoh kings chiseled, on immovable stone buildings, throughout the kingdom of ancient Egypt, religious writings that stated the god Ra supported and blessed the ancient Egyptian kings, which helped to "officially institutionalize" popular support of the ancient Egyptian kings. An ancient Egyptian citizen could not oppose their king politically without presumably incurring the wrath of the sun god Ra. No subversive citizen could destroy these stone carvings without lots of time and super-human effort, because soon after a citizen began to begin to begin to erase these carvings, pharaoh soldiers would detect and execute that subversive goofball. Eventually, the Christianity god paradigm developed, in which there was another God, who contradicted the ancient pharaoh religion by politically opposing the ancient pharaoh kings, and politically supporting the ancient Israelites who were trying to wage war against the ancient Egyptian pharaohs. To further support these politics, there was another lord in the Christianity god paradigm, known as Jesus, who was a house builder by trade, and who himself was by coincidence an Israelite. The Christianity god paradigm could potentially undermine the politics of the pro-pharaoh political religion, that was intimidatingly chiseled into massive stone carvings--still viewable today--all over ancient Egypt.

Ideally, a calendar system would reinforce the concept that the universe is potentially (or, at is least practically) infinite in time. Human generations, wars, political cycles, wealth generation cycles, and vast numbers of other phenomena occur in cycles, or occur ad infinitum. The fact that a person is part of an infinite cycling and recycling of universe events helps provide a more rational conceptual backdrop for interpreting things like ambition, moral behavior, and war, compared to viewing time as starting at a "spiritually significant" zero year in a calendar. One could in theory create a calendar system with the zero date set as the birth of the universe, or the day the posited "Big Bang" occurred, but the vast expense of time (13.8 billion years) from year zero to the present makes use of this calendar system to be awkward. How would we describe the year of the writing of the Declaration of Independence of the United States (1776 in today's calendar)? 13.8 billion years plus 1776? 13BY+1776 for shorthand? A more contemporary time anchor would be more practical.

A calendar system could be universally adopted that chooses as a zero date an event that does not intellectually induce a perception that time itself has a starting point. This zero date even should be datable with reasonable scientific accuracy, at least to the extent that an arbitrary date can be assigned to the event, and the zero date event should be proven to have existed and, ideally, there should still be proof existing to the present day that the event actually occurred, and this physical proof ideally should be capable of continuing to exist for thousands or millions or years. One suggestion would be to create a global calendar system that uses the construction of the great pyramid of Giza in Egypt as the zero date of the calendar. This pyramid still exists, and is datable to approximately 2,550 years before the birth of Jesus Christ.

The great pyramid of the ancient king Cheops is technically a religious artifact. However, this pyramid represents the ancient pharaoh religion, a god paradigm that is obsolete and that is not observed in the present. The pharaoh god paradigm is not, for most people, an emotionally significant god paradigm, and is considered an infidel god paradigm by many.

In addition, Cheops' pyramid seems to have originated as an egotistical construction task, driven by an egotistical king (Cheops) who wanted to live immortally by constructing a gigantic tomb for himself that would help to bring him into the afterlife. If the pyramids were constructed today, they would be considered by many people and journalists to be a waste of resources, partly because, unlike Buckminster Fuller's geodesic dome (Fuller, 1963), there is minimal internal living or sheltering space within the pyramid, in proportion to the vast amounts of costly building materials and expenses needed to create the structure. Also, if the pyramids were constructed in the present, questions would be raised about whether or not the public funds used to build the pyramids were being spent in a spirit of corrupt, political egotism. The philosophy motivating the construction of the pyramids would be widely ridiculed. It is only due to dumb luck, not considered in the calculations of the original builders, that the pyramids have, in hindsight, paid for themselves many times over due to their being a perennial tourism revenue generator.

The rather pointless motivation to create the pyramids makes many people feel a level of detachment or derision towards the pyramids, which may induce people to see the pyramids in emotionally detached ways, as geometric constructs that could be scientifically and mathematically described. This would make a calendar system, with a zero date set at an arbitrarily chosen date of the pyramid's construction, to not intellectually distort people's concept that time is infinite, because Cheops' pyramid is not an object of much emotional or religious significance to most people. With the Gregorian calendar, many people are emotionally gripped by the association of the first year of that calendar with the birth of Jesus Christ, which may intellectually distort peoples' sense of time. The pyramids also exist to this day, and are durable enough to continue existing for thousands or millions of years, serving as a perennial landmark of time orientation.

The Human Motivation to Gain Assets

What is an asset? Why do the laws of physics permit assets to exist? These questions are important because much of human thinking involves developing strategies for acquiring assets, and in developing strategies to compete with other humans, insects, non-human mammals, and reptiles, to obtain limited assets on the planet earth. Those who die wealthy are sometimes envied for having lived a comfortable life, and obtained a bigger share of wealth than the average person or the "little guy."

An asset is anything that an organic mind thinks is valuable, given how that organism's mind tends to value things, said tendency being determined partly by the genetics of the organism's body and mind, and partly by learning behavior after being born. Typically, given how most organisms have evolved, an organic mind tends to consider things to be assets if these things improve the survival of the body to which that mind is attached, or improve the ability of that body to reproduce. This is primarily due to the laws of thermodynamics, that dictate that organic bodies, and the minds attached to them, are thermodynamically unstable cohesions of atoms and molecules, or energy

151

concatenations, and require a continuous input of food energy to maintain the existence of their intrinsically unstable body forms. Also, these thermodynamically unstable bodies require strategies for reproduction, because there is apparently no way for these thermodynamically unstable body forms to avoid catastrophic disintegration (i.e. death) in the long run, despite consuming energy in the short run. A thing that improves the survival or reproduction of a species may be perceived by that species' minds as being an asset.

There is also some kind of conceptual relationship between what is considered moral and what is considered an asset. The common moral belief to "do unto others as you would want them to do unto you," or that "moral behavior consists of striving to provide the greatest good for the greatest number" implies that moral behavior is related to providing assets or a fair distribution of assets to others. Humans generally consider it to be immoral to murder someone, because via murder one takes from another person their life. Humans often consider their own life to be their most valuable asset, and it is highly adaptive for humans to have evolved this belief. Legal systems universally make murder illegal and severely punishable, which is perhaps the most universal example of legal systems coinciding with moral beliefs. Here, the moral belief that it is wrong to take someone else's life originates in it being adaptive for humans to think that their own lives are their most valuable asset. It is also adaptive for a human to feel that the idea of personally being murdered is tremendously horrifying, and this idea invokes tremendous fear and/or anger. In addition, humans generally consider it to be horrifying for their own relatives, who carry their own genes, to be murdered. These beliefs in turn has evolved in people the tendency to support making murder illegal and severely punishable.

Different minds between species consider different things that improve survival or reproduction to be assets, as do different minds within the same species. The evolution of minds that show variations in what a particular mind perceives to be an asset, is a way by which natural selection evolves minds that are able to exploit different life support and reproduction niches. Some variations are not valuable in adding to a mind's ability to survive and reproduce its genes, but with luck variations occur that are valuable in these ways, which give members of a species access to new or different survival and reproduction niches relative to members of that species. Some assets can be considered by an organic mind to be valuable because they are emotionally pleasurable, but may not directly seem to improve survival and reproduction. Food, shelter, water and access to reproduction opportunities are generally considered to be the most valuable assets by most organic minds. From where do these assets originate?

Water, and the atomic and molecular components of materials used to produce the asset of shelter, such as rocks, silicon, and cement bases, are all provided by the universe generally, and the planet earth locally. Metals, such as iron, that can be used for building materials, can be produced in nuclear reactions that occur in gravitationally collapsing suns, or in supernova explosions occurring in the universe. Food consists of molecules, that are edible or digestible to a specific species of animal, that are automatically generated on the planet earth as a result of chemical synthesis reactions, occurring in plants, that are mostly powered by solar energy, and that involve storage of solar energy in the chemical bonds of the edible food molecules.

The origin of the concept that shelter is an asset lies in the thermodynamic instability of the human body. The human body ideally operates at a body temperature of about 37 degrees on the Celsius temperature scale. This is an ideal body temperature for facilitating the broadest range of the bio-chemical reactions in the human body that permit the body to maintain the cohesion of its thermodynamically unstable atomic and molecular form. Shelters are an asset because shelters facilitate the ability to protect the human body from temperature fluctuations, which helps to keep the body at this 37 degrees Celsius temperature. Shelters also protect humans from insects and predators, which try to eat the atoms and molecules of the human body, since the atomic bonds within the molecules contained within human flesh contains stored energy from the sun, which insects and predators can, by consuming, use to maintain the thermodynamic stability of their own thermodynamically unstable body forms. Humans do not want to be eaten by insects and predators, even if this fate would be "nothing personal," since consumption by a predator or an insect is simply an energy equilibrium phenomenon occurring in the universe.

Food assets, and wood that can be used to make shelter assets, originate fundamentally from plants. Plants use photosynthesis to chemically synthesize their plant bodies, and to create wood, which is the main structural support of trees (and countless shelters). Cellulose and lignin are the main strength-forming molecules in wood. Wood can be precisely cut and shaped using human power, that is leveraged by hand axes or machines. Wood makes a good construction material because wood is strong enough to hold up trees, giving it high strength per unit of volume, and wood is relatively insulating, which helps to protect shelters from temperature extremes of hot and cold. Wood can be joined into elaborate structures using screws and glue.

Photosynthesis uses energy from the sun to power plant growth. This solar energy also give plant bodies the energy inputs that plant bodies need for their cohesive atomic and molecular body forms to be thermodynamically stable. Earth's sun is a nuclear reactor in space, that provides a continuous input of light energy to the planet earth. Earth rotates around the sun in 365 earth-day cycles, and around earth's axis in 24-earth-hour cycles, which illuminates most of earth's surface for half of the 24-hour day with sunlight that powers photosynthesis. Each cycle of solar illumination to the planet earth provides a net addition of free energy that powers synthesis of food molecules within plants (Fuller, 1982). The continuous and cyclical growth of plant food molecules provides perpetual energy that perpetually powers the life cycles and the stages of growth and development cycles of the plants and animals on the planet earth. This continuous energy and continuous plant food molecule growth also results in a continuous resurrection of the motivation to find food energy generation after generation among the animals of the planet earth. Earth also tilts towards and away from the sun on earth's axis, which results in different levels of sun energy reaching earth's surface at different times of the year, typically in 3-month time clusters known as "seasons." The existence of these seasons also causes the origination of all of the human concepts, scientific and poetic, associated with "seasons."

The sun's automated power output, the cyclical rotation of the earth around the sun, the earth around its own axis, and the photosynthesis reactions on planet earth that result in plant matter forming continuously, are examples of automatic movement phenomena occurring in the universe, arbitrarily caused by the laws of physics. Since these automatic movement phenomena generate plants that can be consumed by animals to improve the survival and reproducibility of animals, these phenomena also originate the possibility that minds will evolve on the planet earth that think of food as an asset. The existence of food on the planet earth is due to automatic movement phenomena in the universe, which in turn originated the concept, that evolved to become encoded within the genes of the homo sapiens mind, that food is an asset. The thermodynamically unstable human body and mind become energized by consuming plant-based food energy, and by consuming animals that themselves became energized after eating plants, and stored the energy of the plants (and the sun) within their body molecules. Powered by energy, humans then used their own human energies to exploit opportunities provided by the universe generally, and the earth locally, to create other forms of assets on the planet earth, such as when a human uses its own body energy, that is ultimately powered by the sun, to lift and position bricks and wood to create a shelter.

Automobiles and other forms of transportation (trains, planes, bicycles, etc) are also assets. The laws of physics and chemistry make it technically possible for these objects to exist and function, which are often directly or indirectly powered using petroleum or natural gas (which are forms of fossilized, ancient stored solar energy) or electricity (which is often originally generated from fossil fuels). The homo sapiens concepts associated with transportation are among the most complex systems of concepts that the homo sapiens mind thinks about. Mechanical maintenance of the transportation objects, legal regulations regarding their use, the engineering designs of transportation objects, the logistics of creating broadly distributed fueling capabilities, and systems for manufacturing, selling and financing these objects, require vast amounts of homo sapiens brain thinking energies.

From where does the motivation originate for homo sapiens to conceptualize the invention of transportation objects and to conceptualize the engineering and logistics associated with them? Transportation allows humans to maintain the thermodynamic stability of their body forms by being able to use the transportation methods to travel to food sources, to farm food (via tractors and harvesters) and to bring farmed food to markets, to move construction materials to areas where shelters are being constructed, to travel to shelters, to travel to areas on the planet earth where reproductory encounters can take place, and to make possible a grid system that arranges houses and businesses in orderly ways on the large expanse of a country's land. All of these advantages fall under the categories of thoughts that improve the human ability to survive and reproduce, which explains the origin or the motivation to think these thoughts. An auto mechanic shop, with its customer service, tools and complex scientific approaches to the diagnosis and fixing of automotive problems, seems like a highly complex invention of the human mind. However, the motivation to create auto mechanic shops is ultimately driven by a human motivation to reproduce, and to maintain the thermodynamic stability of the human body form, and this motivation is ultimately caused by the tendency of the universe to move towards energy equilibrium.

When assets automatically come into existence on the planet earth due to the automatic growth of edible plants, and due to the energy contained within the chemical bonds of the molecules within these plants powering the creation of other objects that humans perceive as assets, the question arises among humans of how the assets on the planet should be distributed. It is highly adaptive for a human mind to ask the question of how assets on the planet earth are distributed, because who gets what determines who gets the most food energy to power their thermodynamically unstable body forms and to keep those forms from disintegrating due to thermodynamic instability, and who gets shelter assets, which are useful as a safe location for engaging in reproduction activities and raising offspring and propagating genes. Almost all people ask this question, and (this is also a highly adaptive thinking habit) use their minds to develop strategies for enabling them to access things in society that are perceived as assets.

If there are no rules regarding how assets are to be distributed, a free-for-all will ensue, where all members of the same species rush to take the assets that are generated automatically on the planet earth due to the automated astronomical cycles that determine the light energy inputs of the planet earth, or that appear due to the use of plant-based energies (that are really sun-sourced energies) to create non-plant-based assets. If there are plenty of assets available to satisfy everyone, the free-for-all situation is acceptable to all. If there are not enough assets, some will lose in the free-for-all race to grab assets. Peace can occur if the losers are content to suffer the lack of assets.

If the losers are not content, however, the losers may try means such as violence, murder, or other acts of evil to take assets from others. What is an act of evil? An evil act is an act whereby a person (or entity) A uses force or fraud to cause another person (or entity) B to transfer an asset from person B to person A, such that person B would not voluntarily have agreed to transfer that asset to person A if person B was objectively informed of, and able to understand, the total gain or loss that would result to person B from the asset transfer. This is in contrast to an act of good. An act of good is an act whereby a person (or entity) A induces another person (or entity) B to transfer an asset from person B to person A, such that person B would normally voluntarily agree to transfer that asset to person A if person B was objectively informed of, and able to understand, the total gain or loss that would result to person B from the asset transfer.

This definition of evil is useful conceptually because it does not ascribe moral value judgements to acts of evil, which makes the definition more objective, since evil and morally are not conceptually inter-twined in this definition. If a crocodile grabs an antelope, drags the antelope into a pond, and kills and eats the antelope, the crocodile is committing an act of evil against the antelope, according this this definition. However, given this definition, it is irrelevant if the crocodile thinks that this evil act is immoral, because this definition of evil does not include a value judgement about whether or not evil acts are immoral. People who commit evil acts may not be aware if the acts are arguably immoral, or may not be able to conceptualize what specific principle of moral behavior has been violated by committing the act of evil, and how this moral principle fits into a general philosophical system of moral behavior. This definition of evil accommodates the possibility that a legal system may function more to prevent acts of evil, than to enforce moral principles, given that the difficulties of proving legal cases with weak or deficient evidence may prevent seemingly "morally acceptable" judgements from being legally acceptable. The idea that evil actions and immorality are inextricably inter-connected is potentially a misleading misconception, and these two entities need to be separated conceptually if one is to understand how the brain works or how nature works.

The free-for-all model of asset distribution may result in a lop-sided distribution of assets that could result in genetically less fit humans reproducing their genes more frequently than genetically more fit humans, if the less fit humans were able to gain a strategic advantage over more fit humans in the free-for-all race to grab assets. The potential problems with the free-for-all model of asset distribution caused the human mind to evolve a tendency to create a wide variety of asset distribution mechanisms to facilitate asset distribution among humans, to prevent there being a free-for-all asset distribution reality. Racism, classism, ethno-centricism, political systems, legal systems, military and police systems, meritocracies, democracies, communist political systems, morality systems, educational systems, money, banking systems, societies and religions are some examples of asset distribution mechanisms that humans have created. Transportation pathways, along with street signs, are also asset distribution mechanisms. Civilization itself is the ultimate, all-encompassing asset distribution mechanism. Civilization makes possible the division of labor on a colossal scale, which permits mass-scale economic efficiency, and permits a money medium of exchange to exist on a massive scale, which permits barter exchange transactions of real assets to occur with extreme precision, but in a standardized and mathematically simple way. It is easier for a barber to pay money for a bushel of corn than to try to barter a bushel of corn for a haircut, if the farmer might not need a haircut at the moment when the barter exchange transaction is proposed. It is also more guaranteed for the farmer if the farmer gets the money now, rather than give the barber the bushel of corn in exchange for a promise from the barber (enforced by trust alone) that later, when the farmer needs a haircut, the barber will provide the haircut.

Every human has a philosophy of good and evil, and a philosophy of to what extent the person's behavior causes the person to gain assets from society, versus contributing assets to society, and under what circumstances one behavior dominates over another, with respect to any particular asset. There is a wide range of such asset-distribution-influencing personal philosophies, due to the fact that a vast variety of such philosophies could exist and be adaptive from an evolutionary perspective, in that having a particular philosophy of good versus evil may improve a human's ability to propagates that human's genes. A particular philosophy may reduce a human's ability to reproduce his or her genes, but still enable the human to generate enough offspring to replace that human after that human dies. A vast variety of such philosophies can exist that can also be adaptive for gene reproduction. Numerous variables that influence the goodness and evilness of human behavior, and the "morality" or "immorality" of a person's behavior, are "tweaked" and "adjusted" by the forces of natural selection. Differences in these variables result in a wide range of evil versus good, or "moral" versus "immoral" behavior patterns among the vast numbers of humans on the planet earth. The distribution and types of these philosophies among humans can determine the "morality" of different societies and civilizations. This "morality" is shaped more by how natural selection evolves the human mind, instead of it being shaped by humans being "conscientiously moral."

Most assets or forms of wealth that humans create are temporary. Food wealth certainly is temporary, since almost all food tends to rot within weeks of its creation, except for some preserved or canned foods. Few foods last for years, such as honey, wine, dried beans, dried corn or freeze dried foods. Non-renewable energy wealth, such as gasoline, natural gas or coal, is destroyed as soon as it is burned to produce energy. Houses made of wood and sheet rock will eventually rot without continued maintenance, which costs money. Concrete structures will also tend to disintegrate within a few centuries without maintenance. Electronics wealth becomes obsolete within a few years. Automobiles tend to wear out or become obsolete within a few years. Houses made of stone, precious metals, undeveloped land, or durable public infrastructure are some examples of assets that can last potentially indefinitely.

However, for various reasons, most human wealth or assets are non-durable and disintegrate soon after their creation. This reality makes it challenging (and in many situations irrational) to try to make stored wealth or savings of any kind to retain their value beyond a few years. This reality also forces generations of humans to continuously expend energy to work to regenerate assets and wealth. This is the origin of the cycle of wealth generation, in that today's workers, after growing old and retiring, must be continuously replaced by a new generation of workers to continue re-generating assets and wealth. The sun, which provides a continuous source of free energy, is the ultimate power source of the never-ending generations of workers who use their body and mind energies to re-generate wealth. This explains the origin of the human mind's concept, and expectation, that working to make a living goes on forever, and that today's children must be trained and educated to eventually become tomorrow's replacer's of today's asset generators.

In Search of Morality

Where does moral behavior exist in homo sapiens societies? Many people think that they are moral, but do significant numbers of people exist who contain within their minds a complete, fully axiom-driven system of morality, applied completely non-hypocritically? It is perhaps questionable if such a system can exist, because no philosopher seems to have invented it by now. There was a famous philosopher named David Hume (1711-1776) who wrote a small book called "An Enquiry Concerning the Principles of Morals," who attempted in this book to create such a system, and yet his system is full of arbitrary value judgements that many would find questionable (Hume, 1777). Even a straightforward system of morality, such as Moses' Ten Commandments, that is also presumably endorsed by a deity, is rarely followed non-hypocritically by anyone in homo sapiens civilization. Thou Shalt Not Kill, yes, but if one is participating in a battle in the context of a state of war that is legally supported or recognized by a government, then it is socially acceptable to kill enemy soldiers, especially if they are trying to kill you. Thou Shalt Not Commit Adultery, yes, but shall you question the wisdom of the parents of one of your hundreds or thousands of ancestors who may have been conceived due to acts of adultery? Charles Darwin, the founder of evolutionary theory, would have hesitated before questioning their wisdom.

Are people moral? Do people honestly believe that human life is infinitely valuable, and that the prevention of human suffering or the prevention of human wealth deprivation are absolutely valuable assets in civilization? Or does moral behavior, or its inconsistently logical hypo-critical forms, arise due to the forces of evolution? Why would the forces of evolution evolve people who have moral beliefs? People would only evolve to contain these beliefs if following these beliefs contributed to propagating the genes of those who hold the beliefs. In addition, people would only evolve a tendency to violate moral principles under certain circumstances if violating these beliefs contributed to propagating the genes of those who violate the beliefs. Just as in politics, one can only understand politics by following the money, one can only understand how human minds evolved to possess moral beliefs (or to violate moral beliefs) by following the gene.

One working definition of morality might be that moral behavior is behavior that contributes to the greatest good of the greatest number of people, or to the members of the homo sapiens species of animal on the planet earth. One problem with this definition is that if everyone follows this behavior pattern, and society becomes happier and wealthier as a result, people may in their prosperity have larger numbers of offspring. This then decreases the per-capita wealth of civilization, which may lead to deprivation, and a possible increase in the amount of murderous violence or war, to reduce to number of people in civilization, to restore the per-capita wealth level to one that provides more life support and gene reproduction opportunities per capita. This is the famous Malthusian argument, which may make sense as a physics phenomenon, if one believes that war or genocide is an energy equilibration phenomena occurring in the universe, due to humans killing each other to increase the per-capita wealth of the survivors, and to increase the per-capita quantity of thermodynamic stability contained within the bodies of the survivors (Malthus, 1798). It would seem that any moral theory that claims that people should work for "improving human life" should contain a caveat that there must be. in addition, ways of preventing excessive population growth resulting from people being too prosperous.

Another problem with this definition is that it is an arbitrary value judgement to claim that human life is infinitely valuable, if one thinks that a human life consists of a temporary concatenation of atoms and molecules, held together by bonding forces, where each atom and molecule has a range of quantum energy states, strictly parameterized by the laws of physics, and functioning as a kind of energy cluster. Before a human was conceived as an initial zygote, that human's atoms and molecules were scattered individually throughout the universe, and no other human cared about this particular human because this particular human did not exist. A woman's womb concatenated that future human's scattered atoms and molecules into that human body, and because that body was born and existed, that body was given an extremely high value by an arbitrary value judgement existing among human minds. Eventually, after that body lived its life and died, its atoms and molecules once again disintegrated, and that body no longer existed as an entity that was assigned with high value. If the matter making up that human body was not concatenated into that living human body form, that matter would be scattered in the infinity background of the universe as atoms and molecules that could be theoretically concatenated into a practically infinite number of other constructs of matter, including lifeless objects. However, to have a morality system that is secular, it is necessary to accept as an arbitrary axiom that human life is infinitely valuable, and that moral axioms should be designed to somehow "improve" human life.

The moral belief, that human life is infinitely valuable, implies that the thermodynamically unstable energy form manifesting itself as a human body is infinitely valuable, and that its existence should be safeguarded. By this definition, morality is arbitrary, since moral beliefs imply that a particular energy structure, that is represented by the energy cluster of a living human body, is the most valuable type of energy structure in the universe. However, it is arbitrary to believe that the energy cluster represented by a human body is more valuable than any other energy cluster in the universe, such as a campfire, a raccoon, a sun, a black hole, or a corn plant.

Another problem with defining moral behavior as behavior that contributes to the greatest good of the greatest number of people, is that it is impossible to predict how a behavior or action that "contributes to the greatest good of the greatest number of

162

people" that is performed now, will affect future historical events. If one assumes that all events occurring now are inextricably part of the chain of events that causes all subsequent future historical events, one must assume that any "morally good deed" performed today will inextricably contribute to any horrifyingly violent or destructive historical event that will occur in human history after the moment when this morally good deed was implemented. Countless poor people were fed in many charitable food pantries by well-meaning people who felt good inside for helping to feed these poor people, prior to the start of World War II, a war in which 50 million people were killed, often quite gruesomely. All of those moral acts of feeding the poor were part of the chain of causal events that caused World War II. If, later in human history, a World War III or World War IV occurs, these moral feeding acts also will, in hindsight, have to be considered part of the chain of historical events causing these wars. Morally good actions can (and have, by the countless trillions) contributed to the chain of historical events leading up to horrifyingly violent events in homo sapiens history. It is impossible to predict what one is optimizing by trying to act such as to contribute to providing the greatest good to the greatest number of people.

Morality commonly is justified from the argument that God requires people to be moral, and to value and help to nurture human life. A secular justification for morality would require arbitrarily assigning an extremely high value to human life. Secular morality could be adaptive based on the practical reality that if someone were to behave immorally, that person may be attacked by others against whom that person behaved immorally, due to an adaptive inclination of potential victims of immoral people to defend themselves against attacks by immoral people. Also, the friends and family of those who are victims of immoral behavior may become angered or upset at the victimization of the victim, and then work to attack the attacker. This would also be an adaptive behavior pattern that adds to the propagation of that family's genes. Therefore, although the ultimate effect of an immoral act on future history cannot be precisely predicted, it can be predicted that the immoral act will cause pain and suffering to the victim and the victim's family, and perhaps contribute to making contemporary societies more toxic places to live in due to the increased "negative karma" from the immoral behavior. Nonetheless, all of these secular arguments may be of little significance, given that there are colossal numbers of historical examples of people who acted morally or immorally in the past in human history, but after these moral or immoral acts occurred, subsequent historical events occurred of which there could have been no way, in hindsight, of predicting that these historical events would follow the chain of causality in which the moral or immoral actions played an integrated role.

What is meant by "improving" human life or well-being? One way to improve human life would be to engineer societies so that societies provide people with whatever it is that people consider worth having. Different people value things differently, so it is difficult to determine what it is that a morally engineered society should be providing to people. There are also the over-arching issues that the environment of the planet earth may be damaged by providing people with what they consider worth having, and this environmental damage may result in mass death of humans in the long-run, and permanent loss of per-capita wealth and of the ability of humans to survive on the planet earth. Much of human "progress," for example, depends on leveraging the enormous energy contained within petroleum fuel sources to generate energy that can be used to power machines and technologies that prolong human life span. However, petroleum energy is practically non-renewable, and burning it has increased the concentration of carbon dioxide in the atmosphere, to an extent that such burning is causing massive retention of heat on the planet earth, and beginning a process of mass extinction, potential global crop failures, and the potential collapse of human populations. Here, technological advances seem to be contributing to the annihilation of vast numbers of humans in the long run. The notion that it is morally good to be a scientific researcher and contribute to developing the science behind advanced technology, or to be a politician or banker who helps develop countries so that these countries are technologically advanced, is certainly questionable in the context of basing the energy economy of civilization on the burning of petroleum fuels as a central energy source.

Perhaps a more refined definition of morality would be to define moral behavior as

164

behavior that contributes to increasing the per-capita wealth (whether wealth of resources, or wealth of health, or wealth of shelter, etc.) of members of the homo sapiens species of animal on the planet earth. This definition would be problematic because it would probably require some kind of civilization-scale social engineering to prevent people who are prosperous from having so many offspring as to make it impossible to maintain a comfortable level of per-capita wealth in homo sapiens civilization. Preventing people from having excess offspring when those people are prosperous enough to support the offspring itself comes with moral problems.

Moral behavior might be defined as behavior that contributes to giving the average person what the average person feels is worth having. There is an emotional component that determines what people consider to be worth having. Today's lower class people possess far more wealth and comfort than the richest kings from hundreds or thousands of years ago. In theory, those lower class people should feel as confident and happy and smug as the richest kings of the past felt when they were sitting on their wealth and power. Yet, lower class people often feel chronically depressed from the realization that they are of low wealth status on societies' dominance hierarchies or "totem poles." The perception of what is desirable may depend on one's perception of where one is ranked in the context of various human-created hierarchy constructs. The possession of an absolute amount of wealth and physical well-being may not be enough to make someone feel that they have satisfied their needs, if there is an evolutionary thought-process operating in their minds that makes them feel emotionally bad if they rank low on the hierarchy within their societies. Both the perception of the hierarchy, and the people who make up the hierarchy, are arbitrary constructs of nature. But, since hierarchy positions are relative, and are irrespective of whatever absolute wealth each individual possesses, where there is a hierarchy, it is impossible to satisfy everyones' emotional need to be relatively close to the top of a hierarchy. Some people will not feel that they posses what is worth having, if they rank low on their societal hierarchy. This makes it difficult to implement a moral axiom that moral behavior consists of providing others with what they value or need most, if that includes valuing being at the top of a hierarchy.

People often consider having a well-paying job to be a coveted asset, and often wish to live in countries where there are opportunities to advance in society through career advancement and development. People often want to see opportunities to obtain some kind of training or advanced education and apply that towards a money-making job that provides them with a career where they can ambitiously rise up in rank and authority in society. Many people are fundamentally motivated by the desire to make money, advance in their careers. and satisfy their perceived needs. If there is money or a perceived need to be acquired, many people will be motivated to work hard, or commute to a place of work or a place where they can buy what they need. Such people would prefer to stay at home and stare at the walls, or waste their time watching TV, rather than pursue an activity where there is no money to be made or no personal need to be satisfied.

Assuming that money-making and satisfying their needs are most desirable, at least to these people, perhaps an argument can be made that that which is morally good provides others with money-making, career advancement and need-satisfying opportunities. In this context, what is morally good is not necessarily what is charitable, but consists of entrepreneurial activities, implemented by well-capitalized, often highly intelligent business leaders, to create opportunities for members of the public to make money, advance their careers and satisfy needs. These business leaders might not themselves care about behaving charitably or morally, but may only be motivated themselves by a desire to make money. It is theoretically possible for all people to feel satisfied solely through such commercially-oriented behaviors. A society where commercial-oriented behaviors satisfy all peoples' perceived needs might be considered morally optimal, and in such a society, charity given for free, which is often commonly thought of as a moral behavior, would be irrelevant.

All of these previously mentioned problems with moral beliefs and behaviors imply that much moral thinking is based on misconceptions. Thinking and behaving in a morally "good" way may not be as obviously beneficial to humanity as it seems. People may be less moral than they think, because most people will violate basic moral principles in some situations, and may not have the mental skills to conceive of and follow a comprehensive system of moral behavior. In addition, some people can gain advantages in life by behaving immorally. Also, many people who commit acts of evil may not necessarily believe that these evil acts are also immoral. They may behave in an evil way, but not have a concept of what is immoral in their minds. Political, military, police, banking and legal systems also do not necessarily, or cannot necessarily, operate along moral principles in all situations. Humans seem to have evolved such that many humans conceptually disconnect evil acts (that is, unfair barter exchange transactions) from moral value judgements regarding these acts. This may be a more rational and realistic way of understanding morality, and may prevent people from making the mistake of expecting moral behavior to occur in situations where moral behavior does not occur in reality.

Yet Another Discussion of Free Will

If I am walking through a random patch of woods, and I am about to starve to death in two minutes, and to my right I see a wild apple tree filled with apples, but to my left I see non-edible plants and trees, I have to decide about which of these two paths, the left or the right path, is optimal to take, if I want to avoid starving to death. If I decided to walk to the right, eat the apples, and avoid starving to death, did I make this decision from my own free will? In this scenario, I decided to walk right towards the apple tree and not walk left because in my genetic ancestral line my ancestors had a higher probability of surviving and propagating their genes if they evolved with a brain-thinking or brain-deciding tendency to walk towards the apple tree and eat the apples if they realized that they were in the situation that I was in. Ancestors without this tendency would have a higher chance of being wiped out of the gene pool, leaving behind those with this tendency.

One argument against the existence of free will is that the universe appears to be driven by automatic movement phenomena, or atomic and molecular patterns of physical or chemical behavior of matter that play out automatically. For example, heat flows automatically from a warmer body to a cooler body, establishing thermodynamic equilibrium between the two, and the converse does not occur without an external energy input.   Table salt, consisting of molecules of sodium and chlorine atoms bonded together in a one-to-one ratio per molecule, automatically dissolves into separate ions of chlorine and sodium when placed in water at room temperature. Solutes move from a higher concentration to a lower concentration when two solutions of different concentrations are put in contact.   Hydrogen and oxygen combine explosively to form water molecules, when hydrogen is heated in the presence of oxygen.   Applying electrical energy to water can separate the hydrogen from the oxygen in a process of electrolysis.   Fatty membrane-bound structures often form spontaneously when fats are placed in water. Every chemical reaction that is known to occur under various conditions of temperature, pressure, etc., is an automated movement phenomena in the universe.   Another example of automatic movement in the universe is protein synthesis.   When a cell uses DNA information to form a chain of amino acids into a protein, the linear chain or amino acids being formed automatically folds into the protein, such as to usually have the appropriate three-dimensional shape and functionality of that protein.   This protein folding process is driven strictly by the laws of physics and the mathematical laws governing how a linear chain of amino acids automatically folds into a protein structure.

The human body seems to consist of an aggregation of automatic movement phenomena occurring at the atomic and molecular level, mostly in the form of a vast variety of chemical reactions that occur automatically if strictly parameterized conditions are in place for the atoms and molecules to react with each other chemically, but also in the form of thermodynamic equilibrium processes, and solute movement within bodily fluids or across biological membranes.   These automated motion phenomena work synergistically together to result in a body system that is in equilibrium.   These automated motional phenomena make the continued existence of the thermodynamically unstable homo sapiens body form possible, as long as food energy is inputted continuously into the system to power the system, and as long as a disease process does not alter the natural energy equilibrium of the body, so that the body's atoms and molecules can continue to be arranged in a coherent body form.   If these automatic movement phenomena unavoidably proceed to their endpoints, how can the mind, which is made up of these automatic movement phenomena, have free will? The forces of evolution evolved minds to have the combinations of automatic movement phenomena that exist inside the minds because having these phenomena are adaptive, given how these processes begin to move automatically in response to sensory stimuli from the planet earth.

Another reason why free will may not exist is that the laws of thermodynamics dictate that a closed system cannot perform work without an input of energy, which implies that thinking and decision-making are not possible unless they are powered by energy. An organic mind's thoughts are caused by bio-chemical reactions within the organic mind, and these bio-chemical reactions cannot occur without an input of energy, assuming that these bio-chemical reactions are non-spontaneous according to what is the Gibbs Free Energy value of each respective bio-chemical reaction involved in generating a thought. If the bio-chemical reactions are spontaneous, they occur automatically anyway.

To generate a thought that seems to be an autonomous or free will decision, the energy that is needed, to power the bio-chemical reactions in the brain that form that supposed "free will" thought, must exist before that "free will" thought can be generated. To make a "free will" decision, a mind must control the source of the energy that powers the bio-chemical reactions in the brain that generate the free will decision thought before that thought is made. However, to control the source of this energy, the mind must generate a thought to control that energy source, and then this thought must be powered by another energy source that the mind must also control, and so on, ad infinitum, without there being an original thought, ultimately directing the "free will" decision, that was not powered from an energy source that was generated automatically, beyond any mind's control. It would violate the first or second law of thermodynamics if a human could generate a thought while simultaneously controlling the ultimate origin of the energy source that powered the bio-chemical reactions in that human's brain that generated that thought.

Can a person use free will to decided to make a cup of sugar water? A person could go to a kitchen, grab a sugar cube, put it in a glass of water, dissolve the sugar, and drink the sugar water. Ultimately, however, the opportunity to make a glass of sugar water is completely beyond any person's control, and is provided by the universe itself. The sugar molecule's structure is determined by the laws of physics, and the atoms that make up the sugar molecule are provided by the universe, as are the laws of physics that cause the automatic movement phenomenon that sugar dissolves in water at 23 degrees Celsius to result in sugar water. The farmer who grew the sugar crop, from which the sugar to make that sugar cube was refined, obtained the seed for that crop from a previous crop, and the seed for that previous crop came from a previous crop, etc., down to the original time when the first wild crop of that plant was first found randomly on the planet earth, provided by the planet earth and the universe. Every element of the chain of causality that ultimately put that sugar cube on a person's kitchen shelf, and the water and the glass in that person's kitchen, used to make the sugar water, traces back to original supply sources arbitrarily provided by the universe. Humans certainly cannot create the sub-atomic particles that make up the atoms of that sugar molecule, and indeed humans cannot even touch a sugar molecule, given that there is always a tiny inter-molecular space between a human's fingers and an object being touched. It is a misconception to think that a person can "make" a glass of sugar water. Instead, a person can only exploit opportunities, provided by the universe generally and the earth locally, to make sugar water, and these opportunities only exist under certain strictly parameterized circumstances and not other circumstances, and these opportunities are strictly limited by the universe generally and the earth locally, and the limitations of the circumstances that provide these opportunities are entirely beyond the control of the person. For example, the laws of physics make it impossible for a human to make a glass of sugar water within a time span of one unit of Planck time. Instead, the laws of physics dictate that a certain minimum number of Planck time units must pass before a human can "create" any glass of sugar water.

All choices that humans may encounter, for which humans may make decisions, are provided arbitrarily by the universe, due to factors beyond the control of any human.

The human mind has evolved such as to have a higher probability of surviving and reproducing if the mind takes certain opportunities, presented to the mind arbitrarily by the universe under certain circumstances, and rejects other opportunities presented under other circumstances. This decision-making is similar to the automated decision-making of a single-celled organism such as a paramecium, which is a purely mechanical molecular machine.

If a food item is nearby a paramecium, and this food item is shedding molecules that can induce conformational changes in molecular receptors for those molecules on the paramecium's outer surface, the paramecium may move towards the food item. The paramecium presumably knows how to move towards the food item because the concentration of molecules shed by the food item increases the closer the paramecium moves towards the food item. This causes greater numbers of molecule receptors to be activated the closer the paramecium moves towards the food item. The paramecium does not have a mind with the free will to decide to move towards this food item (which was provided to it arbitrarily by the earth locally and the universe generally). Instead, the paramecium evolved such that it has a higher chance of surviving or reproducing if it follows molecule trails of molecules that can function as food items towards increasing concentrations of the food molecules, in various circumstances where such opportunities occur. This is an automated, robotic, chemotactic response to the detection of food items provided by the universe, that are provided to the paramecium due to factors entirely beyond the control of the paramecium (Lampert, 2011).

Do computers have free will? The answer is no. Humans created the minds of the computers, and humans dictate how different computers think or process information by designing the micro-processors of the computers, by applying the laws of physics to micro-processor design, where said laws arbitrarily exist in the universe. Humans also provide the data inputs that direct the computer what to think about or process. The computer is forced to think in a precise way, dictated by how electrons move along the human-designed microscopic pathways inside the silicon micro-processor driving the computer. Humans also provide the energy that drives the computer's brain, by generating electricity in power plants, that sends electrons, driven by energy, into the computer's micro-processors, where said electrons follow the laws of physics in moving from path to path to generate solution outputs.

Computers can play the game of backgammon with expert skill. During the computer's turn, the computer generates a range of possible move choices, and ranks the move options from best to worst, and then executes a decision using the best option. There is a point where the computer transitions from ranking the best options to executing the decision to move and making the actual move. Here, an array of possible choices is generated, an optimal choice is chosen, and there is decision-making execution and action, but there is no free will. The computer is programmed to only choose the most optimal choice among all of the choices that the computer calculated are possible given the current dice roll, given how the computer calculated the rankings of these choices from best to worst. The computer has an array of choices, but is forced by its program to only choose the best choice. Here, decision-making and decision execution can both exist independently of free will. The computer's decision is driven by the laws of physics, by human programming, and by human-supplied electricity, and is beyond the computer's control.

But if computers do not have free will because humans control the creation and functionality of the computers' minds, does that not mean that humans have free will because they created the computers? Humans were only able to create computers because the laws of physics, that humans cannot control, make computers possible, and because the natural resources (metals, plastics, glass, silicone, etc.) that humans use to make the computers are arbitrarily provided to humans by the universe and the planet earth. Humans cannot control the factors that determine whether or not computers can exist, or the factors that determine if the natural resources exist on the planet earth to be able to manufacture computers. In addition, the laws of physics dictate that computers cannot be made all the time on the planet earth, but can only be made at certain times, in certain places, and in certain quantities, and this is subject to limitations of how many resources exist on the planet earth to make computer-production possible. In general, the laws of physics dictate that computers with microchip minds can only be manufactured in factories with highly precise environments, where materials are assembled using a variety of tools to manufacture the computer. A person cannot manufacture a computer microprocessor while sitting in an easy chair sipping tea, for example.

Humans "created" computers not out of human free will, but because the universe programmed humans to create the computers. The tendency of the universe to move towards its own equilibrium causes automatic phenomena such as natural selection, which is an energy equilibration phenomenon, to cause the evolution of thermodynamically unstable humans, who need energy to maintain the existence of their thermodynamically unstable body forms, and who must reproduce due to the laws of physics making it impossible for a human body to exist forever. This evolution then induces humans to create computers, that can help humans survive and reproduce on the planet earth by generating mathematically optimal calculations that humans can use to improve their ability to survive and reproduce on the planet earth. Therefore, the motivation to create computers is a system of thought that falls under the categories of thoughts that improve the ability of humans to survive and reproduce, and the motivation of humans to think thoughts that improve survival and reproduction was installed in the minds of humans by the universe, via the universe-driven energy equilibration phenomenon of natural selection, that ultimately evolved the human mind, in the context of an automatically equilibrating, thermodynamically disequilibreated universe,

However, if free will might not exist, then why do so many people (or most people) believe that they have free will? The idea that people have free will is widespread, and indeed is a conceptual foundation of almost all human thinking, and is so pervasive in human thinking that it is difficult to escape the conceptual clutches of free will, or to imagine how the mind could in theory operate without free will. Indeed, the laws, rules and/or regulations of criminal justice systems, legal systems and penal systems all presume that free will exists, as do numerous religions and political systems. If free will does not exist, then the belief in it must be a misconception. But why would the misconception that free will exists be so widespread in human thinking, and integrated in the rule systems of so many societal structures? The answer is that there must be some natural selection forces at work that make it adaptive for human brains to evolve such as to believe that free will exists, even if such a belief was a misconception.

There potentially are man-made causes of natural selection forces that select for people who believe that free will exists. One possible causative factor is religion. In the Christianity and Islam god paradigms, for example, there is the concept that God gave people free will and the choice to live life either in a good way or an evil way, and that after dying, a person is judged by God whether that person was morally well-behaved enough in life to deserve to go to heaven, or was evil enough to go to hell. A belief in free will would be required to believe in this judgement day concept. Many people only choose sexual or marital partners who are of the same religion as they, and will not sire offspring with someone of a different religion. Not believing in free will might make one not believe in religion, which could reduce one's ability to reproduce if large numbers of potential mates in that person's society would not mate with someone who was not religious. Historically, people who did not believe could have been persecuted or executed by government forces, religious authorities or by civilian peers, which would help to remove from the gene pool those who did not believe in free will and who might as a consequence not be believers.

In god paradigms, whether these paradigms are monotheistic or polytheistic, it is presumed that gods have free will. Having godly free will would require that gods be capable of forming thoughts without requiring energy to power those thoughts. If a god's thoughts required energy, then the energy needed to power the thought of a god would have to exist before the thought was generated, in which case the god would not have free will because the god would not be able to control the origin of the energy that was powering that god's free will thought. This would make it impossible for gods to have free will thoughts (a necessary condition to being a god) unless gods could generate thoughts without requiring energy to generate the thoughts. Since generating thoughts without an energy source to power the thoughts would violate the first law of thermodynamics, religious people would have to, by faith, believe that gods have an intrinsic ability to function without their being subject to the first law of thermodynamics. The first law of thermodynamics would not apply to the thoughts of gods, which would give gods free will, but also, if gods could operate without their being subject to the first law of thermodynamics, in theory gods would have unlimited power, such as the power to form the earth and the lifeforms in it, or the power to generate lifeforms that actually had free will. The ability of gods to exist in violation of the first law of thermodynamics must be regarded as a miracle to be accepted on faith. This miracle may also give gods the power to create humans who, at least in that aspect of their mind functionality that determines free will, can generate free will thoughts without requiring the energy to power the free will thoughts to exist prior to forming the thoughts. This is one workaround for making free will possible within a physics and thermodynamics framework, and would make the Judgement Day elements of god paradigms workable.

Government legal systems are another potential man-made source of natural selection forces that select for people who believe that free will exists. The concept that criminals should be punished or penalized or executed for committing crimes implies that free will exists. If free will did not exist, a criminal would not be blameworthy of committing a crime, and therefore would not deserve punishment for the crime. It might be justifiable for society to control and restrict the criminal's movements to prevent the criminal from accessing future opportunities to commit crimes, by hiding the criminal from society by incarcerating the criminal, to prevent the criminal from accessing mainstream society to commit another crime. However, punishing the criminal for committing a crime would be illogical if free will did not exist. Also, if free will did not exist, there would also be no justification in continuing to incarcerate a guilty prisoner if it could be somehow proven that the criminal would never again commit any more crimes if the prisoner was put back into mainstream society. Suppose, for example, that an incarcerated criminal somehow gained access to a chainsaw and cut off both of his or her arms and legs, and survived this episode. The criminal, who would now be only a torso, could not possibly commit another crime in the future, and it could not be justified to keep that criminal incarcerated in the context of a legal system where free will was acknowledged to not exist. That criminal

175

would need to be released from prison immediately, even if the crimes for which the criminal was originally incarcerated consisted of murdering dozens of people.

However, if punishing a criminal is irrational because criminals cannot have free will, than there is no rational justification for having a penal system, built into a legal system, to punish criminals. It would only be justifiable for society to sequester the criminal from mainstream society (such as by incarcerating the criminal in a pleasant prison environment, without implying that the criminal is being punished) to block the prisoner from committing another crime. A person who does not believe that free will exists may not accept a government's penal system or recognize a government legal system containing a penal system. That government might then view that non-believer of free will to be politically subversive, and imprison, persecute or execute that individual, potentially reducing that individual's ability to propagate that individual's genes.

Religious systems, and government-backed legal and penal systems, that both explicitly promote, or imply, the concept that people have free will, are powerful peer pressure forces that obligate people to believe that free will exists. These systems can limit the ability of those who do not believe in free will to survive in societies with these systems, or to obtain money, food energy or gene reproduction assets. This is particularly true in human epochs prior to the mid-twentieth century, in which societies, civilians and governments were particularly autocratic, and people in general less educated, which facilitated herding people under the common umbrellas of religious and legal systems that implied the existence of free will. Religions that imply that free will exists promote and enforce the establishment of government legal systems that imply that free will exists, and vice versa. In addition, if there a large number of people, particularly powerful or rich business people, within society who honestly believe that free will exists, the existence of this large number of people also will provide natural selection pressures in favor of evolving people within society who honestly believe that free will exists. Although a belief in free will might be a misconception, the belief of the free will misconception would be adaptive. Indeed, it can be adaptive for a mind to have mental illness, irrational beliefs or personality flaws.

Is Rational Thought Adaptive?

Anyone who has met significant numbers of people will conclude that many, and perhaps all, humans are not completely rational thinkers, and do not emote in completely appropriate ways. Of course, it is difficult to define what rational thought is. One might say, perhaps arbitrarily, that rational thought consists of a rational understanding of the principles of mathematics, plus an ability to perform in the mind computations complex enough to simulate (and therefore rationally understand) any natural phenomenon such as a hurricane, or an internal combustion engine, or a paramecium, in motion, down to sub-atomic precision. By this criteria, no human who has ever lived has been rational. Rational thought might also be arbitrarily defined as thought that consists of a reasonable balance between improving personal survival or welfare versus improving the survival or welfare of offspring or of the public in general. This definition would be subjective, although people are more likely to be rational in this sense, than rational in a purely mathematical and computational sense. Another possible definition of rational thinking is to think in a way that is free of mental illness, such as depression, schizophrenia, bipolar disorder, etc., although it can be subjective to define what is "mental illness," or what would be considered a reasonable or socially-acceptable balance balance between mental illness and functionality within society. Also, some mental illnesses do not necessarily hinder the ability to think in rationally logical or mathematical ways.

One may wonder why irrational behaviors are so prevalent in human societies, when it would seem that a person would profit most in life, and survive best and make the most money, if the person was perfectly rational or mathematical. There have been politicians who have waged destructive wars that resulted only in the maintenance of the political status quo that existed before the wars, or people who have stayed in abusive sexual relationships, or people who understood geometry but failed at calculus, or who failed at both, or who lost vast amounts of money gambling because they wrongly believed that they were competent at playing poker or blackjack, or people who were so paralyzed by fear of doctors that they died early in life of easily curable diseases because they were too anxious to visit doctors, etc. Does the common prevalence of irrational behaviors, thoughts and feelings among people in society imply that irrational behavior can be adaptive, and that purely rational behavior may in fact not be adaptive?

There may exist evolutionary selection pressures that would select in favor of various forms of mental illness or forms of irrational behavior among people. Governments can be a source of such selection pressures. Throughout history, there have been governments led by egotistical individuals who valued their own survival above that of anyone else in their society. Some dictators in history have killed thousands or millions of their own people to quell dissent, or merely to eliminate those suspected of possibly being a threat to the dictator's absolute rule. People who publicly question their governments, journalists who write convincing, structured criticisms of government officials, people who in small public gatherings, or even in private gatherings, mildly or strongly criticize government leaders, could be attacked and killed by such egotistical dictators. Individuals who question governments might reproduce less frequently compared to those who do not show such behavior, or compared to those who might show such behavior but have a behavioral tendency to keep their government criticisms to themselves. Such individuals may show behaviors, such as the inputting of information and knowledge to use to make a rational assessments for purposes of decision-making, or the ability to decide on optimal choices when making decisions, or the ability to convincingly communicate to the public of what are the more optimal alternatives for answering certain questions, that would make that individual to be more likely to be viewed as being rational, and would make that individual a more competent and ideal student at a higher-ranked university. If a government dictator wipes those individuals from the gene pool of his or her society, the survivors might have fewer intellectual skills.

In addition, people who are mentally ill, but who voice government criticisms, might escape government attack if the criticism is publicly discounted because the voicer of the criticism is known to be mentally ill. This theme is suggested by William Shakespeare in his play Hamlet, in which Hamlet is not killed outright for possibly being a threat to the king, but is merely followed and spied upon, because Hamlet seems to be acting in a harmlessly crazy way when he shows possible suggestions of aggressive or subversive behavior (Shakespeare, 2005 edition). A schizophrenic individual, who criticizes a government in a way that seems at least partially irrational, voices a less convincing criticism, that may be less threatening to a government, such that the government may not attack this individual, so that this individual may become capable later on of having offspring who have schizophrenia genes. Some people may be unable to rebel against a government because they may be too mentally ill or too physically weak to participate in such resistance, and these individuals might be less likely to be identified as a threat to governments and might be more likely to escape government retribution and might be more likely to propagate their genes in the gene pool.

Some people with schizophrenia have possessed great analytical skills and creative skills, and were able to create works of art, music, science or literature. Often, people with schizophrenia show paranoia, such as thinking that someone is trying to poison them or speculating that others are persecuting them. Perhaps this kind of paranoid thinking is adaptive, since if a schizophrenic individual possesses extreme competence at being able to analyze, critique or mathematically understand ideas, that individual may be able to formulate a strategic plan, or develop critical analyses, that could be used to undermine a government, a powerful religious establishment, or a rich and powerful or dangerous businessperson, and enable that person to take over the power position of such individuals. This might make that person potentially a target of these powerful forces, since he or she would be stepping on too many toes or asking too many uncomfortable questions in applying his or her analytical skills. Being a bit paranoid, and hyper-cautious that others may be preparing to attack such a critical thinker, might be adaptive to those with extremely sophisticated analytical abilities. There may in general be a linkage between having great analytical skills or critical thinking or creativity skills, and being suspicious or paranoid that a person may be attacked for asking too many deep questions, and this linkage may have evolved because it would be adaptive to have it in a world of dominance hierarchies.

A particular combination of rational and irrational thinking patterns can direct a person towards some jobs and away from other jobs, which influences what life support niche a person occupies in their life on the planet earth. For example, if a person is irrational in mathematics beyond simple arithmetic, but is rational at showing houses, that person will not become a mathematics professor, but may become a real estate agent and obtain access to a money-making resource-acquiring niche on the planet earth this way. Someone who can master physics at the expert level, but lack the "emotional intelligence" or "emotional patience" that is needed to deal with people in customer service transactions, may be more likely to become a paid physics teacher or professor, instead of a manager of a business. A person who likes scholarship and quietude may be more likely to become a librarian than a sportscaster, while a macho person, who ridicules scholars and does not understand topics beyond the middle school level, may more likely to become a hockey player than a librarian.

The business world also can create selection pressures that may help to prevent the evolution of rational people. Some businesses require that employees are more rational and emotionally stable compared to other businesses. For example, leadership positions in businesses, or positions as doctors or lawyers in business structures, often require more rational and emotionally stable people. However, other jobs, such as pumping gas for a living, or washing cars, may require less sophisticated rational thinking and emotional sophistication skills. There are fewer jobs available in society that require very high-level rational thought and refined emotional control, compared to jobs that do not require these traits to an extreme extent. This creates evolutionary selection pressures that reduce the adaptability of being rationally and emotionally refined. The lack of a market demand, or a carrying capacity, for jobs requiring rational people who are able to input vast amounts of technical information, limits the extent to which it is adaptive to have a mind with such capabilities. If a society consisted solely of people with such talented minds, there would be no competitive advantage of having such talented minds, while, at the same time, all assets in society would be quickly acquired, titled, and "locked up" by the talented people, which would prevent any class mobility in that society, and potentially force the average person to live in poverty. This would create an incentive to use things other than talent, such as crime or violence, to gain a competitive advantage in such a society.

Character flaws, lack of initiative to pursue higher education, lack of talent to pursue higher education, emotional illness, lack of energy to concentrate for long periods of time, an inability to gain large amounts of knowledge by remembering large amounts of information, lack of intelligence, and other mind limitations can limit the ability of a person to compete for assets in human societies. People with such mind limitations may be unable to develop strategies for competing against other humans to acquire assets within their respective societies, or may be unable to apply these strategies, or follow through on them consistently over time. Consequently, such mind limitations may be viewed as asset distribution mechanisms that are imposed on people, by being incorporated into their genes via natural selection and evolution. These mind limitations are a disadvantage because they limit a person's access to assets, such as to force a person to only be able to access an average or below-average share of assets within his or her respective society. However, such mind limitations may be adaptive, or at least not non-adaptive, if, in spite of being able to only access a below-average share of societal assets, a person nonetheless is still able to generate a number of offspring that is comparable to the number generated by wealthier individuals who had fewer mind limitations that prevented them from gaining assets in society. It would also be adaptive if, in spite of feeling bad emotionally due to having a below-average share of resources, a person continues maintain his or her will to live, and to live long enough to generate significant numbers of offspring. In addition, however, such mind limitations can be adaptive because, by forcing people into only being able to access an average or below-average share of resources, and by forcing people to be incapable of out-strategizing the richer and more powerful people in society for assets, these mind limitations prevent these people from threatening the power and wealth of the rich and powerful in their societies, so these people are less likely to be attacked and killed by those more powerful people. Since it is more practical for people to have the ability to gain an average or below-average share of societal assets, versus being able to form and apply strategies for gaining a huge fraction of societal assets, evolutionary selection pressures select for people who have weaker asset-acquisition capabilities. If a gene pool consisted entirely of people who all had the mentality of kings, i.e., who were all extremely egotistical, extremely greedy, extremely intelligent, psychologically stable, able to manage and command armies and governments, and experts at forming strategies to out-compete other humans for assets, the societies formed by people with that gene pool would likely consist of endless and violent power struggles, driven by egotism and greed. There might be so much violence in such societies as to reduce the overall birth rate of those societies, which would not be adaptive.

Many people instinctively feel emotionally uncomfortable reading books. After reading just a few books, an individual may encounter plausible ideas that may contradict those ideas promoted by powerful government, business and religious leaders. Reading many books may cause a person to encounter, or piece together, entire systems of thought that are different from those promoted publicly by powerful government, business and religious leaders. A feeling of discomfort may come over the reader, in that since this reader now knows of a better vision of how societies should be structured, compared to the ideas promoted by powerful society leaders, this reader may get into trouble by publicly explaining these opposing viewpoints. The origin of a feeling of emotional discomfort felt from reading a few books, and especially from reading many books, may originate from many historical examples where critical thinkers were attacked by powerful peoples within societies, leading to evolutionary selection pressures, driven by civilization-structured dominance hierarchies, for evolving people who have an instinctive dislike of reading books. The advantage of reading large numbers of books, namely the possession of critical thinking skills that can enable one to make large amounts of money and become relatively more successful, and higher ranked in socio-economic status in life, must be balanced against the possibility of being attacked and destroyed by powerful societal leaders who view the sophisticated book reader as a threatening competitor to their status. Evolutionary selection pressures may flip-flop between evolving people with either of these two extremes of liking to book-reading or disliking book-reading.

Those who read large amounts of books and display unconventional knowledge sometimes will be subject to derision, insults or ostracism by others in society. An adaptive fear, of the public display of knowledge that contradicts an average core of beliefs projected by societies, governments, business leaders or religious leaders, may lead people to attack those who display such knowledge. This prevents the attackers from appearing to be friendly with the more knowledgeable, and therefore potentially more subversive, knowledge-inputting book-readers. It can be adaptive for a person to have a tendency to not want to appear to be friends with those who are targeted by powerful societal leaders. A disdain, to various degrees, of extensive book reading is so common globally that there must have been very strong selection pressures throughout history to evolve people who have such disdain. It may be evolutionarily adaptive for people to have some degree of fear or contempt of those who read large numbers of books.

The evolutionary tug-of-war between evolving egotistical minds with better abilities to secure their own personal survival, versus collectivist minds that work to enhance government collectivist goals, is shown by people who evolve in a resource-sparse, desert environment, such as in the Middle East. The resource-sparse desert environment creates strong selection pressures to evolve minds with personality traits that make the people egotistical, independent-minded, resistant to collectivist behaviors, and perhaps a bit predatory and deceptive towards other members within their societies, in order for each mind to best be able to extract sparse resources needed for survival from the desert. However, the governments governing these people create selection pressures favoring the evolution of minds who obey the governments, and are willing to participate in collective military actions. The two evolutionary selection pressures in many ways contradict one another, resulting in people who are mostly egotistical, but also who seem to arbitrarily possess traits that, at least superficially, induce them to work towards achieving government collective goals. If traits for egotism evolve to be extremely prevalent in a desert society, governments may feel that their power is threatened by excess egotism, and a violent ego-driven civil war may occur. Excessively egotistical people may be killed off by these civil wars, and a form of "cutting the grass," or reducing the amount of super-egotistical people within a generation, results. The resulting surviving populations are more collectivist in their mentality, but the evolutionary selection pressures of the desert, that select for egotistical behavioral patterns, would still be present, and eventually would increase the proportion of egotistical people within the population, leading to another cycle of ego-driven civil war and "cutting the egotistical grass" that will occur in the future. In the desert, it is "rational" to have an egotistical and independent-minded mentality, but now and then this mentality can be anti-adaptive if it results in death by powerful entities requiring a minimal level of collectivist compliance.

Explaining Partying Behavior

Why does partying behavior exist among animals, or why is partying behavior adaptive? Partying behavior might be defined as a temporary concatenation of members of the same species within a geographically small-area space on the planet, such that these members are not necessarily directly engaged in reproductory or survival activities, but are in close enough proximity to one another to project information to one another about their body and mind characteristics. Examples include a group of iguanas or walruses congregating on the beach, or humans having a dinner party or a cigar party. Parties can be a source of platonic pleasure, if free food is offered to guests at the party, or if jokes, games and other communications are originated and experienced during the party, the mind-inputting of which results in the release of pleasurable neurotransmitters in the minds of the party-goers. The emotional pleasure that results from these platonic communications may not directly contribute to survival or reproduction. However, platonic idea structures that, when stimulated, release pleasurable neurotransmitters, do exist in the minds of most or all humans, since it is adaptable for minds to randomly evolve variations in thinking abilities, just in case one of these random abilities by luck increases the probability of survival or reproduction of the species on the planet earth. The activation of these pleasure-inducing platonic-thought-generating neuron circuits, and the resulting feelings of platonic pleasure, is one of the things that attracts people to parties. Some of the analytical or motor skill elements involved in playing a pleasure-inducing game at a party, such as hitting a pinata, or playing chess, can be applied to other life skills that do generate survival or reproduction advantages, which also shows the rationale as to why platonic thinking patterns generating pleasure can be adaptive in minds.

Partying behavior can be adaptive, and can improve survival or reproduction of a species on the planet earth, simply because a party-goer may by luck find a reproduction partner at a party, or find a new friend who can direct that party-goer to resource-gaining activities like new jobs, or to other people connections that result in jobs or mates. Partying behavior, then, is adaptive because it functions as an access point for accessing random and unpredictable opportunities to find mates and gain resources.

Partying behavior tends to arise among species that can afford to party, where the energy costs of partying, or the energy losses of lounging around and not doing anything, are less than the value of the potential adaptive gains of partying. A low-metabolism iguana, or a fat and sluggish walrus, can afford to spend hours lounging around not doing much of anything. Humans have been able to leverage the mass production of food via complex agricultural systems, and the energy of petroleum fuel sources, and also renewable solar-powered, wind-powered or hydro-electric energy sources, to access more energy than they could access without these technologies, which enables humans also to afford to spend hours expending energy in partying behavior that does not directly improve survival or reproduction, but which may do so indirectly.

What is technology?

A "technology" is an object, that is altered by an organism, via the organism using one of its body parts to directly or indirectly apply energy to that object, such as to alter the energy level, molecular shape or constitution, or position point on the planet, of that object, such that such alteration improves the ability of that organism to survive and reproduce, or provides a platonic entertainment, but generally without the organism directly eating, or mating with, that object. "Technological behavior" might be defined as the exploitation, by an organism, of an opportunity, provided by the earth locally and the universe generally, for the organism to use its body part or body parts to apply energy to an object in the organism's external environment, such that altering that object improves the ability of that organism to obtain food energy, increases its ability to propagate its genes, improve its ability to regulate its temperature, or generally improves the energy equilibrium of that organism, but generally without the organism directly eating, or mating with, that object. By these definitions, all shelter-building by animals or insects is technological behavior. A chimpanzee sticking a twig into a termite nest, pulling out the twig, and eating any termites clinging to the twig, also is showing technological behavior. An otter using a rock to smash open a clam that the otter placed on the otter's stomach is also an example of technological behavior. A killer whale creating a wall of bubbles around a school of fish to funnel the fish into a concentrated spot to be more easily caught and eaten is also an example of technological behavior. A spider generating spider silk from its own body and then using that silk to create a spider web shelter and bug-trapping device in its external environment is also technological behavior, even if the spider silk strand objects originated from inside the spider's body, because after its origination the spider silk strand became an object in the spider's external environment. Lice-picking or tic-picking grooming behavior is also technological behavior, since this reduces disease levels and thereby improves the organism's thermodynamic or energy stability.

Organic minds can only implement technological behavior if the universe is in a state of thermodynamic disequilibrium. The thermodynamic disequilibrium makes possible the ability of an organism to have the energy needed to transport itself to a location in the universe where technological behavior is possible, and to be able to apply energy to a form of matter such as to be able to use that form of matter in a technological way. This limits technological behavior to only those behaviors permitted by the laws of physics and the thermodynamic state of the universe, which makes technological behavior a more automated process that is not driven by free will.

Complex machines are also forms of technology. Of all the animal minds on the planet earth, only human minds can "create" complex machines or show any major sophistication in altering the shape of matter to form more useful technological objects. Humans do not "create" or "invent" technologies. Instead, the human mind exploits finite, limited opportunities, provided by the universe generally and the earth locally, that are provided in ways that are strictly parameterized by the laws of physics, to obtain, and alter the energy states of, various forms of sub-atomic, atomic or molecular matter. These realities contradict the notion that technology-developing behavior among humans is driven by human free will or creativity.

The ultimate origin of any complex machine or other product of advanced technology, such as a computer micro-processor chip, consists of a human body part directly applying energy to matter to make that machine and its parts come into existence. A simple example of this is using a human body part to grab a piece of copper ore and then making a fire to smelt the copper from the ore. A micro-processor requires complex machinery and a complex manufacturing environment for the micro-processor to be created, but the raw materials needed to make those machines and manufacturing environment originally were obtained by using human body parts to directly contact the natural raw materials from which these machines originated. Human body parts are used to apply energy to buttons and levers that are used to control the machines, but ultimately no part of the machine originated except through direct contact of a human body part with the matter that eventually would become a part of that machine, or a part of the things that generate the energy to run the machine. This shows that the ability to create technology is strictly limited to opportunities provided arbitrarily by the universe generally and the earth locally to apply body energy to matter existing on the planet earth that can be used to create these sophisticated technological products.

Humans therefore are not exercising free will when creating, discovering or inventing technology, but are only exploiting opportunities that were provided to them due to factors beyond their control. Humans can only exploit technologies that are theoretically possible, but cannot control the laws of physics that dictate what technologies are theoretically possible. Humans by luck evolved with minds that sometimes are able to locate conceptual access points for "discovering" these technologies, or for discovering simple ideas that can be built upon to discover more complex layerings of ideas. Humans also have no ability to alter the most fundamental sub-atomic constituents of matter, which are presumed to be vibrating strings of energy, according to string theorists. Humans can exploit opportunities, provided by the universe, to apply energy to matter such as to alter the energy states of matter, and perhaps alter how fundamental sub-atomic particles are combined to create larger clusters of matter. However, humans cannot alter the most fundamental sub-atomic constituents of matter, and humans cannot create opportunities to alter matter, but must follow strict parameters, provided by the universe, for exploiting opportunities to alter matter. A simple example of this is that if a piece of smeltable copper ore is located five meters away, and a furnace is located 8 meters away, a human located these distances from these objects at a certain moment of Planck time cannot, according to the laws of physics, smelter that copper ore object at that moment of Planck time. Instead, the laws of physics dictate that the human must travel a minimum distance, that requires a minimum number of Planck time units for such travel to occur, before that human can grab the copper ore and bring the ore to the furnace. The strict parameters that the universe imposes on humans, that dictate under what circumstances humans can apply energy to matter to create technological objects, prevents humans from having free will to "freely invent and create" technologies. The abilities to know how to exploit those opportunities originally occurred in the human mind ultimately due to luck.

The "technology-inventing" behavior of humans is commonly viewed as being too complex and "soulful" for such behavior to result from purely automated brain-thinking. However, technology-invention is a purely stochastic, or chance-determined process. Much technological or scientific discovery is documented to have resulted from pure luck, due to the inventor luckily finding the discovery. If a discovery seems to have been planned in some way, such as the way that Russian chemist Dmitry Mendeleyev "planned" how to fill in gaps in the periodic table of the atomic elements, there must exist some kind of pattern of thinking in the mind of the scientist, that is analogous to the problem-solving plan used in the discovery, before the planning to make the discovery can exist. This pattern of thinking either developed in the scientist's mind by luck, or by the scientist learning that pattern from a source or teacher that ultimately obtained that pattern from pure luck. This is reflected in the saying that "one recognizes only what one already knows," which is an impossible statement to disprove. Technological discovery by humans is analogous to an Easter Egg hunt, where children randomly search for hidden eggs scattered in their local earth environment.

What is a University or a School?

This is an important question because much structuring of human lifestyles consists of sending humans into multi-year educational programs or systems. The fundamental purpose of a university of school, and educational materials in general, is to induce changes in the neuron structures of the minds of students, generally by installing into the minds of the students expansions of their libraries of objects that the students are aware of, and the axioms pertaining to how those objects can be used, or what can be obtained from these objects, such as to improve life support or gene reproduction on the planet. It is unknown and mysterious why humans chose what they chose to function as educational materials, or as neuron-structure improvement facilitators. Some things in the universe facilitate neuron-structure improvement in human minds, while others do not, for reasons that vary with different human minds and which may be arbitrary. Why does watching an instructional video improve neuron structure in some watchers but not in other watchers? Why are some educational materials capable of imparting improvements in neuron structures of some students, but not in others? Why did humans exploit the opportunities provided by the universe to create schools and universities as the main facilitators of neuron structure improvement in minds?

A university or school is a building or set of buildings, with chairs and a centralized blackboard where an instructor can write down communications for an entire class of students to read. The instructor is generally needed because the mind of the instructor possesses (in principle) an understanding of a topic being taught that is more sophisticated than that of the students, and the instructor can inform that student that the student is wrong if the student communicates an incorrect understanding of the topic being taught. The instructor provides something that often cannot be obtained from non-human teaching materials, which is the ability to understand the student's argument, using non-linear human mind thinking, and to exactly correct the misconceptions that students may have about a topic. It is precisely this ability that makes the instructor a uniquely advantageous pedagogical factor in human-interactive learning environments.

Apparently, the human mind's learning ability cannot escape the need for another human instructor who can customize error-correction to each particular student. Somehow, auto-didactic learning does not generally impart a more sophisticated neuron structure to a student's mind compared to instructor-facilitated learning. The school or university is also apparently the best tool for mass-educating large populations of students, but it mysterious to explain why the laws of physics result in this phenomenon being true. It is mysterious to explain why the human mind evolved such as to exploit the opportunities provided by the universe generally and the earthy locally to create schools and universities as the standard tools for mass-producing human mind learning.

Why do Political Systems Exist?

A political system is a situation on the planet earth where one or more members of a species of animal has the power to decide how much of, and to whom, a specified asset is distributed among another members of that species. For example, if a group of boy scouts is seated around a campfire, and one of them tells an offensive joke, and the others berate that boy scout for telling the offensive joke, and the boy scout submits to and accepts this derision, the group of boy scouts is forming a political system. The assets being distributed are acceptance by the group, and the right to tell offensive jokes. The group has the power to withdraw its acceptance from any one member of the group, with this power being backed up by peer pressure. The berated boy scout accepts the derision of the group because the power of peer pressure compels the boy scout to do so. If the boy scout attempts to fight back by beating up the group members for berating him, the boy scout may be beaten up by the group in a counter-attack, and/or the boy scout may lose the acceptance that the group provided.

"Politics" is the mechanism that determines who has the power to decide how a specific asset is distributed on the planet earth. Who holds political power can be counter-intuitive. "Officially recognized" politicians may hold all political power, or the political power of official politicians may be diluted by rich businesspeople in society, influential journalists, government military leaders, rebel military leaders, grassroots activists, published scientists, book writers, etc.

Gorillas form political systems in the form of alpha-male dominance hierarchies, where an alpha male gorilla has exclusive rights to mate with a harem of females. The alpha male excludes other males from access to the harem mating rights assets, by being stronger than other males, such that any rival male who attempts to muscle in on the alpha male's territory is beaten up by the alpha male and is forced to move away from the alpha male's dominance hierarchy harem structure. This alpha-male dominance hierarchy political system evolved in gorillas' minds as a symbolic logic way of behaving such that the genes of the most powerful, healthy and robust alpha males propagated through the gorilla gene pool. This political system is like a game that gorillas play, where the rules are instinctively known to the alpha male, the females of the harem, and the male rivals to the alpha male. These three groups of gorillas interpolate their minds with one another in playing the game. The females understand that they will generally only mate with the alpha male, after the alpha male wins the contests deciding which male is stronger by violent physical fighting. The loser males understand that they should move away from the harem after loss of the physical fight. The alpha male understands himself to be the winner of the fight and the owner of the exclusive rights to mate with the harem females. The evolution of the instinctive understanding of this political game, an understanding that is distributed and standardized among multiple gorilla minds, is an adaptive mechanism for ensuring that only big, burly, healthy, muscular alpha males reproduce their genes within the gorilla gene pool.

There are countless forms of political systems. Wherever there is an asset of which one person has the power to influence the distribution of that asset to another person, there is a political system. A housewife refusing to cook for her husband unless her husband stops his alcohol habit is one example. A mother denying her child a lollipop unless the child eats his peas is another.

The need for assets evolved in the human mind due to the laws of thermodynamics, which determine how the possession of assets influences the equilibrium and stability of the atomic and molecular cohesive body forms of humans, and the ability of humans to reproduce on the planet earth. The value of assets may result in the evolution of people who are willing to inflict acts of evil on other people, using force or fraud to confiscate assets from other people. This may result in some people getting a larger proportion of assets, and other people getting fewer assets and also being killed and injured in the process of being forced to surrender assets to other evil humans. To prevent this outcome, people want to be led by governments, to provide rule systems for asset distribution that prevent acts of evil and associated injury, violence and death. Since governments are the originators of rules and rule enforcement within country perimeters, there is no theoretical limit as to how much a government may confiscate from the people ruled, in any particular epoch or geographic area on the planet earth. The advantage of governments providing this rule system is balanced by the potential disadvantage of submitting to government rule, with submission to government rule generally being more attractive than societies in which civilians force other civilians to give away their assets, or societies where people try to survive in a state of nature.

Government political systems are probably the most complex of all political systems. It would be difficult to program a silicon computer to "invent" or "discover" the concept of a government political system, because government political systems are conceptually multi-faceted. The first step to analyzing why a political system exists is to identify what specific asset or assets is the political system distributing, who is distributing the assets, and to whom are the assets being distributed?

Government political systems exist because land is life support. Dry land is the surface on which plants, that can provide energy to thermodynamically unstable human bodies, can grow and be harvested. Dry land is also where animals can exist, that can be hunted or farmed as sources of nutrients for thermodynamically unstable human body forms. Land can also be used as sites for shelters, that can help to maintain optimal temperature environments that help to maintain optimal thermodynamic stability of the human body, and that shelter the human body from thermodynamically destabilizing energy-siphoning attacks by insects and predators. Land is also a potential site of fresh water, which is a molecular matrix that is required to make possible the bio-chemical reactions and osmosis behaviors that enable the human body to exist. Since land is so valuable, humans without a central government are prone to not recognizing land ownership boundaries, or to being confused as to what exactly those boundaries are, or to injuring or killing other humans to take over ownership of land and its associated life-support qualities. It is adaptive of humans to evolve a tendency to support being ruled by a government that parcels out land usage in a formal way, which prevents a human civilian from experiencing sudden and unexpected death in a land dispute with another civilian. "Free-for-all" scenarios where people rush to obtain assets, without a centralized rule system for deciding who gets what asset, can lead to violence and death among civilians, which may not be adaptive for human genes.

A government's primary function is to use centralized force, mediated by military and police forces, and also legal forces such as lawyers, judges, legal rule systems and court systems, to define and enforce the geopolitically circumscribed macro-perimeter of a country, known as the country's boundary. Governments also divide up the geopolitical macro-land-mass of the country into land parcels, with various use designations (residential, farming, transportation pathways, gas and electric pathways, commercial, military etc.), recognize a precise measurement system for measuring the land parcels, and enforce a centralized system for titling these land parcels, guided by a logical, written legal system, that is enforced by the government enforcers. This prevents land parcel titling and boundary disputes, and prevents civilians from killing one another over land disputes. Governments also designate the grid system that connects land parcels with gas and electric and water piping systems, and road systems. Governments also are needed to centralize military and police forces, to prevent the existence of factions capable of using violence to enforce their own land parceling systems. Only a team of enforcers can define and preserve the country's declared border. A single person cannot control huge amounts of land. Necessarily, then, a government must be a team, to which civilians belong.

The cost of surrendering to government rule is less than the cost of not having a centralized government, which is generally the rationale of why civilians consent to government rule. The centralized parceling and gridding of land tends to increase per-capita wealth, and make possible the division of labor that increases efficiency of asset production, which also increases per-capita wealth, compared to if governments did not exists to perform these functions. The submission to government rule is generally adaptive, and improves wealth and gene-reproducing capabilities of individual civilians. One potential downside of government rule is that governments may demand that some civilians endure costly sacrifices to uphold the stability of the government, such as through taxation or through military conscription. Governments may also become tyrannical, that is, governments may excessively confiscate societal wealth in order to improve the wealth of government officials. There is also no theoretical limit as to how selfish government officials can be, because technically government officials can unilaterally decide how force is used.

The complex intelligence of the human mind causes humans to form highly abstract concepts of land parceling and use, that are far more sophisticated than concepts of land use held by non-human animals. This causes humans to conceptualize the concept of a government overseer of the geo-political macro-perimeter of a country. From an evolutionary standpoint, there is a tug-of-war between evolving minds that have characteristics that make human minds submit to government, and evolving minds that have characteristics that make human minds rebel against governments. This tug-of-war can cause wide swings in the genetics of human minds over many generations. Humans with rebellious minds may prosper, and acquire personal wealth while being less likely to surrender wealth to governments, without being killed by governments in some epochs, but may be killed en masse by governments in other epochs. Corresponding changes in the genes of mind that determine attitudes towards governments may show up in the human gene pool. Humans who have mind traits that make them more likely to submit to government rule are less likely to be killed by

194

government forces, but are more likely to become participants in government wars and be killed as a result, and are more likely to lose wealth to taxation. In different epochs and countries, different degrees of rebelliousness and submission towards governments may be adaptive, with corresponding influence on the gene pool. No one attitude of rebelliousness or submission is optimal in all epochs and countries, leading to continuous changes over time in the parts of the genes of the human mind that determine humans' attitudes towards government rule.

The Triviality of Opinions

Is a sense of achievement rational? Many an accomplished person on their deathbed has died feeling satisfied with their achievements in life. Such accomplished individuals might feel satisfaction at having raised several children, or established a successful business, or invented something useful or written a book. A determination that one has "achieved" something in life is a value judgement that originates either in the mind of the achiever, or in the minds of other people besides the achiever who believe that value judgement. Both the achiever and those who accept this value judgement will eventually die, which may render the value judgement irrelevant. New generations of people may be born who may share this same value judgement and then, in hindsight, perhaps look up the history of the deceased achiever from a previous generation and praise that individual for his or her achievement, and this may "resurrect" the contemporary "validity" of the value judgement, but eventually these humans of the new generation of judgmental people will die as well. Can this cycle of new generations of people forming the same value judgements and praising that same deceased person from the past continue ad infinitum? Probably not, simply because the number of generations of humans that can occur is vast, producing vast amounts of human-centered information over generations that is too colossal in scale for any one human brain to begin to memorize. The memories of the most famous people of the present will eventually be erased, or reduced to a caption in an obituary page. Without people to form judgments about the good and bad aspects of an achievement, there can be no value to the achievement.

195

A person's "achievements" in life often require the continued existence of specific people on the planet earth in order for the achievement to be definable. A successful business, for example, exists because of the specific employees and employers running the business, and because of the specific customers purchasing the products and services of the business, to such an extent as to enable the business owners to afford to stay in business. Eventually, the business owners, employees and customers will all die and disintegrate, forcing the disintegration of the business and its associated achievements. Sometimes, the business may continue to exist legally after the deaths of the original employers, employees and customers. However, the business will be a different business, because a business is essentially defined as a cult of personalities of the employers, employees and customers associated with the business. Winning a sports trophy is irrelevant unless people exist who recognize the existence of the sports trophy and the achievement represented by the trophy. One cannot "feel a sense of satisfaction at achievement" if one is the only member left in the world of one's species. Those who recognize the trophy and its respective achievement are themselves subject to eventual death, or disintegration into the infinity background of the universe. Eventually, the entire human species will also go extinct, especially given that the planet earth is predicted by scientists to be destined to be destroyed by the sun within a few billion years.

Achievements accomplished today influence all subsequent future events, and this technically results in the achieving having a permanent effect on the future, and never ceasing to be relevant as a causative element in causing future events. However, since it is impossible to predict the world pathways taken by all sub-atomic particles in the universe after the date when an achievement was accomplished, it is impossible to predict what the actual effects will be of the achievement. There is therefore no way to precisely assess the value of an achievement.

Events that occurred in the past are essentially impossible to re-access, either in the present or future. This is because an event that occurred in the past involved an ultra-parameterized concatenation, and change over time while the event was taking place, of the sub-atomic particles making up that event. The probability of these exact same sub-atomic particles from a historical event coalescing again into the regeneration, in the future, of this exact same event is astronomically low, given any particular combination of location on the planet earth, and epoch in the history of the planet earth, and this same event is also unlikely to recur in the history of the known universe. Therefore, when a person remembers an event of the past, the person is remembering a concatenation of sub-atomic particles, changing over time, that is impossible to re-access. In this sense, a person in the present tense is dissociated, to an infinite extent, from any event of that person's past, even if the event happened yesterday. Can there be any justification for reminiscing with fond nostalgia about past events from which a person, in the present, is infinitely dissociated? Is there any difference between remembering and talking about an event that occurred a month ago, and discussing an event that took place 1 billion years ago, if a person is equally dissociated from both events, and equally incapable of accessing the concatenation of sub-atomic particles that made up both events? The exact concatenation of sub-atomic particles, plus their quantum energy states, that made up both events are equally inaccessible to the person remembering or discussing the past events. This makes it trivial or pretentious for one to remember events in one's personal past, even though people in general have a powerful instinctive motivation to reminisce about events of their past, and to form a sense of identify from their experience of those events. The total inability to access the combinations of sub-atomic particles that resulted in events of a person's past essentially forces a person to exist only as an entity in the present, since both the future and the past are inaccessible.

One cannot use a time machine to travel back in time to re-access the concatenation of sub-atomic particles that resulted in the event. Time machines currently do not exist and time travel into the past may be prohibited by the laws of physics. Even if a person could travel back in time, the act of traveling back in time would almost certainly alter the path of history such as to prevent that person from being born in the future. Introducing a body from the future into the past might also violate the first law of thermodynamics, since this would add or create new matter or energy into a world system in the past.

Also, the things that a person can achieve in life, such as starting a business, usually will break down and disintegrate relatively soon after the achievement is created. On rare occasions, scientific, artistic, or publication achievements can be remembered continuously for generations, but then again, being remembered for generations is not an asset for the achiever once the achiever dies. The death of the achiever results in catastrophic destruction of all of the identity elements that made up that achiever's identity construct, such that, in dying, the achiever no more owns his or her achievement than any other matter or energy construct, alive or dead, "owns" this achievement. In addition, given that all people are made of matter, and matter is mostly made of empty space, and that the state of "being a human organism" is defined more in terms of bonding relations of sub-atomic matter, than a definitive "solidness," it is difficult to see how either the achiever or the judges of the achievement's merits possess an identity to begin with. In addition, all matter and energy that is altered by the achievement changes form continuously, and within short periods of time this matter will tend to completely disintegrate and become reconstructed into different matter and energy structures that cannot be recognized as being part of the original achievement. The value judgements that praise achievements tend to be part of homo sapiens culture on the planet earth, with such cultural constructs not necessarily generalizable or considered acceptable generally in the universe or on other planets with living creatures possessing cultures that could theoretically exist in the universe.

Are political achievements are significant, either for the politicians who achieve them or the soldiers who fight for the achievements? What do political achievements optimize? One major problem with political systems is that, because they affect entire countries and populations, they influence the histories of colossal amounts of sub-atomic particles. This makes it computationally impossible to predict, to sub-atomic precision, what will be the ultimate results of the political achievements. Political hierarchies are also strongly influenced by the personalities of the people within the hierarchies. These hierarchies change continuously, as politicians within them die, or lose creativity as they age. Political information rapidly becomes obsolete due to the continuous changes occurring within political hierarchies. Rarely is political information valid for more than a decade, due to alterations in the personnel of political hierarchies. Political achievements can become rapidly obsolete if the political hierarchy that originally achieved the achievement changes into another political hierarchy that does not espouse the political philosophy that originally motivated achieving the achievement. Soldiers who fight to enforce one political hierarchy's policies may find that, due to alterations of that political hierarchy's personality complex within a few years, due to additions, removals and changes to the personnel content of the hierarchy, that the original political motivation for the soldier's fighting has become obsolete. This applies to both the political hierarchy to which the soldier owes allegiance, and the political hierarchy of enemy politicians.

In "The Decline and the Fall of Roman Civilization," a classic history book by Edward Gibbons, large numbers of cycles of human war and peace are documented, suggesting that cycles of war and peace run ad infinitum, without those cycles necessarily evolving into progressive or predictable historical outcomes (Gibbons, 1790). World War I, the "war to end all wars," is part of the chain of causality that lead to World War II (an event that could not be predicted because it is impossible to predict the world pathways of all sub-atomic particles on the planet earth, given their initial conditions immediately after the end of World War I), while World War II is also an inextricable part of the chain of causality that lead to the Vietnam war in the 1950s, 1960s and 1970s, and the (relatively progressive) internet era of the late 20th to early 21st centuries. Of course, labeling historical epochs or events as "progressive" or "non-progressive" is trivial because it is impossible to predict, to sub-atomic precision, the chain of causal events that will result from "progressive" or "non-progressive" historical events.

It is also not clear how living organisms, and the matter and energy structures that make up the epochs in which those organisms exist, all of which are made mostly of empty space, can be defined as constituting "progressive" or "non-progressive" epochs. Certainly, no prediction, made by any major political power player involved in World War II, about the outcome of World War II, included events such as the subsequent

Korean or Vietnam wars, or the internet epoch of the late 20th to early 21st centuries. Therefore, neither government leaders, nor scientists, nor the soldiers of World War II were able to predict the outcomes of soldiers' participation in World War II.

Is it rational to have judgements about the morality of historical events? If all historical events result in subsequent historical events that are unpredictable, due to the impossibility of predicting the later world pathways of all sub-atomic particles existing at the conclusion of a historical event on the planet earth, it follows that it is irrational to form judgements about whether a particular contemporary historical event is "moral" or "immoral," or "progressive" or "non-progressive." It is also irrational to form judgements about whether past historical events were "moral," "immoral," "progressive," or "anti-progressive," because of the inability to predict all possible events that result from the chain of causation of which the past historical event in question is a part. This shows (nihilistically) that it is rational to view all historical events as being acceptable, and that no historical event is morally better or worse than another. All historical events evolve into an infinite chain of subsequent historical events, and it is unpredictable if those events will turn out to be "moral," or "immoral," or "progressive," or "anti-progressive."

All meetings of people that have occurred throughout history, whether they were scientific meetings, meetings to make logistical decisions for businesses or institutions, government political meetings, etc. consisted of temporary states of matter. The atomic and molecular concatenations making up the people at these meetings, and the environments of these meetings (tables, chairs, room walls, etc.) were all temporary states of coherent matter that eventually would disintegrate, according to the laws of thermodynamics. A meeting may have been intellectually interesting or emotionally gripping, and may have resulted in seemingly important decisions being made, but the ultimate results of these decisions, made by temporary states of matter, were and are unpredictable. Since these states of matter making up meetings are ultimately arbitrary ways of concatenating atoms and molecules according to the arbitrary laws of physics, every aspect of the meeting, including the questions, premises, observations and other paradigm elements discussed during or associated with the meeting, and feelings felt during the meeting, were themselves arbitrary and destined for disintegration. Ultimately, then, meetings are "much ado about nothing," except that these meetings are elements of the chain of causality of completely unpredictable future events in the universe.

Another problem with having opinions or attitudes about historical events is that all historical events are an inextricable part of the chain of causality that led to the improbable event of the sperm containing a specified person's chromosomes uniting with an egg containing that person's chromosomes, resulting in the zygote that resulted in that particular person's existence. Since this event is so astronomically improbable, all historical events preceding this event had to occur exactly as they did occur, in order for this event to occur. A person who considers any historical event occurring prior to that person's conception to be negative, or an event that should never have occurred ideally, is essentially denying the justification for his or her existence, which is arguably irrational. In addition, it is pointless to condemn any historical events occurring after a person's conception, because this would be like a person essentially denying the justification for the conception of any relatives of that person who were conceived after that person's conception, or after historical events that that person condemns. Therefore, these condemnations would also be irrational. The conclusion from this is that all historical events are absolutely wonderful and desired, no matter how violent or murderous the historical event, because it would be absurd to negate the justification for one's own existence, or the existence of one's relatives who were conceived after one's own conception.

A person might think that, if a horribly violent and mass-murderous historical event was part of the chain of causality that was necessary for that person to eventually have been born, that this person might be, in theory, willing to not have been born in the first place, and to sacrifice his or her life, if that would have been what was needed, to prevent that horribly mass-murderous historical event from occurring in the first place. However, even if one were willing to sacrifice one's own existence as a price for eliminating from the past an undesirable historical event, the laws of physics do not give a person the ability to make a decision to eliminate an event from the historical past. Even if one could perform such magic, one would, by preventing the occurrence of that horrible historical event, also prevent the births of billions of people whose births depended on a chain of causality that included that horrible historical event. That person would be deciding to prevent the existence of billions of other people, and instead exchange the existence of those billions of people, who were born due to the chain of causality resulting from that horrible historical event, with the existence of other billions of people, who would be born if that horrible historical event did not occur, but with no guarantee that the replacing population of billions of people would form a better history than the population replaced by the magical ability to erase an undesirable historical event. Of course, if string theorists are correct and an infinite number of universes exist, all of these possible outcomes would occur anyway, which would make a hypothetical action of erasing a horrible historical event from the past to be of no advantage whatsoever, because that event would eventually occur somewhere and sometime within one of the infinite universes, as would the non-occurrence of that historical event in another one of the infinite universes (Greene, 1999).

Conscious Awareness and Cultural Memes

Unique among animals, humans are able to record their thoughts in thought-recording mediums that can outlast the lives of the originators of the thoughts. While a human, if lucky, may live up to approximately 100-125 years of age, a book consisting of ink on paper can last for over 800 years with decent storage conditions. Words written on fired or hardened clay tablets, or chiseled in stone or painted on cave walls can last for thousands of years. Words laser-etched on slabs of nickel and encased in a durable plastic resin or amber can last for hundreds of thousands of years, even if thrown out into the open wilderness. Some works written on papyrus paper and stuffed into mummified crocodiles, or dumped in the open sand of the dry Egyptian desert, have been readable after two thousand years, outlasting the destruction of the ancient Library of Alexandria and outlasting the 1,000 year dark ages that preceded the Renaissance. Recording words in long-lasting recording mediums allows the thoughts of previously deceased people to be learnable by currently living people, which permits the buildup of knowledge over generations.

Knowledge is difficult to originate because luck is needed to originate knowledge, either by the originator being lucky enough to possess the mathematical or scientific pattern of a thought in the mind prior to generating the knowledge thought, or by the originator experiencing a life experience that contains the theme of the knowledge thought. Knowledge, when recorded, obviates the obligation to acquire knowledge by luck alone, by being lucky enough to encounter a representation of a piece of knowledge in one's environment, and also being lucky enough to contain a neuron structure in one's mind that is capable of detecting that knowledge element when that element was presented by one's environment to one's mind. The Ten Commandments of Moses, which is a pretty good basic system of morality, if applied non-hypocritically, was not invented by Moses, but was known in various forms by people thousands of years before Moses was born. These ten moral principles tend to become generated automatically whenever there are societies or civilizations, because sooner or later conflicts arise where the themes or behavior patterns summarized by these principles become relevant. Still, one needs first a society to conceive of the principles, and societies require concatenations of large amounts of human activity and energy to come into existence. It is therefore much easier to simply study pre-existing written summaries of previously originated knowledge such as systems of moral principles, that might have required vast amounts of time and energy to originally become discovered or encountered, rather than attempt to be the originator of the knowledge. It is far easier to simply study Shakespeare's plays, than to actually be Shakespeare, and wander around society, and wander inside existing libraries, and collect thousands of axioms, then arrange them into a publishable iambic pentameter form that, miracle of miracles, make millions of human minds consider those writings to be instructive and thought-provoking.

It is difficult to explain why the laws of physics make this concept, that it is easier to learn pre-existing knowledge than it is to generate knowledge originally, to be true. Certainly, however, many people find that in their own lives, it is somewhat rare and lucky to experience an experience where a theme or a principle can be extracted from the experience. It is also impossible for any one human to generate, from their own personal life experiences, all of the ideas, themes, concepts and mathematics that apparently can exist in the universe. The concept that 2+2=4 might be generated systematically, just by a person experiencing the difference between holding 4 fruits in hand, versus 3 fruits. A concept like the pythagorean theorem, however, is a more abstract concept that requires several integrated bits of knowledge before the general principle can be developed. A land surveyor or farmer or home builder might encounter this theorem in their line of work, where a precise ability to calculate land areas is important for performing one's work, but discovering the pythagorean theorem is considerably less likely than discovering that 2+2=4. There is a lower probability of discovering more abstract principles like the principles of Quantum Mechanics compared to discovering a "down-to-earth" idea like the pythagorean theorem.

The recording and storage of acquired knowledge results in a buildup of knowledge of objects and axioms pertaining to objects over time and over generations or humans. This makes it possible, via learning and studying, for the newest generations of humans to gain expanded libraries of objects and axioms pertaining to objects that exceeds that of previous generations of humans, by rapidly and efficiently studying vast amounts of accumulated knowledge that required hundreds or thousands of times more time to originally generate than the time that is required to study the generated knowledge. There may also be a kind of "survival of the fittest" natural selection mechanism that determines which ideas, or definitions of objects and axioms pertaining to objects, become installed in which minds through learning, simply because some learned knowledge will more likely improve a person's ability to survive and reproduce compared to other learned knowledge (Dawkins, 1976). Librarians curate collections by storing in the collections every general idea represented among human scholars, but only a small fraction of the ideas contained within this "idea supermarket" becomes installed in any one particular mind through learning or studying. This leads to the idea that conscious awareness consists of an accumulation of culturally acquired memes, or units of knowledge previously generated by typically now-dead humans (Dawkins, 1976; Dennet, 2017).

This meme idea is simplistic, however, because while a knowledge base can feed into and shape that entity called "conscious awareness," that knowledge base is not conscious awareness itself, but functions to make conscious awareness more complex, by incorporating into conscious awareness a library of objects and axioms pertaining to objects, that is far larger than is possible if humans, like other non-human organisms, did not record their thoughts in relatively permanent mediums, and were not informed by the thoughts of previous generations of now-dead members of the same species. This results in a wide variety of thoughts being thought by a human mind, where the system of thoughts thought is essentially the "conscious awareness." Another problem with the "meme" idea is that it does not explain why some memes become installed in some minds, but not in other minds. Why do some people like Beethoven's fifth symphony and poker, but not football, while other people like poker and football, but not Beethoven's music in general? Why do some people like to knit and play canasta, while others do not like knitting, but like fishing, and hate canasta? A human public library jumbles together thousands of millions of different human cultural memes, but why has the human mind evolved such that it is only capable of remembering a small fraction of the memes contained in a human library, and why can human minds contain thoughts that are not human-created memes, such as thoughts about trees or rivers? The meme idea is akin to claiming that a vast amount of human cultural memes have been created, and it is implied that humans "simply" pick and choose the ones that they will remember and incorporate into their "conscious awareness." However, there is absolutely nothing "simple" about what the factors are that make people choose certain memes to be installed in their minds and not other memes, and this tendency to incorporate some ideas and not others is a profoundly mind-influencing mechanism that has evolved via natural selection forces, and works to diversify human mind functionality. In any theory of mind, this tendency cannot be ignored or implied as being too obvious to need explanation.

Also, human cultural memes are essentially inaccessible to non-human minds, which makes the "meme" idea anthropocentric, and is akin to implying that only human minds are "consciously aware," or implying that there are not some fundamental atomic or molecular mechanisms that are common to all minds, human and non-human, such that human mind-stuff is part of a continuum of all mind-stuffs in the universe. If a raccoon dips a piece of pizza, obtained from a human garbage can, into a pond to wet it to make it more digestible, objects like pizza and human garbage cans may be human cultural memes that become part of the raccoon's conscious awareness, but the act of dipping the pizza into pond water is a primitive behavioral element of the raccoon's mind and is not a cultural meme. Also, however, pizza food molecules consist of fats and carbohydrate molecules that are common to vast numbers of other different food items. If the food molecules are generally natural and universal, how can pizza be a "cultural meme" if it is made up of these same natural food molecules? Pizza may seem to be a "cultural construct or meme," but it is made up of natural molecules that arbitrarily result from the arbitrary laws of physics.

Some Science of Mind

Is Reincarnation Possible?

Since each organism consist of atoms and molecules, that are theoretically describable, at any moment in Planck time in the life of that organism, using precise parameters of atomic quantum energy states and atomic and molecular bonding relations between those atoms and molecules, reincarnation is possible in principle. If the parameters of the specific proportions of atoms and molecules, atomic and molecular energy states, and bonding relationships, of an organism at a specific moment in Planck time were precisely known, an exact copy of that organism could, in theory, be constructed, as long as there was some kind of machine or atom assembling device capable of precisely duplicating those parameters. In practice, no such device exists. It is possible to clone the DNA of such a parameterized organism, and put this DNA into a zygote, and then put the zygote into a womb, which is essentially the only device known to be be able to assemble the atoms and molecules of an organism from a DNA instruction template, and create an exact DNA copy of the organism. However, this DNA copy would not contain the specific protein and lipid structures that this organism developed within itself and within its mind as a result of its life experiences up to the moment in Planck time when its body and mind forms were such that it was desired to reincarnate them. One can, using today's practical technology, clone a DNA copy of a person, but not the memories that the person gained in their life.

Cloning the person and their memories would require precise knowledge of all of the parameters making up that person and his or her memories at that moment in Planck time when that person's body consisted of an aggregate combination of quantum energy states such that that person's reincarnation was desired, plus a device (as yet non-existent) for synthesizing an exact copy of this person according to the parameters existing within that person's body at that moment in Planck time. This perhaps might be possible if it were possible to genetically engineer DNA so that it not only directed an exact genotype copy or clone of the previous individual, but if also the fat and protein structures that made up the learned memories of that individual, up to the point in that person's life when it became desirable to reincarnate that person, could be also programmed into the DNA. It is not known, however, if the protein and fat structures of memories could explicitly be programmed in DNA such as to exist in the resulting organism whose structure the DNA directs. Perhaps, in theory, this is possible, in that, if DNA can program a bird to have a pre-existing instinctual knowledge of how to make a nest and how to engage in sexual reproduction, then perhaps a super-parameterized system of memory and identity constructs can be programmed in the DNA to exist in a human whose reincarnation is desired.

In nature, it would not be adaptive for organisms' DNA to program such a super-parameterized concept of identity in an organism. This is simply because the information contained within the memories of friends and family among other members of a species, and memories of pets, places, things, experiences, etc., would have long become obsolete by the time that organism containing DNA encoding these memory structures matured into an adult. The subjects and objects within these memories will have by then changed beyond recognition, or disintegrated altogether. Such memories would then not be applicable to improving survival or reproduction of the resulting matured zygote. All of these memories would be memories of constructs of matter anyway, and would be themselves arbitrary. Often, such memories consist of low-information-content representations of the vast amounts of information that existed in the real life events that originally formed the memories.

Another way of reincarnating an individual is via a "statistical" way, in that one can wait until enough time has passed, in the history of the universe, that an exact copy of that person, at that moment in Planck time when their reincarnation was desired, arises by pure luck somewhere else in the universe. The probability of this occurring by luck at any one time-space location in the universe is, of course, too astronomically low to bother calculating, although this probability is not quite zero. To have the same essential memories as the individual whose reincarnation is desired, such a "statistically reincarnated" human would not only have to have the same DNA, but probably would have to exist in the same environmental context, with the same concatenations of matter and people and environmental parameters that originally shaped the protein and fat structures of that person's super-parameterized memories. The probability of both an exact copy of both an individual and that individual's environment arising somewhere in the universe is ultra-astronomically unlikely, but is also not quite zero. Actually, if, as string theorists suggest, there are an infinite number of universes, each representing every theoretically possible combination of matter and energy allowable by the laws of physics, then the probability of this happening is 1, and indeed such super-parameterized, statistically reincarnated individuals will arise an infinite number of times among the infinite numbers of histories of the infinite numbers of universes (Greene, 1999; Hawking, 1996).

Doctors and the Laws of Physics

Why do the laws of physics allow doctors to exist, or allow diseases or healing procedures to exist? These are important questions because so much of human thinking consists of the motivation to seek out health care and thoughts about health and doctors. One way to begin to answer these questions is to explain why diseases or medical problems in general exist. A full explanation of this topic is too extensive to cover here, but a few basic points can be made. Medical problems generally reduce the body's ability to maintain its thermodynamic energy equilibrium. The laws of physics arbitrarily make it possible for numerous different kinds of manifestations of energy disequilibrium to exist in a human body. A genetic disorder can cause mental retardation or physical disorders, which may reduce a person's ability to use their mind or body to access to life support or gene reproduction niches. Genetic disorders often result in generalized problems in the way the body chemically synthesizes the proteins or fats needed to create a thermodynamically stable body. Pathogens such as bacteria or fungi, that are themselves thermodynamically unstable and require food energy to maintain the cohesiveness of their atomic and molecular body forms, gain access to the human body and then extract energy from the energy stored within the body's molecules. The body and its molecules can be used as energy, by pathogens that can digest the body's molecules. The body is like a delicious piece of meat moving around the planet earth, and the only reason why the body is not immediately eaten and digested by bacteria and fungi like a piece of meat is because the body's immune system is always on high alert, ready to attack any pathogens that contact the body. Viruses penetrate body cells and genetically alter the genes of those cells, so that the energy of the cell is used to create copies of the virus and the virus's genes, which damages the ability of the attacked cells to maintain their thermodynamically unstable energy forms.

Poisons are molecules that can block chemical reactions from occurring in the body, that are necessary for the body to maintain its energy equilibrium. Cyanide, for example, paralyzes breathing, so that oxygen, which is necessary for many energy equilibrating chemical reactions in the body, can no longer be available to oxygenate a body's blood supply. Bacteria that infect a body can also produce poisons that can prevent a body's ability to maintain life support.

Bio-mechanical body problems can manifest as arteries blocked by arterial plaques, or arteries that tear due to a lifetime of wear and tear on the artery walls, which helps prevent blood flow to various body parts. Without blood flowing to the body's cells, and providing cells with nutrients and oxygen, cells cannot maintain their energy equilibrium and may disintegrate on a mass scale. Some bio-mechanical body problems, like damaged knees or damaged spinal discs, hinder mobility, so that a body cannot easily move towards food sources or places where reproduction activities are possible.

Some infectious agents, like bacteria and viruses, or foods to which a person may be allergic, may cause the release into the body of proteins and other molecules that are foreign to the body's own proteins and molecules. These foreign molecules can trigger a powerful immune system attack on the foreign molecules, and this immune system attack itself can damage the body's own cells, such as to compromise the body's ability to maintain its thermodynamic equilibrium. Cancer results from a person's body cells mutating genetically, such that the cells begin to multiply uncontrollably, and reduce the ability of the body to maintain its thermodynamic equilibrium.

The fact that the laws of physics permit these various forms of energy disequilibrium to occur in the human body, potentially compromising the ability to survive or reproduce, is the origin of the concept that a person may need to obtain the services of a doctor to facilitate survival and reproduction, and that it is adaptive for people to believe in this concept. Doctors are defined as humans who know how to identify and heal medical problems and have the supplies and tools to be able to implement cures.

Why do the laws of physics permit healing procedures to exist that doctors in turn can implement? One reason that healing procedures are physically possible is that bacteria and viruses require numerous bio-chemical reactions to occur, in order for those bacteria and viruses to be thermodynamically stable entities while they are pathogens infecting a body. There are some chemicals that doctors can use that will disrupt the bio-chemical reactions needed for some bacteria and viruses to grow and exist. The laws of physics dictate which chemicals are useful for disrupting which bio-chemical reactions. The penicillin molecule, and antibiotic, blocks the bio-chemical reactions that allow bacteria to form a protective cell wall around the bacteria, so that bacteria cannot maintain equilibrium with the surrounding body fluids, causing the bacteria not be able to maintain the solute/water molecular balance within the bacteria, which results in death of the bacteria. Chemicals can also be used to poison the chemical reactions occurring in cancer cells. Chelating chemicals pull toxic metals from the body and put the metals in a form that the body can excrete as waste products.

Bio-mechanical problems like worn knees can be solved by replacing knees with artificial replacements. These replacements can be made from metals mined on planet earth, that are provided by the earth locally and the universe generally, and melted, as is allowed by the laws of physics, to form into the shapes needed to replace the worn body parts.

One simple way to heal a disease is simply to cut out the disease. Applying the physics principle that pressure equals force per unit of area, an extremely sharp knife or cutting tool, made of metal provided by the universe, provides enough force per unit area to break up the chemical bonds and inter-molecular bonds that enable a pathogenic mass, such as an isolated cancer clump, bacterial clump, skin mole, etc. to be attached to the body part to which it is attached. The doctor can cut out the disease clump and cure the disease, provided that the clump of diseased tissue is the only location in the body where that diseased tissue exists, and that the doctor can see the clump of diseased tissue completely with the doctor's eyes, either with unaided vision or with magnification, and provided that the body is capable of healing, by itself, the wound created by the removal of the disease. A doctor could also sometimes use an artificial material to re-build that empty wound area (such as when a dentist drills out a cavity, and creates a hole in a tooth where the cavity was, and fills in the hole with an artificial filling material). Not every disease can simply be "cut out" to cure it, but "cutting out" a disease is a simple cure-all that most doctors can do with excellent and predictable results, as long as the earth and the universe provide the raw materials or metals needed to create the tools that can be used to apply enough force to break up the atomic and molecular bonds along the perimeter of the disease clump, to break the clump free from the body part to which the clump is attached.

Another general way of for doctors to heal is by reducing, as much as is technologically possible, the level of pathogens causing a disease, without necessarily being able to completely remove all of the pathogens, to make it as easy as possible for the body's immune system to target and kill off the remaining pathogens, and then rely on the body's natural healing processes to reconstruct the remnants of the wound site with molecular precision. For example, doctors can drain abscesses and flush out abscessed areas with saline to reduce bacterial levels, and also cut away dead tissue that the bacteria is consuming in the abscessed area, which reduces the bacterial food supply, allowing the immune system to come in and kill of the small amounts of bacteria that are left, and the body's healing processes to reconstruct the area. Here, doctors are not necessarily precisely targeting the bacteria. In many diseases, only the immune system can precisely target bacteria with molecular precision, using substances called antibodies, and other immune system chemicals, that thanks to the laws of physics are capable of attacking bacteria by chemically interacting with the molecules on the bacteria's surfaces. In this sense, the immune system shows precision in targeting and killing specific pathogens that doctors can barely access or understand.

Once the bacteria or virus pathogens have been eliminated, the resulting wound site is reconstructed with molecular precision by the body's healing processes. Here, as well, doctors do not have the technological ability to reconstruct wound sites to molecular precision, such as to duplicate the required protein, fat and carbohydrate structures of healthy human tissue, and the precise inter-molecular and intra-molecular bonding relationships between these molecular structures. Many medical cures rely on the body's natural immune system and natural healing processes to ultimately cure the disease process. This also occurs when doctors use radiation to kill off cancer cells. Radiation is a form of energy, allowable by the laws of physics, that is capable of killing off cancer cells. The radiation can damage many normal human cells as well, and the doctors hope that the body's natural healing processes will clean up the mess caused by damaging the non-cancerous body cells during the radiation treatment. There is a certain technological crudeness to modern medicine, given that doctors rely so much on the body's natural immune system and healing processes to target disease and to repair diseased tissue to molecular precision, yet doctors themselves cannot with existing technology target disease as precisely as does the immune system, or reconstruct tissues to molecular precision.

The Motivation to Drink Water

An organic mind's motivation to drink water is somewhat difficult to explain in a reductionist way. Water is a matrix that permeates the dry matter of an organism's body. Water permits blood circulation and osmosis to occur, which move nutrients and energy sources and ions between cells and cells, and cells and the environment. Water also is a "universal solvent" that dissolves atoms and molecules without necessarily altering their chemical structures. Water, by permeating the dry matter of an organism, permits various bio-chemical reactions, necessary for life, to occur in that organism, at certain energy levels, that otherwise would not occur without water permeating the organism. When an organism seeks out water, it is not seeking out an energy source, but it is seeking out a certain molecule, the water molecule, to input into its body, since the laws of physics require this for the body to function properly. The specific physics reasons why water is necessary for organic bodies to function is complex and beyond the scope of this book, but can be found elsewhere. The fact that water is continuously being lost or evaporated from organic bodies is a major cause or origin of the mental motivation to continuously need to seek out water for drinking. The critical need for water for the organism's body to function properly is another major cause of the origin of one of the central components of conscious awareness, that water exists, and that if an organism does not drink water, it will feel very uncomfortable emotionally due to feeling thirsty, and that this organism will eventually die without water. Ultimately, it is a kind of arbitrary "magic trick" of the laws of physics that water exists and that water is such a central part of organisms' lives and thought processes.

Emotions

What is the purpose of emotions, or feelings of physical pain or physical pleasure felt inside the brains of humans and other animals? Emotions provide the human mind with a way to quantify the value of thinking certain thoughts but not others, due to feeling different feelings of physical pain or pleasure, that is felt inside the volume of the brain, when thinking some thoughts versus other thoughts. Emotions therefore induce humans to think certain thoughts more frequently than others, because humans will tend to think thoughts more frequently that feel pleasurable emotionally, and to think fewer thoughts that feel emotionally painful. Humans also think thoughts that simultaneously are both emotionally painful and emotionally pleasurable, but where the emotional pleasure felt when thinking such thoughts outweighs the emotional pain of thinking such thoughts, which provides an overall motivation to think such thoughts. Each personality can have a tendency to feel different emotional reactions in response to having various different thoughts, resulting in people differing from one another in terms of what emotional motivations they have for thinking certain thoughts but not other thoughts, resulting in people differing from one another in their respective personality patterns, with some patterns being more adaptive than others.

The emotions felt in response to thinking certain ideas can motivate a person to think one idea more than another, if thinking about one idea elicits more emotional pleasure than another. This might happen if large amounts of pleasurable dopamine are released as an accompanying event if a person thinks about a certain idea or topic or axiom. For example, suppose a person feels euphoria while playing chess, but feels bored while changing the oil in a car. That person will tend to play chess if he as an opportunity to do so, and to avoid changing the oil of a car if that opportunity presents itself. Suppose another person feels euphoria while playing chess, but this feeling only lasts for about an hour, and then the person gets bored of playing chess. That person will tend to play chess for an hour at a time, then stop and engage in some other thinking activity. Suppose that same person, in playing chess, uses up the supply of dopamine contained within the neurons that release pleasurable neurotransmitters in response to his playing chess, after about an hour, and then it requires three days for those neurons to replenish their supply of dopamine. This person will tend to play chess for 1 hour, then stop playing, and then not "feel like" playing chess for another three days, after which the person will play chess for another hour, and this chess-playing habit or cycle may repeat for years.

Emotions result from the release in the mind of neurotransmitters that induce emotions. Human emotions can range from the extremely painful, such as the emotional pain that might be felt by a human if the human was being eaten alive by a saltwater crocodile or a pack of hyenas, to the extremely pleasurable, such as the emotional pleasure that a human may feel in response to an orgasm, with a wide range of feelings in between, including the "neutral" feeling of boredom or ordinariness, that one might feel when looking at what is typically thought of as an everyday object such as a table or a spoon. There likely exists a limited number of emotion-inducing neurotransmitters. However, given that humans feel a wide variety of nuanced emotions, consisting of subtle combinations of emotional pain and pleasure, it seems that emotion-inducing neurotransmitters are combined in various ways, like the individual colors of a painter's palette, to give rise to shades of emotion (Turner, 1999).

Works of art, whether works of painting, music, literature, sculpture, etc., can induce highly differentiated feelings in humans, encompassing highly parameterized combinations of pain and pleasure feelings, particularly music, which is a purely abstract and emotional art-form. The feeling of highly differentiated emotions in response to experiencing works of art can invoke philosophical ideas, since intellectual ideas may be experienced that correspond to or "match" the highly differentiated emotions felt from the artworks, in the sense that a particular intellectual idea may itself invoke and be associated with a highly parameterized pain/pleasure combination emotion. It is presumed that human emotions are more nuanced and complex than the emotions of non-human mammals or reptiles, which contributes to the increased intellectual complexity of human thought compared to non-human mind thought.

What makes humans "spiritual" may be that each person's mind feels different emotional feelings in response to the detection of specific objects and specific axioms pertaining to the objects, depending on what objects and axioms are being thought about or observed in the present tense. For example, looking at a banana may elicit certain feelings, such as feelings of boredom, or perhaps feelings of humor given that a banana has a shape that makes it look cute or funny to many people. Eating a banana may elicit different emotions compared to merely looking at the banana. Participating in sexual activities can elicit powerfully pleasurable feelings in people and in non-human animals. It is likely that humans feel a wider range of emotions, of a wider range of complexity, than non-human animals, and this leads to increased emotional subtlety associated with human thinking activities. The ability to detect a wider range of energy fingerprints emanating from a correspondingly wide range of different objects, and the ability to detect a wider range of energy fingerprints associated with axioms pertaining to objects, that is, associated with what can be done with or obtained from different objects over time, coupled with a wider range of emotional subtleties in the emotional responses that humans feel in response to thinking about objects and their related axioms, provides the human mind with more complexity than the minds of non-human animals, leading many to think subjectively that humans are more consciously aware than animals.

Theoretically, the human mind could have evolved so that it does not feel emotions, but rather would use a non-emotional "numerical" way of rank-ordering the "value" of thinking certain ideas versus other ideas, without feeling emotions as the motivator for thinking certain ideas and not other ideas (Dawkins, 2009). However, a purely mathematical abstract representations of emotion might not be practical from an evolutionary standpoint, because the human brain seems to have limited brain energy resources to use for thinking in purely abstract mathematical ways. Too many damaging free radicals are formed when thinking in purely abstract mathematical ways for such thinking to be practical for most human minds if done for long periods of time. The human mind is not like a computer that can perform vast numbers of mathematical calculations without being damaged by free radicals generated from such thinking. An emotional way of quantifying the emotional value of an idea is therefore more practical than a purely abstract mathematical way of quantifying the emotional values of ideas. An emotional system is required in general among humans, however, since this serves as a way of making humans think some thoughts more than others. Natural selection forces can tweak the emotional values of thoughts programmed in human genes, such as to induce the evolution of human minds that tend to think thoughts that are adaptive, in that these thoughts improve survival and reproduction.

One particular category of human behavior, sexuality, is best motivated by emotional feelings instead of "abstract, numerical representations of emotional values." A human is more likely to reproduce if the human feels emotional pain from not reproducing, and emotional pleasure from reproducing, versus the human registering a non-painful, abstract low emotional "value" in response to not reproducing.

A computer can in theory be programmed to have a digitally simulated emotional system. This is possible by assigning digital emotion values to various different computer thinking tasks. For example, if a computer is playing backgammon, the act of thinking backgammon might register as a 60 on an arbitrarily programmed emotion scale that ranges from 0 to 100. Playing chess might be arbitrarily assigned a value of 49, and playing a screensaver might be arbitrarily assigned a value of 17, while displaying a word processor document might be arbitrarily assigned a value of 80. The computer is then programmed to only perform those thinking tasks that register as a 50 or above on the emotional scale. This would be comparable to a human only thinking thoughts that the human feels like thinking, if emotions that are 50-100 are pleasurable emotions on the scale, but emotions that are 0-49 are painful emotions on the scale. To add complexity to the emotional scale, the assigned emotions could be dynamic. The backgammon emotion values can change randomly, or decline at a steady rate over time, then rebound to 100 at a steady rate over time. In addition, a "general well-being" emotional scale can be added, where the computer is programmed to assign a number, representing a digital emotion, that represents the overall well-being of the computer, which would be an emotional value that is always on, in addition to the emotions that the computer assigns to various thinking tasks. A computer can be programmed to acquire a low well-being value if the computer spends too much time thinking things that generate low scores on the emotion scale. For example, the computer might develop a low score of 10 on the well-being scale if the computer spends half a day for the next week carrying out logic operations that rate below 40 on the emotion scale. The computer would register the low 10 emotion value continuously, while registering other digital emotions due to things being thought. This would simulate the phenomena of a person becoming generally depressed or developing post traumatic stress disorder, which is also a continuously negative feeling of emotion felt during day-to-day living, if the person experiences too many events with painful emotional feelings associated with them.

What is Intelligence?

Intelligence involves being able to detect the energy fingerprints of different kinds of objects in the universe, and being able to detect energy fingerprints associated with how these objects change over time when implementing axioms pertaining to what can be obtained from of done with objects over time. An object can be living, like a person or non-human animal or a plant, or non-living like a rock or an apple. An object can exist if the laws of physics permit the object to exist, that is, if the laws of physics permit sub-atomic particles cohesively concatenate into that object, given what physics conditions of temperature, gravity, energy, etc. are required for the object to exist, according to the arbitrary laws of physics. Axioms pertaining to objects also exist due to the laws of physics.

Why do the laws of physics allow intelligence to exist? Minds that are "intelligent" can detect the energy fingerprints of patterns of automatic movement phenomena in the universe, which is essentially why the laws of physics make intelligence to be possible. To be able to do this, an an organic brain may need to be able to anabolically generate a neuron structure that is capable of somehow mimicking or reflecting an axiom pertaining to how a specific object can be altered, or what can be obtained from that specific object, or a neuron structure that can detect what multiple energy fingerprints emanate from an object as that object changes in a patterned way over time.

It is automated, arbitrary and outside of free will whether or not a person will detect a specific kind of pattern. Countless schoolteachers have attempted to teach specific patterns to specific schoolchildren, but failed in the attempt because the schoolchild simply "could not get" that pattern or concept. It is arbitrary why a schoolteacher can write a mathematics formula like 3+2=5 or the pythagorean theorum on a blackboard, and some schoolchildren "get" the formula, but others do not. The ones who "get" the formula have brains that are able to react to the simulus of seeing the equation on the blackboard such as to generate anabolic neuron patterns that reflect that pattern. Some brains have these pattern-generating anabolic capabilities, with respect to certain patterns, and others do not. Each brain acquires a combination of patterned anabolic neuron structures through learning processes while learning things during life. The brains that collect the most patterns with the widest diversity may become the most sophisticated brains on the planet, and the leaders of the planet.

A computer can be programmed to be able to play the board game of backgammon, and possess a component of intelligence by being able to use logic to play backgammon. A game of backgammon occurs automatically, once the objects (15 checker pieces, 24 position points of the board, and 6-sided dice) are brought together into a common space, and the rules of backgammon are imposed on the objects in the context of that common space, and dice are rolled to begin the game, so that the outcomes of the game can occur automatically according to the logic of the backgammon game. A computer can be programmed to mimic the logic of backgammon through the programming of an electronic set of Boolean algebra logic gates that mimic the game. The laws of physics permit the logic of a specific game of backgammon to play itself out in an automated way, if this logical playing out of that specific backgammon game follows parameters, dictated by the laws of physics, that specify under what circumstances it is possible for a backgammon game to exist. This playing out of a backgammon game can only occur if the universe is in a state of disequilibrium, such that this particular game of backgammon can play itself out, from beginning to end, as part of a group of automated motion phenomena that is part of an over-arching automated tendency of the universe to move towards its own equilibrium. The playing out this specific backgammon game, and all other phenomena in the universe that play themselves out logically, which are also put in motion by the automated tendency of the universe to move towards its own equilibrium, make possible the existence of specific kinds of logical patterns, and the existence of intelligence which occurs in minds capable of detecting specific kinds of logical patterns.

It seems that automatic movement phenomena, such as the movement of heat from hot bodies to cold bodies and not vice versa without an external energy input, or the automated conversion of wood to carbon, in an atmosphere containing significant amounts of oxygen, when wood is burned at sea level on the planet earth, can only exist if the universe is in a state of disequilibrium. The disequilibrium state of the universe causes automatic movement phenomena to occur in the universe, because essentially all of these automated movement patterns are part of overall systems of automated patterns that ultimately result in increasing the universe's equilibrium. As long as the universe is in a state of disequilibrium, automated movement phenomena can exist, because equilibrium processes can continue to exist in the universe. The status of the universe being in a state of disequilibrium allows intelligence to exist, where intelligence is a mind property that detects patterns of automated movement in the universe, and can locate opportunities provided by the universe to use automated movement phenomena to improve the survival and reproducibility of the organism capable of thinking intelligently. Once the universe reaches a state of equilibrium, no more automated movement phenomena can occur in the universe, and intelligence can no longer exist. In addition, thermodynamically unstable cohesive organic living body forms, that require a continuous input of food energy in order to be able to maintain their thermodynamically unstable body forms, cannot exist if the universe reaches a state of equilibrium, nor can the minds of these thermodynamically unstable bodies exist, nor can the associated functionalities of their minds exist either.

Essentially, the laws of physics specify what kinds of automatic movement phenomena can exist in the universe and under what circumstances these automatic movement phenomena can exist. For example, at room temperature on the planet earth, sugar can dissolve in a glass of water automatically, but on the surface of the sun, sugar cannot dissolve in a glass of water, because the sun's surface would be so hot as to completely atomize the atoms and molecules of the glass of sugar water. However, at room temperature on the planet earth, sugar automatically dissolves to its saturation point in a glass of water, which gives rise to the ability, in theory, to know of the concept that sugar can be dissolved into water to create sugar water. A person who is aware of this concept is more intelligent than a person who is not aware of this concept, at least with respect to this one concept. Since the laws of physics permit a glass of sugar water to exist, and for sugar water to be automatically createable, at room temperature at sea level within the environment of the planet earth, the various patterns of this automatic movement phenomena of dissolving sugar in water at room temperature on the planet earth can be represented as an intelligent concept. The ability to conceptualize the process of how to make a glass of sugar water, and to be aware of the existence of sugar water, may evolve in a mind if such knowledge is adaptive to improving the ability to survive or reproduce. The specific way by which minds can evolve with the ability to possess this knowledge, and the means by which a mind can be aware that a glass of sugar water is possible, are currently not known to scientists.

The objects that a mind can be aware of can, in theory, consist not only of inanimate objects like rocks or trees, but matter-constituted or energy-constituted, but relatively intangible, objects like a planet's atmosphere, or living objects like animals or plants or other members of the homo sapiens species of animal. Any thing that can emanate an energy fingerprint that can differentiate that thing from all other things can be grasped by the mind as a specific object. That is, the mind can grasp a definition of an object by possessing sensory inputting mechanisms that can input the unique energy fingerprints emanated from specific objects, or unique combinations of energies emanated from specific objects, and then send signals reflecting these specific input patterns to the mind.

One of the problems of defining intelligence is that no organic mind knows about every object and every axiom-pertaining-to-a-specific-objects that are theoretically possible in the known universe. All minds contain a tiny subset of this total body of knowledge, and lack other aspects of this total body of knowledge. In addition, it is difficult to define what an object is. For example, if a person shaves a small splinter off a wooden table, is the table without the splinter still a table? How does one know that the table exists, if the table is made mostly of atoms, which are mainly empty space? How much of the subset of total knowledge in the universe must a mind contain before the mind can be considered "intelligent?" Is a honeybee "intelligent" because it is an expert on the paradigm of the life-support and gene-reproduction aspects of the honeybee insect, but is not aware that pickup trucks exist? Is a computer "intelligent" because it can play chess, even if the computer is not programmed to be "aware" that it exists on the planet earth, and that it exists in a wider universe?

Is a human billionaire considered to be super-intelligent because he or she was able to outsmart most other humans and make a billion dollars? Such a billionaire would be probably be an expert of the logic of how people think, and of the logic of how homo sapiens societies work on the planet earth, or else the billionaire would not have succeeded in the ultra-competitive world of money-making. However, are not these elements, of the billionaire's mind paradigm, arbitrary information constructs existing in the universe, that are only applicable in the highly parameterized environment of homo sapiens civilization on the planet earth, and that would not be applicable as money-making paradigms anywhere else in the universe? One cannot, for example, market cotton diapers to humans, if one exists on a hypothetical planet named Elba, populated by hypothetical aliens called Droogs, that are all allergic to the molecule cellulose, which is the main molecular constituent of cotton.

Of course, no mind is aware of every possible definable object that can exist in the universe, and every possible axiom that can be associated with a defined object. It is not necessary for a mind to possess such all-knowing intelligence in order for a mind to possess enough intelligence for that intelligence to optimize the ability of that mind's body to occupy a life support niche, and a gene reproduction niche, on the planet earth. The fact that all human minds are different from one another demonstrates that minds obviously input different combinations of awarenesses of defined objects, and different combinations of awarenesses of axioms pertained to specific defined objects. There is no one definitive "conceptual collection" of awareness of sets of defined objects, and sets of axioms pertaining to objects, that optimizes a mind's ability to occupy a life support and gene reproduction support niche on the planet earth. When the natural selection forces of evolution evolved human minds to be able to possess a wide variation among minds' respective "conceptual collections" of conceptualized objects and axioms-pertaining-to-objects, these humans became more

223

able to distribute widely across the planet earth and occupy a wide variety of life support and gene reproduction niches on the planet earth. This helped to ensure the historical survival of the homo sapiens genome.

What is the difference between intelligence and conscious awareness? Computers can play the complex board game of backgammon better than any human, with superior ability to choose the most optimal decision among the choices provided by the dice at every turn. Does this ability to play backgammon expertly make the computer "intelligent?" The computer understands the logic of backgammon and can make optimal decisions given the logic of the game. However, the computer's ability to play backgammon is an isolated intellectual skill, one existing independently of a wider sense of awareness of the universe. When a human plays backgammon, the human plays the game with an awareness of how playing the game fits into an overall awareness of that human's life on the planet earth. For example, a human may play a game of backgammon with a friend, feel emotional pleasure resulting from the friend's company, and think that the human must now go home to meet the wife, and then the next day go to work to be able to make money and pay for that human's shelter. On one hand, the computer is "intelligent" because it can play backgammon better than any human, but on the other hand, the computer is "stupid" because the computer does not realize that it exists on the planet earth, that is illuminated by the sun, with a moon rotating around the earth, and green grass and trees. Here, a distinction, it is presumed, is made between "intelligence" and "awareness," or perhaps, one might presume that a thinking mind cannot be considered "intelligent" unless it is both "intelligent and aware." Yet, if a human plays backgammon less intelligently than a computer, how can a human be more intelligent than the computer? Can a human be more "intelligent" than a computer because the human is aware that the human exists in the context of life of the planet earth, even if the human's conscious number-crunching capability is vastly inferior to the super-rational super-mathematical number-crunching computer mind? The "awareness" that humans have of how their existence is oriented to the existing planet or surrounding solar system or universe is arbitrary, because these orienting surroundings exist due to

224

arbitrary reasons, and in the infinite time and space context of the universe, a human can only use arbitrary criteria to specify when or where these orienting elements exist in the history of the universe.

Given that intelligence approaching human or primate intelligence rarely has evolved in the animal kingdom, it seems that having human-level intelligence may not be a very adaptive trait among animals. Intelligence may benefit an individual's ability to gain survival and reproduction assets (Gabora, 2011), but may possibly reduce the overall ability of the species to which that individual belongs to propagate its genes over evolutionary time. Intelligence as a trait may interfere with the ability of other traits within a species to contribute to the reproduction of that species' genes over evolutionary time. It would require complex mathematical simulation to determine what would be the "optimal" mix of traits within a species, of which intelligence would be one possible trait, that would contribute to the gene reproduction of that species, given the energy niche that this species occupies within a food chain.

Alligators and crocodiles use the same basic techniques for capturing and killing their prey animals that they have used for tens of millions of years, and the prey animals seem to be susceptible to being captured and killed by these techniques perpetually in their evolutionary history. Why do the prey of alligators and crocodiles not evolve ways to outthink the alligators and crocodiles? One possible answer is that if the prey of alligators and crocodiles evolved improved mind function that allowed them to avoid being eaten by alligators and crocodiles, that there would occur overpopulation of these prey animals, and this overpopulation can result in murderous fighting by those animals against one another, as they compete for scarce resources, since the per-capita resources of these prey animals has declined within their ecological niches due to their increased populations.

Increased intelligence may also interfere with herd behavior, where such herd behavior can be adaptive. For example, a herd of wildebeests could, in theory, when attacked by a lion trying to pick off a wildebeest from the outer periphery of the herd, change their herding movements such as to create a wide circular opening in the outside perimeter of their herd pool. This might fool the lion into going inside the circular opening, after which the wildebeests could use slightly higher intelligence and calculation to coordinate their movements to quickly close the circle in on the lion, and trap the lion inside the herd of wildebeests, after which the wildebeests can easily trample the lion to death.   However, the increased mathematical and common sense intelligence that wildebeests would gain by evolving minds that contained this strategy could increase the independent-mindedness of wildebeests, such as to reduce the tendency of wildebeests to move as a cohesive herd.   Moving and thinking as a herd can offer evolutionary advantages. For example, if a wildebeest is moving in a herd, since the outer perimeter of the herd, where lions could attack and kill a wildebeest, is a very small area compared to the safer inside of the herd, the probability is such that a wildebeest in a herd most likely will be immune to attack from a lion, even if the wildebeest does not use a calculated, intelligent strategy to try to keep itself inside the herd.   In addition, giving lions an opportunity to kill off some wildebeests, by wildebeests herding-behavior creating that vulnerable outer perimeter, can be helpful to the wildebeest's genes, if a lion tends to kill off the weaker and sicker members of the wildebeest species.   Low-intelligence herding mentality offers protection to the wildebeest and the wildebeest's genes. The evolution of wildebeest intelligence that can induce a wildebeest to be more independent-minded and less herd-minded may overall reduce the genes protection available to that mutation of wildebeest. There are other factors besides intelligence that can contribute to the gene reproduction of a species, and this may lock a species into evolving to possess a "package" of gene traits that may not change much over evolutionary time, due to that package being an optimized mixture of traits that optimizes the ability of that species to survive and reproduce within its energy or ecological niches.

Memory

All memory formation is automated, since memory formation is caused by bio-chemical reactions in the brain, that only occur if strict physics parameters exist, that make these bio-chemical reactions occur. The ability to form any memory is entirely beyond the control of the human. The energy to form a memory must exist before the bio-chemical reactions that form the memory can occur. Humans, however, cannot control the sources of the energies that power the bio-chemical reactions that occur in their minds. This is because, in order to "control" something mentally, the energy that is needed to form the mental control thought must exist before that thought is initiated. Humans cannot control the source of the energy that initiates that thought.

Organic human brains only record an extremely tiny fraction of the information about the event that a brain is remembering. This is because any event that is to be remembered is made up of countless numbers of sub-atomic particles, that are interacting with one another in countless ways, over the vast numbers of Planck time units over which this event takes place. It is impossible for an organic human brain to put forth the colossal amount of number-crunching that is required to track the world pathways of all of these sub-atomic particles while the event is happening. Of course, most of these sub-atomic particles exist underneath the external surfaces of the objects involved in the event being remembered, so that there is no way for the information about these sub-surface sub-atomic particles to be inputted by a human brain, and even if the brain was aware of all of the sub-atomic particles that make up an event, there is no way to computationally track the world pathways of each particle. Humans, therefore, can generally only remember an event in terms of the activities of the sub-atomic particles that are visible on the external surface of the objects involved in the event. Even then, the brain cannot detect all of these surface sub-atomic particles, and also cannot begin to computationally track all of the world pathways of these only these surface sub-atomic particles during the course of the event. Therefore, the amount of information remembered about an event is an extremely tiny fraction of the total amount of sub-atomic particle information that is required to completely understand what happened during the event, down to sub-atomic detail. Clearly, human memories are extremely superficial representations of the events being remembered, and this makes one wonder what the selection criteria is for the organic brain to select what specific, extremely limited details are included in the memory of an event. If a beloved grandmother bakes a delicious apple pie that warms one's hearts, the computational number-crunching power required to track the world-pathways of all of the sub-atomic particles just in that apple pie is far beyond the human brain's computational power.

The human mind's ability to form memories depends on anabolic bio-chemical reactions occurring in the mind. "Anabolic" chemical reactions are reactions that form proteins, fats and other complex biological molecules in the mind. Such anabolic reactions are needed to form the molecular structures that encode memories in the mind. One can only form a memory of a real-life event if the event projects energy fingerprints that induce the energy-fingerprint-inputting structures of the five senses to initiate bio-chemical reactions that send signals to the brain, so that these signals direct the anabolic chemical reactions that form the memories of information that triggered these signals.

It is energy-intensive for thought-conducting particles to be continuously flowing through nodes within a circuit or molecular relaying pathway in order to maintain the existence of a thought result or answer. As a result, the ability to form memories evolved in biological minds. Memories are a low-energy way of storing thought results, so that the thought-conducting flow of thought-conducting particles can be turned off, but there would still exists a low-energy memory of the results, that requires minimal energy to maintain, which amounts to far less energy than would be needed to continuously maintain that thought result via an active flow of thought-conducting particles through the neuron nodes that cause that thought result. The function of mind memory systems in general (whether those minds are computerized or biological) is to be a low-energy way of storing computed results, to avoid the high-energy need to continuously flow thought-conducting particles through circuit nodes to maintain the existence of the results.

Another demonstration of how the mind is an automated thinking device, and that memories form through automated molecular behavioral patterns, is that the mind remembers the past and the present but not the future. The late Stephen Hawking, who was the Lucasian professor of mathematics at Cambridge University, explored this topic in his book, "A Brief History of Time." Essentially, time in the universe moves forward in the time direction where the universe is expanding, and where the universe tends towards increased thermodynamic entropy. This "arrow of time" transitions (or seems to transition) from the past to the future, and not from the future to the past (Hawking, 1985 and 1996; Heinrich, 2016; Ellis, 2013). That is, the universe is expanding and continuously evolving towards a state of increased entropy in the time direction from the past to the future, and not in the time direction from the future to the past. Consequently, the human mind can only observe universe phenomena such that the universe is continually expanding, and the entropy of the universe is continuously increasing, over time. This requires that the human mind only remember the past and present, but not the future. It has also been shown that all operations that cause the creation of memories, whether these are biochemical reactions that result in biological brain memories, or electron movements that result in silicon computer mind memories, cause an increase in the entropy of the universe (Bennett, 2003; Street, 2016). Human memories are automatically constrained by the laws of physics to only record memories in a way to that increases the entropy of the universe, and are automatically constrained by the laws of physics to only remember the past and present, but not the future.

Information

Information can be defined as energy that reaches an energy-inputting molecular mechanism, that is capable of relaying the energy to a pathway, circuit or relaying mechanism, such as to send energy to a node within this pathway, circuit or relaying mechanism, such as to generate a thought as a result of energy moving through that node. This broad definition includes phenomena such as light information entering the eye and sending a signal to an organic mind, or an electron signal sent to a computer microprocessor silicon mind, or a chemotactic signal sent to a paramecium, which can alter the behavior of the paramecium, due to whatever physics and chemistry changes occur within the paramecium due to the signal. Information is a subset of energy. All information is energy, but not all energy is information, because not all energy reaches an energy-inputting molecular mechanism, such as to alter the energy state of that molecular mechanism, such as to cause the molecular mechanism to relay the energy further to other thought-generating pathways, circuits or relaying mechanisms. Since information is energy, information is subject to the same laws of thermodynamics (Pepperell, 2018) that apply to energy.

Unlike energy in general, energy that is defined as information cannot, by definition, exist independently of a detecting device that is capable of detecting the information energy. For example, if one asks, what is the minimum amount of information that is needed to describe a Hydrogen atom, the answer is not "one proton and one electron orbiting the proton," or some other answer that is strictly limited to describing the sub-atomic particles that make up a hydrogen atom. The answer must also add, in addition to this number of bits, the minimum amount of information that is needed to describe the detector of a hydrogen atom. It is also ambiguous what is meant by a "detector of a hydrogen atom." Hydrogen atoms can be "detected" in different ways by different energy-inputting molecular mechanisms. A hydrogen atom can be "detected" by a molecular mechanism such that this hydrogen atom can be absorbed through a biological cell membrane and sent to a location within a cell to become part of a chemical reaction. A hydrogen atom, more abstractly, can be detected as an object consisting of a proton and an electron, and as one of the atomic elements that is detectable by the homo sapiens mind. This is a more abstract definition, and the ability to describe this definition requires much more sophisticated mind functionality, containing of a wider range of object-detecting molecular mechanisms, than a molecular-sized detector of a hydrogen atom that moves that atom towards the site of a bio-chemical reaction. Much more information would be needed to describe the hydrogen atom and its detecting molecular mechanism/s in that more abstract sense of detecting a hydrogen atom.

Information energy alters the quantum energy states of the atoms and molecules that make up the system that is inputting the information energy. Light energy, for example, consists of photons of varying degrees of frequency and intensity, which can impart energy onto the parts of a human eye that receive light energy, providing an energy input that increases the total quantum energy of the body receiving the light energy. These parts then expend energy to relay that light energy signal to the brain,

230

and then the brain expends energy to process the signal and decide whether or not to behave differently in response to the signal. All of these energy expenditure functions change the quantum energy states of the atoms and molecules within the homo-sapiens body system that are receiving the photon energy input. Other inputs, such as taste inputs, touch inputs, sound energy inputs also directly project energy to the homo-sapiens body form receiving those forms of information energy, and alter the energy state of that body via energy expenditures needed to relay the information to the brain. However, there is no guarantee that the homo-sapiens brain understands what energy is, so there is not guarantee that the homo sapiens brain understands what information is.

What is a Question? What is Desire?

From a common-sense standpoint, a question may be defined as an information-seeking action, broadly categorized into questions such as who, what, where, when, why or how. However, what does a question mean in atomic or sub-atomic terms? Why do the laws of physics permit questions to exist? Neither questions nor answers are possible unless the universe is in a state of disequilibrium, such that local environments that are in a state of disequilibrium can occur in the universe, such that automatic movement phenomena, driven by the disequilibrium state moving towards a state of equilibrium, are possible, which makes it possible to match a question to a rational answer that represents a patterned, pre-ordained movement phenomenon permissible by the laws of physics.

Questions like "where" or "when" seem simple enough, in that they essentially ask for the location of a specific object or objects within some kind of 4-dimensional coordinate system of X, Y, Z and Time (here, we are assuming for argument's sake that there are only these four dimensions in the universe, and ignoring for the sake of convenience the possibility that there may be eleven dimensions in the universe according to the modern physics theory of String Theory).

The question "who" asks for information about people, and the answers to "who" questions are essentially arbitrary, human-created cultural constructs that describe a person, such as a person's name, ethnicity, religion, style of dress, or other characteristics that describe the characteristics of a specific person that result from the arrangements of matter that are possible in a person's matter structure, given what the laws of physics permit, such as what is that person's physical gender or eye color. Other answers to "who" questions are similar to "where" or "when" question answers, in that these answers describe the person's X,Y,Z and T coordinates at various points during that person's life.

(The "T" or time coordinate used when describing people typically refers to a date in the Gregorian calendar system, the most widely used calendar system, where the year 1--there is no year zero--is set at the posited birth year of the Israelite Jesus Christ, who is designated as a lord in the god paradigm known as Christianity, where this first "1 AD" year was determined by a Christian religious scholar named Dionysius Exiguus in the year 525 of the Gregorian calendar, although it is uncertain exactly how Dionysius determined the posited exact year of the birth of Jesus Christ.)

Questions such as "why" or "how" are more complex to answer than "what" or "where" questions, with answers requiring much larger amounts of information and often some understanding about how objects change over time. For example, one answer to the question of "why do trees exist?" is that trees come from seeds, and that tree seeds, when planted, begin growing over time to eventually form trees, using a complex growth process driven by the laws of physics. A question like "how does one chop a tree down safely?" requires answering how to use a tree-cutting tool to cut a tree over time, in such a way as to make the tree fall in a direction away from people or animals who may be injured or killed by the falling tree. The answer to a "how" question is often a sequence of actions where an object applies energy to another object in a step-by-step manner, permissible by the laws of physics, that results in some kind of alteration in the energy state, atomic structure or position point on the planet earth of the objects. The answer to a "how" question cannot be rational unless the laws of physics permit that answer to occur, given the initial conditions of matter in the system pertaining to which the "how" question was asked. In this respect, the ability of an answer to a "how" question to be true is pre-ordained by the laws of physics, and the laws of physics only provide a finite number of opportunities in the universe such that a particular true answer to a "how" question is physically possible.

One reason why "where" questions exist is that not all real objects in the universe, existing in a present time, can emanate an information fingerprint to a mind, such as to make that mind aware of an X,Y,Z,T coordinate location for every object in the universe. A reductionist mathematical explanation explaining why the laws of physics result in this phenomenon being true is perhaps too complex to provide. From a common sense standpoint, it is obvious that not all energy that emanates from an object can be detected by an energy inputting molecular mechanism that can detect that energy as a distinctive energy fingerprint emanating from the object. Light reflecting from an object can be blocked by another object, so that this light cannot reach an organic light energy detector. A mind can be physically located too far away from an object for any energy (sound energy, light energy, touch, taste, or smell energy) to be capable of altering the energy state of an energy inputting receptor that sends signals to a mind. Where emanating energy fingerprints can be blocked, unknowns can exist, and where unknowns can exist, questions can also exist. There are vast numbers of unknowns all around the minds on the planet earth. If a person is inside in a room, for example, the walls and window frames block light, so that any object (i.e. 99.99999999999% of the objects on the planet earth) existing outside of the room may be blocked by the walls and window frames from emanating light energy that reaches that person's eyes.

Most of the components of the life support and gene reproduction niches that will be occupied by an organism after it begins to exist cannot be predicted prior to the existence of the organism. For example, the locations on the planet earth of the food items that an organism needs to survive, and who are the members of that organism's species with whom that member must interact in order to obtain life support and gene reproduction assets, are not predictable prior to the existence of that member. Hence, a member of a species cannot be born with an evolved, pre-programmed concept of exactly where on earth are located the specific water sources and food items needed for survival, or the exact descriptors of the fellow members of the species with whom the

233

organism must interact to gain life support and gene reproduction assets. Instead, the organism must be born with a genetically programmed mind ability to learn how to discover where these food and water sources exist, and to learn how to discover which members of its own species, if any, can be interacted with such as to obtain life support and gene reproduction assets.

Some organisms are instinctively programmed by their genes to ask specific questions pertaining to these assets. For example, human babies instinctively ask who their parents are, since their parents are the only sources of life support assets during a human babies first years of life. After developing into sexual maturity, sexual hormones begin to circulate in a human's body, which may make the human look around and ask, of the people around me, who might be a partner in a gene reproduction activity? The laws of physics prohibit predicting these and many other bits of similar knowledge prior to the existence of a body and the mind attached to that body, but the forces of natural selection can evolve in an organism a behavioral tendency to find out this kind of information after being born. An entire system of specific "fill-in-the-blanks" unknowns, like an unfinished "Madlibs" game, might be pre-installed in an organism's mind by its genes, along with a behavioral tendency and learning ability to find answers to fill in these blanks after gaining knowledge through the experience of roving around the planet earth.

Instinctive behaviors and knowledge can be genetically programmed into some organisms, such as with the instinctive knowledge that a bird possesses to build a nest, or the instinctive knowledge that a crocodile may possess concerning how to hunt, kill and eat various animals. It would be adaptive for a species' genes to cause the installation of instinctive behavioral patterns in an organism's mind if the planet earth, in a practically endlessly repeating cycle, provides structures or life support or gene reproduction niches such that these instinctive behavioral patterns are perennially adaptive for a specific species.

If a ribose molecule contacts an MCP signal-inputting molecule on the surface of the E. coli bacterium, that is capable of undergoing a molecular shape-change that results in the sensing of an energy fingerprint emanating from the ribose molecule, a chain of molecular reactions occurs that transfers energy to a node within the E. coli bacterium, such that energy traveling within this node causes the E. coli bacterium to move flagella in an attempt to move towards other ribose molecules. The E. coli bacterium swims in one direction, and if no more ribose molecules are detected, the bacterium begins to swim in another direction, and if no more ribose molecules are found, the bacterium changes direction and swims in another direction, until it is swimming in a direction such that more ribose molecules are encountered, that cause energy changes in the E. coli's molecular mechanisms that input energy fingerprints from ribose molecules. The initial detection of the ribose sugar molecule results in the E. coli bacterium searching for more ribose molecules, by moving in random directions, in a trial-and-error way, with the objective of the bacterium putting itself at a location such that more ribose molecules will be detectable by the ribose-molecule-energy-fingerprint detecting MCP molecules on the surface of the E. coli bacterium. The E. coli's initial detection of a ribose molecule activates a question within the E. coli thought-generating mind, in that the detection of that ribose molecule activates a molecular mechanism within the E. coli that causes the E. coli bacterium to try to position itself, using random motions, such that energy flows across increased numbers of the E. coli's ribose-molecule-energy-fingerprint detecting MCP molecules.

This illustrates one way of defining a question. A question can be a molecular mechanism, initiated by energy passing through a node in a circuit or conduit or relay chain, such that the molecular mechanism causes the body attached to a mind to move, such that the signal-inputting mechanisms that input the energy fingerprint of a specific kind of object, that were not receiving energy inputs emanating from that specific kind of object prior to the move, now can receive such energy inputs, due to the mind moving towards that specific kind of object that actually exists at the present time, such that that specific kind of object, existing in reality, emanates an energy fingerprint to the energy-fingerprint-inputting mechanisms specific for receiving the energy fingerprint of that specific object. Here, the "question" answers where an object can be located in reality. That is, the question answers where in a specified

X,Y,Z,T coordinate space can the mind be located such that a specific object, existing in reality, can emanate energy, at a distance that is close enough to that mind, such as to project an energy fingerprint to the energy-fingerprint-inputting receptors that receive the specific energy fingerprint associated with that specific object, and that relay that energy, indicating detection of that object, to that mind.

The body attached to that mind can use random motions to try to position the mind where this energy-fingerprinting can emanate such as to change the energy states of the receptors receiving this energy fingerprint, as in the case of the E. coli bacterium. Some minds can narrow down the possible locations where an object has the highest probability of existing, and only move towards these locations in attempting to locate the object. This is a more efficient way of answering a "where" question compared to moving in random directions in hopes of randomly finding the desired object. For example, an egret that is asking the question of where fish can be found to eat will position itself at a body of water to look for the fish, and not attempt to look for fish on dry land.

The process of forming a question and then obtaining an answer to the question cannot happen instantly, but must happen over a period of time. A minimum number of units of Planck time must pass before the bio-chemical reactions that result in a question-leading-to-an-answer phenomenon can occur.

The answer to a "where" question pertaining to a real life object would result in the object appearing close enough to a mind such that the object can emanate an energy fingerprint identifying that object to a sensory receptor or set of receptors capable of inputting that energy fingerprint and relaying the energy signal to that mind. This would result in energy moving to a node within a circuit that conducts this energy signal. If the object is not emanating such information, energy will not pass through that node. A mind can detect if energy is passing through that node. If there is no energy passing through that node, this lack of energy may induce that mind to position itself until it is close enough to the object for the object to emanate an identifying energy fingerprint to that mind's sensory receptors that can input this fingerprint. Here, a "where" question can also be defined as any molecular mechanism that is triggered by detection, at an initial time point A, of a lack of electricity at a node that would normally be electrified, if a specific object was emanating an energy fingerprint to sensory receptors capable of inputting this energy fingerprint, such that this molecular mechanism causes a mind to move, at a time after time point A, towards an X,Y,Z,T coordinate position, such that this object would be close enough to send an energy fingerprint to the node. The verbal asking of a question is not the question itself, but is rather a translation of the actual question, which is the aforementioned molecular movement-causing mechanism. The verbal asking of a question is a tool for communicating the question to other minds capable of hearing the question. Also, asking the question to oneself is a redundant activity, since the question exists already as a molecular mechanism that causes movement.

Minds that can ask questions probably evolved because the physical ability to move evolved in bodies. Asking questions provides an evolutionary advantage only if the organism asking the question is motile enough to position itself to where the answer to the question exists, if the answer to the question is an actual physical object that can emanate an energy fingerprint to that mind, that this mind can detect. Questions also are possible because unknowns are possible. An unknown is any object that could, in theory, stimulate an energy-fingerprint-detecting mechanism that was capable of inputting an energy fingerprint emanating from that specific object, but which is not doing so at a present moment of Planck time. The answer to a question is one that results in the stimulation of that energy-fingerprint-inputting mechanism by that object.

A mind usually knows intuitively what answer it wants or what thing it desires. In other words, the mind knows exactly what neuron pathways and nodes in neuron pathways that mind wants energy to flow through, such that if energy flows through those nodes and circuits, the question answer, or the desired thing, will be obtained. How does the mind know what neuron pathways it wants to become energized, which would be the answers to the questions or the things desired? How does the mind know that it wants to eat a banana, or, in other words, that it wants the various energy-fingerprint-inputting mechanisms, that input the various energy fingerprints that are emanated from a banana while the banana is being eaten, to be energized with the energy emanating from those energy fingerprints? How does the mind know that it wants to experience a real-life reproductory activity, where the multiple energy-fingerprint-inputting mechanisms, that receive various energy-fingerprint-inputs that emanate while a real-life reproductory activity is being experience, actually become energized by receiving those energy-fingerprint inputs? It is unknown scientifically what are the molecular mechanisms operating in an organic mind that makes the mind intuitively know exactly which neurons pathways and nodes it wants energy to flow through.   Perhaps the lack of energy flowing across these nodes itself triggers a molecular mechanism that sends energy to a node within the neuron circuits that generates a thought, or a molecular mechanism, that functions to make that mind position itself such that those other nodes have energy flowing across them. Sometimes, of course, humans don't know what they want. They say, "I'm not sure what I want here, but I'll know it when I see it."

What is the difference between asking a question and having a desire? A question will not have been answered until energy is flowing across nodes in a neuron circuit such that a thought emerges, resulting from energy flowing across those nodes, that consists of the answer to the question.   Similarly, with desire or wanting, the desire is not fulfilled until energy is flowing into nodes within neuron circuits that become activated when the thing that is desired is being "obtained." Generally, when a mind wants something to be true in reality, it wants to be in a position where the desired thing exists in reality, such that the desired thing is projecting energy fingerprints to the sensory inputting mechanisms that input the energy fingerprints from that desired thing, such that the inputting of that energy fingerprint sends energy to nodes within the mind that result in thoughts being generated at those nodes, those thoughts being representations of what that mind originally wanted. The mind wants to go from a point A, where those nodes are not being energized, to a point B, where energy is flowing across those nodes.

A "desire" or a "question," when generated as a thought, by energy passing through nodes within mind circuits that generate the "desiring" or "questioning" thought, may also result in energy flowing into other nodes that result in an emotion being generated alongside the generation of the "desire" or "question." Often, this emotion is painful, and this emotional pain may continue to be felt until the desired thing or the desired information is obtained. When the desired thing or answer is obtained, the flow of energy across the nodes that generate the thoughts of the answer or the desired thing may then result in energy flowing to other nodes that generate a pleasurable emotion, which is often common sensically felt as a feeling of relief and fulfillment from obtaining the answer to the question or the desired thing. This general mechanism may explain aggressive behavior, in that a desire to behave aggressively, or to inflict pain, injury or death on another organism, may be triggered by a thought of emotional pain resulting from not being in a state where the organism is inflicting pain, injury or death on another organism. When the organism positions itself to be in that state of aggression, that is, when the organism is in a state such that it is inputting the energy fingerprints that are emanated by a target organism while the target organism is being injured, put in pain, or killed by the aggressor organism, the aggressor organism feels a thought of emotional pleasure, and no longer feels the thought of emotional pain that preceded the act of aggression.

It is possible to illustrate the concept of desire, at least hypothetically, as a structure of matter. Suppose one has a light bulb electric circuit, with two switches connected in series, such that both switches must be closed in order for electrons to move through the circuit to the lightbulb to light up the lightbulb. This lightbulb circuit is by definition a "mind," since this circuit is a "thought-generating entity," since if electrons move to the node in the circuit where the lightbulb is located, a "motion" will occur in the form of the lightbulb lighting up, said "motion" itself being a "thought," according to the definition of what is a "thought" as put forth in this book. Now, if one or both switches are open, the light bulb will not light up, or the thought will not occur. This illustrates a Boolean logic circuit where two conditions must be met for the thought to occur, or where the thought can only occur if two things happen. Now, suppose a voltage detecting device is attached to the circuit. The voltage detection device will display a "zero" if either of the switches are open, and will display a voltage value if both switches are closed and electrons can pass through the circuit. Note how the voltage detecting device is also a "mind," in that it is a thought-generating entity that generates thoughts consisting of a "zero" display or a "voltage value" display depending on if electricity (i.e. a cloud of electron particles) is passing through the circuit. Here, two mind mechanisms are connected with one another and are interacting with one another.

Now, suppose this lightbulb circuit was actually a neuron circuit. Suppose the lightbulb lighting up was not a lightbulb "thought" but a pleasant emotional feeling "thought." Suppose the two switches would be activated and permit energy to flow across the circuit if two conditions were met, such as if that the person whose brain contained that neuron circuit made a million dollars and also believed that he or she had a good sex life. This would illustrate an example of a desire, of a hypothetical person who felt a negative feeling of lack of fulfillment in life if both conditions were not met of making a million dollars and having a good sex life. If those two conditions were not met, no thought-conducting molecules would travel along the neuron circuit to the node such as to generate a positive happy emotional feeling thought. Now, supposed that there is another neuron mechanism attached to the circuit that detects if there is some kind of voltage or flow of thought-conducting particles moving across the circuit. If no such voltage or flow is detected, the detector sends energy to a node within that person's mind that generates a painful emotional feeling, corresponding to a painful feeling associated with a common-sense thought of having a lack of fulfillment in life. Instead of having a voltage detector reading "zero," as in the lightbulb circuit, the voltage detector, after sensing a zero voltage on that neuron circuit, would induce the sending of energy to a node within the neuron circuit that would generate a painful emotional feeling "thought." If the person became lucky and actually made a million dollars and acquired a good sex life, both conditions would be met, and electrons or thought-conducting particles would flow across the neuron circuit, and the voltage detection mechanism attached to that neuron circuit would register a positive voltage value across that circuit, and would send energy to a node within the person's neurons that would generate a pleasurable feeling.

Depending on how the person's neurons were structured, the painful emotional feeling associated with not meeting these two criteria of success might be continuously felt as long as that person was not both a millionaire and a possessor of a good sex life. These painful emotions possibly would become perpetually inactive after the person achieved both achievements in life. This would create in that person a lifelong desire to try to make a million dollars and to try to acquire a good quality sex life. To generate the painful emotional feeling of lack of fulfillment with respect to a certain achievement in life, there would have to be a voltage detector of some kind that registers lack of energy flowing across a neurological circuit that would otherwise have energy flowing across it if the achievement occurred in reality. An achievement would be perceived as having been accomplished if the accomplishment of the achievement projects energy fingerprints to the mind that can prove to that mind's satisfaction that the achievement has occurred.

A desire for a real-life reproductory activity might generate severe emotional pain in some mammals, but this pain may end, and be replaced by pleasurable emotions, if the reproductory activity occurs in reality, resulting in energy passing through nodes as a result of energy-fingerprint-inputting mechanisms inputting multiple energy fingerprints that, as a collective group of inputted energy fingerprints, prove to the sexual over-brain that a real-life reproductory encounter has occurred. Eventually, the feeling of pleasure diminishes after a single reproductory act. Emotional pain from desiring another real-life reproductory activity may occur again after the reproductory encounter, and the cycle of seeking out more real-life reproductory activities may again occur.

Painful emotions may be motivators to obtain answers to questions or to obtain desired things. However, motivators to obtain answers to questions or to obtain desired things may not be emotional in some cases.. A typical computer's motivation to obtain information and ask questions is driven by purely logical mechanisms, such as when a computer "asks" a video game player to input his or her name if the video game player scores an all-time high score in the video game.

Organic Minds versus Inorganic Computer Minds

How is an organic mind different from a computer's mind? An organic mind evolved to be capable of receiving energy inputs, consisting of energy fingerprints (sound energy, light energy, touch energy, smell energy and taste energy) that emanate from objects in the environment on the planet earth, which so far is the only planet we know of where organic minds exist. The organic mind evolved to have thought reactions to detected objects that enable the organism attached to that mind to maintain the atomic cohesiveness of that organism's thermodynamically unstable body, since the organism's thermodynamically unstable body will disintegrate without a constant input of food energy. The organism also needs to reproduce because the disintegration and death of the organism is (apparently) unavoidable in the long run, given the physical and chemical instability (in the long run) of biological organisms. The laws of thermodynamics caused the evolution of organic minds.

A computer is mostly not programmed to be able to receive energy fingerprint inputs emanating from objects on the planet earth, but instead receives inputs from a computer mouse or keyboard or other common computer input device. The computer is not thermodynamically unstable, as are organic minds and bodies, because the computer is made of silicon, metals and plastics, which do not require a constant input of food energy in order to maintain the cohesiveness of the atoms and molecules that make up the computer.

Unlike a computer mind, an organic mind will quickly be irreparably damaged if its neurons are deprived of a continuous flow of oxygen for a short period of time, such as 5-20 minutes. This requires that an organic mind is always turned on, so as to control the heart that pumps oxygenated blood to the organic mind's neuron tissues. A computer mind is made of vast numbers of microscopic silicon logic gates, constructed according to principles of the Boolean algebra method of describing logic operations, through which an electron cloud moves, and the silicon logic gates are far more stable than organic neuron logic structures. A computer mind can be turned off completely, but its silicon logic gates will not be damaged, but an organic mind must be on all the time, in order for oxygen to be distributed continuously among the organic mind's neurons, or else those neurons will be damaged.

A computer has a calculating "mind," but the computer is much more stable thermodynamically than an organic mind, so the computer is not designed to calculate the best way to maintain the thermodynamic stability of the computer's body form. The computer instead thinks differently from organic minds in that the computer mind is a pure number crunching or calculating device. An organic mind has minimal conscious ability to perform pure mathematical or number crunching activities, but uses its conscious cognitive mind primarily to figure out how to obtain the energy, from objects in earth's environment, that is required to maintain the thermodynamically unstable form of the body to which that mind is attached, and to figure out how to propagate the organism's genes.

The thoughts that a computer has at any particular present tense moment are determined by the human who is directing the computer about which thought to think about. A human might, for example, use a mouse to click on the icon for the game of backgammon on a computer desktop, which would make the computer think backgammon thoughts once the backgammon program booted up. The thoughts of organic minds are mostly initiated by those minds inputting energy fingerprint patterns emanating from objects in those minds' planetary environment, although some organic mind thoughts can originate from energy sources inside those minds.

Unlike organic minds, which use atoms and molecules, and perhaps sub-atomic particles like electrons, as the medium for relaying signals, the computer uses clouds of electrons only. The energy fingerprints that an E. coli chemotactic mind inputs are energy fingerprints emanated by ribose molecules, but the objects that the computer uses as inputs are electrons. The computer mind receives unlimited energy to power its mind through an electric power source to which the computer is plugged, so it would not need to be aware of the laws of thermodynamics to facilitate its own existence or to obtain the energy needed to power its mind. The computer can calculate a wider array of decision possibilities, with more precise mathematics, than an E. coli chemotaxis mind because the computer contains millions of microscopic boolean logic gates, whereas the E. coli chemotaxis mind probably contains few elements that can be described as Boolean logic gates.

Both the computer mind and an E. coli chemotactic mind are driven by the automatic movement of sub-atomic, atomic or molecular particles, driven automatically because the laws of physics dictate that their mind particles will move in automated, patterned ways given the physical circumstances or environmental contexts in which these particles operate. Both minds do not have free will. With both minds, it is difficult (or perhaps impossible) to define exactly how it is that the individual atomic, sub-atomic or molecular particles that participate in the mind functionality of these minds are "unified and cohesive" into a "unified and cohesive thinking entity." Also, how are the atoms, molecules and sub-atomic particles involved in the aforementioned E. coli ribose chemotaxis mind, that participate in the chain of events beginning from the ribose signal to the movement of the E. coli, via flagella, towards increasing concentrations of ribose, "unified into a cohesive cloud that forms a mind mechanism?" How can individual particles of matter be "unified into a mind mechanism?" Perhaps there really is no unity, and that which is called "mind" is only a temporary state of matter, where matter particles interact to cause "mind functionality," but without being in any way "unified."

An E. coli ribose-detecting mind mechanism does not have a memory system, which limits the complexity of its thought-generating structure. A typical computer uses memory in its processing, and has what is termed a "von Neumann architecture," consisting of a central processing unit, a control unit that contains an instruction register and program counter, memory that stores data and instructions, an external memory storage hard drive, and input and output interfaces (von Neumann, 1945). It is not known exactly how organic brains use memory to influence their own thought-generating behaviors.

A computer mind is an example of how mind functionality, resulting from an input that generates an energy signal, and leads to the generation of multiple options for possible decisions, and an optimal decision being chosen, and a movement action being directed by the choosing of the optimal decision, can occur in a way that is understood in a purely reductionist way by humans, since humans designed the computer mind.   However, although the outputs of the computer minds are understandable by human minds, there is no proof that human minds actually can understand reality, so humans cannot be exactly sure what they are creating when they create things known as "computer minds."

Quantum Mechanics and Minds

Do quantum mechanics phenomena influence how organic minds work (Wang, 2013)? The main problem with the idea that quantum mechanics influences organic minds is that all known forms of organic minds on the planet earth operate at temperatures well above absolute zero, so that these minds operate at too high temperatures for any wave functions formed within the mind to not collapse instantly.   Within an organic body, there are countless bio-feedback mechanisms operating, that continuously cause molecules or atoms in the body to be "pinged" by vast numbers of energy units. Each pinging operation can potentially collapse any wave function within the body (Nauenberg, 2007). Therefore, according to Heisenberg's Uncertainty Principle, it is not possible for any biofeedback mechanism in the body or mind to detect the position and momentum of a particle simultaneously, because any bio-feedback pinging mechanism, or any heating element in the body, alters either the position or momentum of the particle.   An organic mind would therefore not be cognitively influenced by a problem or phenomena that might have multiple simultaneous solutions. Schrodinger's Cat is either dead or alive in an organic mind, and not both.

A threory, called the "Orch-Or" theory, claims that micro-tubules in biological cells contain quantum computing computational devices that are the basis of quantum mechanics-influenced organic mind-thought (Hameroff and Penrose, 2014; Hameroff, 1998).   This is a rather extraordinary claim, akin to claiming that pink polka-dotted elephants exist that can balance their bodies on their tusk tips. Although this claim is not necessarily false, a claim like this obviously needs to be supported by experimental evidence (which does not exist), or at least with a theoretical model explaining how this is possible (which also does not exist; for this model to exist, every type of atom and molecule within a micro-tubule must be known, and a model must be made to explain how all of these individual atoms and molecules interact to form this quantum computer, and what are the thought-conducting particles that operate in this computer, and what are the circuits and nodes within this computer, and where do the inputs for this computer come from, and where do the outputs go). Biologists consider micro-tubules to be structural components of cells, and not mind components. It would seem, instead, that all body bio-feedback mechanisms, and all mind functionality, exist in the context of collapsed wave functions.

However, there are papers that claim that that photosynthesis might be partially caused by quantum mechanics phenomena that involve multiple energy states existing simultaneously. This would be a remarkable example of how quantum mechanics phenomena could exist in plants, which operate at a temperature well above absolute zero (Panitchayangkoon, 2010). If these claims are true, this would lend credibility to the idea that a mind operating at well above absolute zero temperature could be significantly or mostly influenced by quantum mechanics effects. However, the literature on this topic is controversial, and physicists are not convinced that quantum coherence can survive long enough in plants operating well above absolute zero temperature for this coherence to affect photosynthesis bio-chemical reactions (Halpin, 2014).

Appendix: The Laws of Thermodynamics and the Gibbs Free Energy Idea

The laws of thermodynamics dictate several important facts about energy and entropy, that are important for understanding biological systems (Garret, 2007), or how the body works, and also for understanding why biological minds (and even computer minds) think as they do.

The first law of thermodynamics, or the Law of Conservation of Energy, states that energy cannot be created or destroyed in an isolated system. Energy in an isolated system can only change form, and in the long run generally changes into heat energy. The energy needed to power the bio-chemical reactions in the body, to power the immune system, and to power the mind, will be quickly used up by a body and converted to heat energy. When the body's internal energy stores are used up, the body, mind and immune system will not be in equilibrium, and the body will not be able to maintain its cohesive concatenation of atoms and molecules, resulting in the eventual disintegration of this cohesive body form. The body can maintain its cohesive form, however, if it inputs energy from its environment. Energy inputs are required, for example, to continuously supply the heart muscle with the energy needed to pump blood, to get the oxygen and nutrients to cells in animal bodies, so that those cells can function with energy equilibrium. Animals also, as another example, require energy to be able to move to sources of water and to drink the water. The water is needed to help atomic ions move to various locations throughout the body via osmosis, and the water also provides a matrix that makes possible different kinds of life-supporting chemical reactions. Blood must be hydrated to become a fluid that can be transported via the heart to provide nutrients to cells.

Large amounts of external energy are also required to fight off vast numbers of bacteria, viruses and predators that are continuously trying to attack and eat a living body. A living body contains vast numbers of energy-containing molecules that are of a higher entropy than a body's external environment. Because of this, vast numbers of other living creatures in the body's environment would like to eat that body, to obtain or hijack the energy contained within the body's cells. Those microbes and predators are also thermodynamically unstable like an animal's body, and need external sources of energy to maintain their own thermodynamically unstable cohesions of atoms and molecules that make up their own living beings. As soon as an animal's body dies, vast numbers of bacteria, insects and other animals swarm onto that dead body and rapidly consume the body's cells, to input into their own beings the energy that was once in that body. A dead body rapidly gives off vast amounts of energy to its environment, by way of that body being eaten by vast numbers of other living beings. Clearly, a living body must hold back a tidal wave of other living creatures, microscopic and macroscopic, that want to eat it. This requires that the body expend vast amounts of energy, by maintaining an immune system, to attack any microbes that want to digest and eat its energy-containing body molecules, that this body formed slowly and painstakingly by directly and indirectly absorbing the energy of the sun over months or years. The body may also have to expend energy to avoid or kill off potential predators that are trying to gain access to that body's energy stored in that body's molecules. All of these attempts by thermodynamically unstable predatory living beings to eat other thermodynamically unstable living being are essentially local pockets of energy equilibration phenomena occurring in the universe.

The first law of thermodynamics explains why ghosts cannot exist, because ghosts by definition can think without an energy input. Thoughts require energy for thoughts to exist, since thoughts are driven by movement of atomic, molecular or sub-atomic particles through circuits towards nodes within the circuits. Movement of such particles cannot occur without an energy input. In various god paradigms, gods are presumed to possess minds that can think and make free will decisions without an external energy input, which would make their existence a miracle, because such mind activity would violate the first law of thermodynamics.

The second law of thermodynamics states that the entropy of any isolated system always increases. If an isolated system has N number of particles in it, and each particle is of the same energy level, then the entropy of the system of N particles is at maximum entropy. Entropy is a measure of the individual differences of energy levels between individual particles in an isolated system. The second law of thermodynamics arbitrarily dictates that, without an external energy input, heat can only flow from a hot body to a cold body, when the two bodies are put in contact, and the reverse cannot occur without an external energy input.

The third law of thermodynamics states that the entropy of a system approaches a constant value as the temperature approaches absolute zero. This law is perhaps too abstract to be of much immediate interest to understanding how the mind works.

There is an equation called the Gibbs' Free Energy equation, which describes mathematically whether or not a chemical reaction, or a biological chemical reaction, can occur, given the energy inputted to start the chemical reaction, and the temperature at which this reaction is occurring. This equation contains variables such as entropy, the environmental temperature, the heat released by the chemical reaction, and the energy inputted into the reaction, in describing mathematically if any particular chemical reaction can occur. Every chemical reaction has a range of Gibbs Free Energy values, that dictate whether or not the reaction will occur, given various combinations of variable quantities, such as quantities of heat released, temperature, entropy and free energy input. Essentially, the Gibbs Free Energy equation takes the various factors associated with the thermodynamics of the chemical reaction (entropy, energy, heat, temperature) and integrates them into a formula for predicting if a chemical reaction or bio-chemical reaction in the body will occur. This equation demonstrates mathematically why energy inputs are required for most body bio-chemical reactions to occur. This equation also shows how it would violate the first law of thermodynamics if many bio-chemical reactions in the body and mind, that are needed to sustain life, occurred without an external energy input. This, in turn, explains the origin of the concept, operating in all living minds, that food energy must be obtained at a continuous rate.

Bibliography

Baars, B. J. (1988). A cognitive theory of consciousness. New York: Cambridge University Press.

Baars, B.J., Banks W.P., Newman, J., Eds. (2003). Essential Sources in the Scientific Study of Consciousness. Cambridge, MA: MIT Press/Bradford Books.

Beckermann, A. The Perennial Problem of the Reductive Explainability of Phenomenal Consciousness – C. D. Broad on the Explanatory Gap. In: T. Metzinger (ed.) Neural Correlates of Consciousness--Empirical and Conceptual Questions, Cambridge MA: MIT-Press 2000, 41-55.

Bell WE, Preston RR, Yano J, Van Houten JL (2007) Genetic dissection of attractant-induced conductances in Paramecium.J Exp Biol 210:357–365.

C. H. Bennett, "Notes on Landauer's principle, reversible computation, and Maxwell's demon", Stud. Hist. Philos. Modern Phys., 34:3;pp. 501–510, 2003.

Blake, W. (1793). The Marriage of Heaven and Hell.

Boole, G. (1854). An Investigation of the Laws of Thought. New York: Dover Publications, 1958.

Broad, C. D. (1925). The Mind and Its Place in Nature. London: Routledge and Kegan Paul.

Chalmers, D.J. (1996). The Conscious Mind: In Search of a Fundamental Theory. Oxford: Oxford University Press.

Crick, F. (1984). Function of the thalamic reticular complex: The searchlight hypothesis. Proceedings of the National Academy of Sciences USA, 81: 4586–4590.

Crick F. (1994). The astonishing hypothesis. New York: Scribner's.

Darwin, C. (1859) On the Origin of Species by Means of Natural Selection, Or, the

Preservation of Favoured Races in the Struggle for Life. London: J. Murray.

Dawkins, R. (1987). The Blind Watchmaker: Why the Evidence of Evolution Reveals a Universe Without Design. W.W. Norton & Company, New York.

Dawkins, R. (2009). The Greatest Show on Earth: The Evidence for Evolution. London: Bantam Press.

Dawkins, R. (1976). The Selfish Gene. Oxford: Oxford University Press, 1976.

Dehaene, S. (1997). The number sense: How the mind creates mathematics. Oxford: Oxford University Press.

Dennett, D. C. (1991) Consciousness explained. New York: Basic Books.

Dennet, Daniel C. (2017). From Bacteria to Bach and Back: The Evolution of Minds, W.W. Norton & Co. 2017.

Dennett, D. C. (1990). "Quining qualia". In Mind and Cognition, W. Lycan, ed., Oxford: Blackwell, 519-548.

Descartes, R. Discourse on the Method of Rightly Conducting One's Reason and Seeking the Truth in the Sciences. In Descartes: Selected Philosophical Writings, ed. and trans. John Cottingham, Robert Stoothoff, and Dugald Murdoch. Cambridge and New York: Cambridge University Press, 1988.

Gabora, L. & Russon, A. (2011). The evolution of human intelligence. In (R. Sternberg & S. Kaufman, Eds.) The Cambridge Handbook of Intelligence, (pp. 328-350). Cambridge UK: Cambridge University Press.

G. F. R. Ellis (2013). The arrow of time and the nature of spacetime, Studies in History and Philosophy of Modern Physics [arXiv:1302.7291].

Eschenmoser, A. (2007). The search for the chemistry of life. Tetrahedron63, 12821–12844.

Foster J. (1996). The Immaterial Self: A Defence of the Cartesian Dualist Conception of Mind. London: Routledge.

Fuller R.B. (1982). Critical Path. New York, NY: St. Martin's Press.

Fuller, R.B. (1963). Ideas and integrities. New York: Macmillan, Collier Books.

Galperin, M.Y. (2018) What bacteria want. Environ Microbiol20: 4221-4229.

Garrett, R.H., Grisham, C.M. (2007) Biochemistry. 3ed. Belmont, CA.: Brookscole.

Gibson, J.J. (1979). The ecological approach to visual perception. Boston, MA: Houghton Mifflin.

Gibbon, E. (1790). The history of the decline and fall of the Roman Empire. London, England. Printed for A Strahan.

Gould, S. J. (2002). The Structure of Evolutionary Theory. Cambridge, Mass: Belknap Press of Harvard University Press.

Greene, B. (1999). The elegant universe: superstrings, hidden dimensions, and the quest for the ultimate theory. New York, NY: W. W. Norton.

Halpin A, Johnson PJM, Tempelaar R, Murphy RS, Knoester J, et al. (2014). Two-dimensional spec-troscopy of a molecular dimer unveils the effects of vibronic coupling on exciton coherences.Nat. Chem.6:196–201.

Hameroff, S. (1998). "Quantum computation in brain microtubules? The Penrose-Hameroff "Orch OR" model of consciousness". Philosophical Transactions Royal Society London, A 356: 1869-96.

Hameroff, S.,and Penrose, R. (2014). Consciousness in the universe: A review of the 'Orch OR' theory. Phys.Life Rev.11(2014),39–78.

Hawking, Stephen. (1996). The Illustrated - A Brief History of Time, (ch. 9: "The Arrow of Time", pgs. 182-95). New York: Bantam Books.

Hawking, S.W. (1985). Arrow of Time in Cosmology. Physical Review D, 32, 2489.

Heinrich, T., Knopp, B. and Päs, H. (2016) Entropy, Biological Evolution and the Psychological Arrow of Time. Journal of Modern Physics, 7, 228-236.

Hobson, A. (1999). Consciousness (Scientific American Library Series). W. H. Freeman & Co.

Hume D. (1777). An Enquiry concerning the principles of morals. LaSalle, IL: Open Court (1930) Pubi. Co.

Jackson, F. "Epiphenomenal Qualia." The Philosophical Quarterly 32 (1982): 127–136.

Jackson, F. (1986). "What Mary didn't know". Journal of Philosophy, 83: 291-5.

James, W. (1890). The Principles of Psychology. New York: Henry Holt and Company.

Johnson AP, Cleaves HJ, Dworkin JP, Glavin DP, Lazcano A,Bada JL. (2008). The Miller Volcanic Spark Discharge Experiment. Science 322:404.

Kirk, R. (2005). Zombies and Consciousness. Oxford, UK: Oxford University Press.

Lampert TJ, Coleman KD, Hennessey TM.2011. A knockout mutation of a constitutive GPCR in Tetrahymena decreases both G-protein activity and chemoattraction. PLoS One6:e28022.

Malthus, Thomas (1798). An Essay on the Principle of Population. London: Printed for J. Johnson, in St. Paul's Church-Yard.

Mayr, E. (1982). The Growth of Biological Thought: Diversity, Evolution, and Inheritance. Cambridge, Mass: Belknap Press.

Melville, H. (1853). Bartleby, the Scrivener. Hoboken, NJ: Melville House Pub, 2004.

Miller SL. (1953). A Production of Amino Acids under Possible Primitive Earth Conditions. Science 117:528 – 529.

Miller SL. (1955). Production of some organic compounds under possible primitive

Earth conditions. J Am Chem Soc. 77:2351 – 2361.

Montagnes, D.J.S., Barbosa, A.B., Boenigk, J., Davidson, K., Jurgens, K., Macek, M., et al. (2008). Selective feeding behaviour of key free-living protists: avenues for continued study. Aquat Microb Ecol 53: 83–98.

Musolino, J. (2015). The soul fallacy: What science shows we gain from letting go of our soul beliefs. Amherst, NY, US: Prometheus Books.

Nagel, T. "What Is It Like to Be a Bat?" The Philosophical Review 83 (1974): 435–450.

Nauenberg, M. (2007). Critique of "Quantum enigma: Physics encounters consciousness". Foundations of Physics 37 (11), 1612–1627.

G. Panitchayangkoon, D. Hayes, K.A. Fransted, J.R. Caram, E. Harel, J. Wen, R.E. Blankenship, and G.S. Engel. "Long-lived quantum coherence in photosynthetic complexes at physiological temperature." PNAS,107:12766-12770 2010.

Penrose, R. (1989).The Emperor's New Mind, Oxford, UK: Oxford University Press.

Penrose, R. (1994). Shadows of the Mind. Oxford, UK: Oxford University Press.

Penrose, R. (2005). The Road to Reality: A Complete Guide to the Laws of the Universe. London: Vintage Books.

Pepperell, R. (2018). Consciousness and integrated energy differences in the brain. arXiv:1804.10508

Pinker, S. (1997). How the Mind Works, New York, New York: W.W. Norton & Company.

Rosenblum, B., Kuttner, F. (2006). Quantum Enigma, Physics Encounters Consciousness. Oxford Univ. Press, London.

Sagan, C. (1997). Comet. New York: Ballantine Books.

Sagan, C. and Druyan, A. (1980). Cosmos. New York: Random House.

Sagan, Carl (1994). Pale Blue Dot: A Vision of the Human Future in Space (1st ed.). New York: Random House.

Salah Ud-Din AIM, Roujeinikova A. Methyl-accepting chemotaxis proteins: a core sensing element in prokaryotes and archaea. Cell Mol Life Sci. 2017 Sep;74(18):3293-3303.

Shakespeare, W., Wells, S. and Taylor, G. (2005). *William Shakespeare, the complete works*. 2nd ed. Oxford [Oxfordshire]: Clarendon Press.

Shannon, C. (1948). A Mathematical Theory of Communication. The Bell System Technical Journal, 27, pp. 379-423, 623-656.

Street, S. (2016). Neurobiology as Information Physics. Front. Syst. Neurosci.10:90.

Treisman, A. (1996). The binding problem. Current Opinion in Neurobiology 6: 171–178.

Turing AM. (1950). Computing Machinery and Intelligence. Mind 49:433-460.

Turner JH. (1999). Toward a general sociological theory of emotions. J. Theory Soc. Behav. 29:133–62.

Wang Z, Busemeyer JR, Atmanspacher H, Pothos EM (2013). The potential of usingquantum theory to build models of cognition.Top Cogn Sci5(4):672–688.

Vandervert, L. (1995). Chaos theory and the evolution of consciousness and mind: A thermodynamic-holographic resolution to the mind-body problem. New Ideas in Psychology13(2):107–27.

von Neumann, J. (1945). First draft of a report on the EDVAC. Ann. Hist. Comput. 15,27–75 (1993).

von Uexküll, J. (1957). A stroll through the worlds of animals and men: A picture book of invisible worlds. In C. H. Schiller (Ed.) Instinctive behavior: The development of a modern concept. New York, NY: International Universities Press.